# Nietzsche and Metaphysics

SUNY Series in
Contemporary Continental Philosophy

Dennis J. Schmidt, Editor

# NIETZSCHE AND METAPHYSICS

*Michel Haar*

Translated and Edited
by
Michael Gendre

Published with the assistance of the
French Ministry of Culture

STATE UNIVERSITY OF NEW YORK PRESS

Originally published in France
under the title *Nietzsche et la Métaphysique*


Production by Ruth Fisher
Marketing by Nancy Farrell

Published by
State University of New York Press, Albany



Printed in the United States of America



For information, address the State University of New York Press,
State University Plaza, Albany, NY 12246

**Library of Congress Cataloging-in-Publication Data**

Haar, Michel.
[Nietzsche et la métaphysique. English]
Nietzsche and metaphysics / Michel Haar : translated and edited by Michael Gendre.
p. cm. — (SUNY series in contemporary continental philosophy)
Includes bibliographical references and index.
ISBN 0-7914-2787-0 (CH : alk. paper). — ISBN 0-7914-2788-9 (PB: alk. paper)
1. Nietzsche, Friedrich Wilhelm, 1844–1990—Views on metaphysics.
2. Nietzsche, Friedrich Wilhelm, 1844–1900—Influence.
3. Metaphysics. I. Gendre, Michael. II. Title. III. Series.
B3318.M5H32 1996
193—dc20

95-12888
CIP

10 9 8 7 6 5 4 3 2

# CONTENTS

# TRANSLATOR'S ACKNOWLEDGMENTS

I wish to thank Michel Haar for his trust and friendship in giving me the opportunity to translate and edit his collection of essays on Nietzsche and Metaphysics. He has read the translation and made various helpful suggestions All editorial changes were made with his knowledge and approval.

I relied on Professor Vincent Avery from Philips Academy, Andover, to complete the editing of this collection. His knowledge of French was instrumental in unlocking some reticent locutions and phrases. Of course, I bear responsibility for any and all shortcomings.

A first version of the first chapter "The Subversion of the Categories and Identities" was first published in *Man and World,* Vol. 4, No. 4, November 1971, trans. Cyril and Liliane Welch, and later in *The New Nietzsche, Contemporary Styles of Interpretation,* edited and introduced by David B. Allison, New York: Delta Publishing Company, 1979, under the title "Nietzsche and Metaphysical Language" (pp. 5–36). In keeping with the author's wish I have revised that earlier version to harmonize it with the rest of the essays.

# Preface

The common thread running throughout these essays[1] is the question of *the overcoming of metaphysics*. Such a question is not imposed upon Nietzsche from the outside by this critic. It is one that Nietzsche himself posed explicitly, "Overcoming metaphysics ... requires the highest effort of human reflection."[2] It marks without a doubt the entire development of his thought from the "overturning of Platonism" to the affirmation of the Eternal Return. Now, before any development, it would be appropriate to define what the properly Nietzschean point of departure is, and to distinguish it from the famous Heideggerian problematic of the overcoming, which entails very different presuppositions. Without reference to any of the specifics of the Heideggerian approach, let me say that what, at the outset and fundamentally, separates Nietzsche and Heidegger is the fact that the former sees the "freeing of oneself from metaphysics" essentially as a task, even a struggle, whereas with the latter no such task could possibly be fulfilled except within a questioning that aimed at determining first "What is Metaphysics?" In a way that may seem cavalier, Nietzsche considers as given and unproblematic the answer to this second question. He takes upon himself the most "popular," and least "technical," definition of all: metaphysics is the belief in "another world," in a world that is ideal and true in itself, or in his own term, it is "Platonism." In one sense he prolongs the Kantian critique of all cognition that claimed to reach beyond the realm of phenomena, but naturally he rejects the reestablishment of faith in a transcendent world as a postulate of pure practical reason. The Kantian noumenon, or Idea, amounts for him to one of the last stages of the extinction of the Platonic sun, "the Idea grown sublime, pale, Northerly, Koenigsburgian."[3]

The overcoming of metaphysics entails therefore for Nietzsche a task of both criticism and reconstruction. It is a task of criticism, for he asks, "How does this belief emerge? What reflexes, impulses, or motivations sustain the negation of the world characterized as 'deceiving' and as merely 'apparent'—a negation that contains implicitly the so called 'completed nihilism,' in other words the complete collapse of all unconditional truth?" Such a collapse does not spare positivism itself or any tendency to idolize scientific facts. It is a task of reconstruction, for he asks, "How can one overcome nihilism, move away from despair ('goals are missing ... there is no longer an answer to the question "Why?"') without falling back into ideals of substitution that are also nihilistic? For example, how can we reestablish 'appearance as a goal' without simply putting appearance, especially the artistic one, in place of truth? What are those new goals?"

This means that the overcoming mobilizes a whole strategy and several approaches, some of which proceed by *retrogression,* and by dint of which we shall have to satisfy two requirements. First, we must understand and "justify"[4] the metaphysical categories and their system of binary oppositions (true/false, essence/appearance, good/evil); second, we must destabilize and subvert the fixedness of such oppositions by having them exchange their roles. Hence, the question raised by Heidegger: "Is it possible to overcome metaphysics by using its own vocabulary and limiting oneself to imposing nothing more than internal displacements and transmutations?" Doesn't Nietzsche remain prisoner to the categories that he overturns, in spite of his efforts to dismantle them? Doesn't he propose a "counter doctrine" (to use his own word)? Furthermore, who could doubt that he is indeed on a quest for his *own* truths (as he says) and his *own* good (he often uses the expression, "my morals")? Doesn't Heidegger minimize the results of the Nietzschean strategy of subversion that does not leave untouched one traditional concept? How can he justify the idea that the *essence* of metaphysics comes out unshaken from this operation, and is not only repeated but also reinforced?[6]

To be sure, let us repeat that Heidegger is right in stressing that Nietzsche concedes without a prior examination that metaphysics is the doctrine of "two worlds," holding it as an originary fact, in itself evident and beyond discussion. Any thought or belief that separates, opposes, or sets a hierarchy between a "world of appearances" and a "true world" is a metaphysics. Such a thought or belief necessarily diminishes this world here as an inferior and corrupt "here under" for the benefit of a "yonder" of the pure Good and the pure Truth, which are understood either philosophically (as the intelligible place of immutable essences) or religiously (as the dwelling within eternal bliss).

To overcome metaphysics for Nietzsche amounts to shedding this illusion, moving entirely within immanence, returning fully to the earth, reaffirming the uniqueness of the world as the Greeks had done before Plato and Socrates. But such a reaffirmation is impossible or in vain without the extremely complex and elaborate critical approach that Nietzsche names *genealogy,* and without a new thinking of the sensible world and the unfolding of appearances. To project the *genealogy of metaphysics* amounts to laying bare the forces which elicit and are satisfied by the values metaphysics promotes; namely: permanence, self-identity, happiness, safety, etc. It amounts to showing why man *needs* that utopia or "fable" of a better or perfect world, that transcends becoming, evil, suffering, contradiction, sensibility, as well as sensuality. It amounts to transforming the purely theoretical or propositional sense of metaphysics in order to make it into the symptom or the symbol of certain types of forces or types of existence.

To think the fullness of immanence requires furthermore a thinking that will be capable of grasping "phenomena as phenomena,"[7] a new thinking of "appearances" which, on the one hand before phenomenology, is able to understand "Being" in terms of appearing, and which, on the other hand, interprets life as the untiring capacity to show oneself in manifold ways, from different points of view, irreducible to a single, centralizing, or totalizing one.

This extraordinary double effort conducted by Nietzsche, his "naive" repetition of the most traditional definition of metaphysics notwithstanding, in no way remains enclosed within his own initial position. His thought cannot be reduced to a mere anti-Platonism. The flaw with the Heideggerian reading of him resides in this: first, it is an easy task to show the extent to which Nietzschean thought results from an overturning,[8] and, second, Heidegger does not see (or pretends not to see) the extent to which both the genealogical approach and the new interpretation of sensible appearances make impossible the restoration, pure and simple, of metaphysics or its "completion," that is to say its absolutization.

To be sure, all Nietzsche originates in this overturning, but nothing in his philosophy can be reduced to it. Thus, the sometimes problematic rehabilitation of some of "the most detested and despised aspects of existence" does not lead him to put "evil" in lieu of "good," but it leads him to a "Beyond ... " Thus, the artistic exaltation of the surfaces of things, their glorification as well as that of manifold reflections—outbursts of joy, peals of laughter, or the no less affirmative breaks contained in tears or grieving—does not lead to an apology of platitudes and superficiality. Instead, the sensible becomes, so to speak, abyssal. What resides on this side is opened up dizzily toward an unlimited slip of levels or points of view that, first, present themselves and, next, are pulled into withdrawal, as if, to use Nietzsche's words, a "cave," a backdrop, could remove itself in order to let another cave, another backdrop, appear, indefinitely[9] ... In the same fashion, the affirmation of the body as "great reason," as "peace and war" in *Thus Spoke Zarathustra,* does not resuscitate a new absolute in Hegel's fashion, but a "new infinite," an infinity of interpretations where none can pretend to be the last, or ultimate, one because all of them are anchored in points of view taken from the most common everydayness: wakefulness/sleep, repletion/hunger, pleasure/pain, health/disease, attractions/repulsions, chastity and sexual activity ... . These differences inhabit our own bodies and inspire all our interpretations up to the most sublime ones. But Nietzsche does not rest content after showing, for example, that fear of the body inspired metaphysicians with the fiction of an immutable world, one inaccessible to error and pain. He tries to give descriptions of the body, of the subject, and of the world that are animated by his love for polychromy, polyphony, and polyvalence. He does not aim so much at rehabilitating appearances against the essence, the multiple against the one, as at reversing the forgetfulness of those discreet truths, at retrieving the unique value of everyday thoughts and gestures, all of them minimal, light-footed, unstrapped by transcendent ends, shimmering in the *chiaroscuro* of simple and ordinary differences. He makes us see what the concern with primary causes and ultimate ends and the quest for the originary and the unconditional dissimulate to us because with them we lose sight of the elementary perspectives of the living being.

However, once more, doesn't the clarification of these "elementary" perspectives of life entail a restoration of metaphysics? It is indeed an originary and fundamental dimension that is being described, i.e., the emotional ground of impulses in which the conscious perspectives, the valuations and ideals, the highest productions of art and science are rooted and from which they all emerge.

But this originary can only be understood as "metaphysical" inasmuch as it is designated under one single name, the "Will to Power," which would refer to an identifiable or distinguishable substance or essence. Now this category or identity itself falls under the general critique of unity as a fiction. It refers back to a latent plurality of impulses, or to complexes of forces in the process of uniting or separating, of associating or dissociating, of acting, of transforming, of interpreting. Indeed, these underground movements of endlessly weaving and unweaving forces in struggle, in equilibrium, in harmony, in disharmony—as the indefinite unfolding of differences (of intensities, of points of view)—constitute what might be an "origin," yet one unpresentable, inexpressible, labyrinthine, unfathomable. In no way could it be viewed as a nucleus of homogeneous and stable meaning or as a foundation that sustains the edifice of knowledge. It designates the movement of self-interpretation of a living being, itself always open to a new interpretation.

Thus, on the side of the "ontology" of the living, Nietzsche is far from restoring metaphysics or leading it to its "completion," because the world of impulses obviously has nothing to do with an ideal world; but neither is it a world or a system of principles and "first causes" to be grasped in and for themselves. For the impulses are not separable "causes": they are intertwined with their effects, and to be discerned or suspected only through the so-callect "effects." It is obvious that there are no longer two worlds.

If an "ontology" perpetuates itself, this takes place amidst some ambiguity. Likewise for a theology. The phrase "God is dead" is not a point of arrival; it is not the final word. It is nothing but the moment of an extreme crisis, where the majority of the countless traditional, philosophical, and religious figures of the divinity unravel: the Supreme Being, the Judge, the Moral God or the God of consciences, the "Christian God," etc. are figures ultimately fusing together or superimposing upon one another. This fusion, or superimposition, in no way amounts to the disappearance or the abolition of the *divine as such*. Dionysos remains one of the most insistent words or motifs of the work. Nietzsche's Dionysos is a living god indeed. The Dionysos of *The Birth of Tragedy* is neither an archeological reconstitution nor the artificial attempt to resuscitate the emblematic and sacred figure of the tragic vision of the Greeks. The Dionysos of the latest texts and the posthumous fragments contains more than the symbol of the unlimited adherence of the living being to life in its totality, which is creative and destructive, joyful and suffering. He is the metamorphosis of a divinity who detaches himself from a backdrop of primitive Pan-like profusion in order to endorse the intimate, personal character of an inspiring Voice Nietzsche calls the "genius of the heart." If Nietzsche's last word takes us back toward a metaphysics of immanence or within immanence, it leads us also perhaps not to the direct reestablishing or validating of metaphysics, but to reevaluating and rethinking its concept, once this concept has been freed of its reactive, negative, essentially pejorative charge and of its status as an obstacle to overcome.

## Chapter 1

# THE SUBVERSION OF CATEGORIES AND IDENTITIES

After a century of commentaries[1] (the most inspired of which—Heidegger's, Deleuze's, and Klossowski's—are as indispensable as they are unforgettable) Nietzsche's work remains enigmatic. It escapes its commentators and keeps its strength of novelty intact. It remains secretive, upsetting, explosive. The astonishing polyphony of its stylistic registers (discursive, descriptive, polemical, aphoristic, poetic) is irreducible to traditional philosophical language and yet, as we shall see, does not steer clear of it entirely. Nietzsche is at the same time translatable and untranslatable into a universal language. He is at the same time a "thinker for everybody and nobody," familiar and distant, assimilable and impossible to assimilate. No interpretation grid could explain the plurality and detail of his contrasts and contradictions, which, to be sure, emerge from the collision within him of twilight and dawn ("I am decadent and at the same time a beginning"[2]): Conjointly he offers the stark assessments of collapse and failure, promises of unutterable metamorphoses, distress and prophecy, mixed bitterness and joy, and so many indescribable tonalities emerging in thought and writing. A succession, an alliance, and a collision take place between subtlety and violence, passion or verve, and analytic coldness, dryness and lyricism, irony and incantation. The most disconcerting aspect of his thought originates in the indefinable mixture of destruction and affirmation (destruction that regenerates and affirmation where all acquired certainty is dissolved and slips away). Far be it from me to claim to provide the key to unlock it, for it necessarily has several "entrances."

Its elucidation however has been made easier today, for many of the earlier mistakes or falsifications have been set aside or have fallen into discredit. Thus, no one thinks anymore of demoting Nietzsche to the level of the literati and the poets, of the brilliant and inconsistent essayists, or of suggesting that madness insinuated itself into his thought (when in fact it interrupted it definitively), or of putting him among the anti-Semites (when in fact he fought against them with extreme vigor), or the Pan-Germanic, or the defenders of a superior race (when in fact he sought to define a new type of humanity that would not be founded on hatred of oneself and of world). We no longer confuse the metaphysical theme of the Will to Power with the vulgar craving for power or the desire to dominate others. We understand more fully now that Nietzsche intentionally took upon himself—and borne—nihilism in order to better analyze it, fight it, and find ways to overcome it. We better understand that his thought is a stupendous experimentation and suffers from its dangers. We now accept the idea that his critique of "humanism" does not propound inhumanity and barbarity, but aims at overcoming a mere anthropocentric focus and man's complacency in making himself a banality and his own idol. In short, we have ceased making Nietzsche into the diabolical. Some of his most daring propositions (on the body or on God) are now mistakenly heralded as self-evident. People have started writing lives of Nietzsche as in previous times lives of the saints were written. He is in great danger of being taken for an edifying author. He himself had foretold with fright: "I have a frightful fear of being canonized one day. ... I do not want to become a holy man, I would rather pass for a buffoon."[3]

To be sure, Nietzsche hides himself behind his very accessibility. For he can be read easily and quickly; so much so that one may have the illusion of understanding him immediately and with little effort because he hardly uses any "technical" vocabulary, and everyone can find favorites to pick and choose from among his aphorisms, depending on the mood of the moment. Furthermore, one can see in him a "psychologist," in the line of the French moralists of the seventeenth and eighteenth centuries, without exactly making an erroneous assessment. In short, it is difficult to stop and take the time to "ruminate" his aphorisms as he invites his readers to do, for it is simply too pleasant to continue reading.

Still, Nietzsche's inaccessibility really derives from something more fundamental, most likely the strange and ambiguous position of his own writing confronting the traditional language of philosophy. Indeed, Nietzsche develops, in direct opposition to the tradition and its language, a language of his own, a form of expression particularly insinuating, insidious, complex and designed for *subversion*. On the one hand, when making use of current metaphysical oppositions (which, for him, all come down to the Platonic opposition between the "true world" and the "apparent world"), he does so with a view to eradicating and abolishing these very distinctions; there is thus inevitably an ambiguity weighing upon his use of terms having a precise meaning within the tradition, terms such as "true" and "false," "good" and "evil." On the other hand, the key words of his *own* vocabulary (Will to Power, Nihilism, Overman, Eternal Return) elude conceptual logic. Whereas a concept, in the classical sense, comprises and contains, in an identical and total manner, the content that it assumes, most of Nietzsche's key words bring forth, as we shall see, a plurality of meanings undermining any logic based on the principle of identity. Insofar as they include significations that are incompatible with one another, these words might be understood as bursting at the seams: a word such as Nihilism designates at once the most despicable and the most "divine" mode of thought. But they function above all to burst open some traditionally accepted identity (e.g., Will, Ego, Man). The recourse to polysemy and the attempt to destroy the great identities of the tradition are based on a theory of language construed as a machine fabricating false identities. And for Nietzsche, every identity is "false," in particular any identity born of conceptualization. As he says, "Every concept arises from identifying what is not identical."[4] Every concept results from a series of metaphorical transpositions (so primeval that they are always forgotten), the "truest" concept being simply the one that corresponds to the identification, i.e., image, which is most familiar and most common (most effaced in its character as a mere image). Far from attaining to the "truth," concepts, like language in general, function as instruments for "gregarious" use, *viz.*, they are identifications for the greatest number.

While the dominant words of Nietzsche's discourse (especially Will to Power and Eternal Return) are meant to subvert, fracture, and dismiss concepts, his overall effort aims at setting in motion the entire logical, semantic, and grammatical apparatus (in which the philosophical tradition has naively taken up residence) in the direction opposite to its most general tendencies; namely, against the assignment of proper nouns, the reduction to identity, and the passage to the universal. In other words, the specific nature of Nietzsche's discourse might well be defined in the first instance as an attempt to encourage disbelief in the laws of logic and the rules of grammar (the final refuge of a defunct theology): it is necessary, he says, to "know how to dance with words," "dance with the pen."[5] This dancing penmanship attempts to rock, to topple, to dissociate, to disperse all conformity, i.e, all truth subjected to the rule of correspondence ("*adaequatio*"). With its various games of irony, parody, interrogation, innuendo—but especially with its ruptures, shifts, displacements, and the like (which it would be necessary to delineate in detail)—Nietzsche's style aims finally at destroying, or at least checkmating, all logical and, especially, dialectical "seriousness," the goal of which is always to establish identities or to reveal the one absolute Identity.

Finally, the method of genealogy, the critical method discovered by Nietzsche himself and presented as the art of deciphering symptoms *ad infinitum*, raises a particular difficulty for the exposition of Nietzsche's thought. Contrary to Plato's method (consisting in gathering sensuous diversity into a unity of essence), Nietzsche's method aims at unmasking and unearthing phenomena, but in an *indefinite* way, i.e., without ever pretending to lift the last veil and to reveal an originary identity or a primary foundation. Thus, the method itself manifests a deeply rooted repugnance for any and all systematization. Hostile to the idea of an ultimate revelation of truth, and rejecting all unique and privileged interpretation ("There is no solely beatifying interpretation"[6]), the method of genealogy is necessarily hostile to all codification of its own results. Moreover, the fragmented, aphoristic, and bursting character of the text corresponds to Nietzsche's own grasp of the world: it is a world scattered in pieces, teeming with explosions; a world freed from the ties of gravity (i.e., from relationship with a foundation); a world made of moving and light surfaces where the incessant shifting of masks is named laughter, dance, game.

Thus, both Nietzsche's language and Nietzsche's method possess an explosive energy: what has vanished in each case is identity, on which every system rests.

However, in each instance the destruction is possible only on the basis of a new and more radical affirmation. Thus, there arises a most penetrating question: might there not be, in Nietzsche, a subtle restoration of metaphysics and ethics (to the extent, for example, that it is difficult *not* to conceive of the Overman as an ideal)? Here we encounter the supreme perplexity that rests permanently at the horizon of my own question: in what sense does Nietzsche "overcome" the metaphysics he combats?

Without doubt, the strictly Platonic structure of metaphysics (based on the separation of true being and lesser being) is abolished, and not just overturned. Every "ulterior world," every foundation, is dissolved, and the final symbol of Dionysos—another word for the Will to Power—summons all the attributes of beings, the "true" as well as the "false," the "real" as well as the "fictitious." Indeed, these terms become interchangeable, insofar as the "true" of which Plato speaks proves to be fictitious and therefore false, and insofar as the real is true if it is taken as false in Plato's sense yet *also* as containing the ficticious within it.

If, however, according to another (more Heideggerian) definition, the metaphysical approach consists of "identifying" beings in their totality—i.e., designating with one name the character of beings as such and in their entirety—is not Nietzsche then still a metaphysician? For if metaphysical thinking is the kind of thought which aims at discovering the unique and ultimate word that seals the character of presence upon every thing present, then it might well be that Nietzsche, by uttering the term "Will to Power," *did* reenact the traditional gesture of metaphysics.

But to what extent is the term Will to Power still an identity? Does it not, like all great themes in Nietzsche, refer back to identities that are broken, disfigured, forever dispersed and unrecoverable? Such are the questions that will serve as a constant background for the present inquiry into the Will to Power, Nihilism, Genealogy, the Overman, and the Eternal Return. This style of approach leaves aside the question of Nietzsche's progressive elaboration of these ultimate themes (and therewith also the problem of distinguishing between the various phases of his work) for two reasons: first, such problems go beyond the limits of the present exposition; second, the exposition is based on the view (not defended here) that the substance of Nietzsche's effort can be found, although in an enveloped, unthought, and veiled way, in the first work, *The Birth of Tragedy,* the work he never ceased to rethink and defend, the one that he was finally to complete.

## The Will to Power

Nietzsche explicitly underscores and affirms in various ways that everything that exists is, at bottom and in its totality, Will to Power: "The essence of the world is Will to Power;"[7] "The essence of life is Will to Power;"[8] "The most intimate essence of being is Will to Power."[9] World, Life, Being, these are not ultimate things, but only formations of the Will to Power: herein we find the "ultimate face."[10]

Accordingly, we must accordingly discard from the very start, as a gross misconception, an interpretation of the Will to Power as *merely* psychological or anthropological. So construed, it would simply be synonymous with hunger for power, and it would be a mere matter of each individual's desiring to dominate others and to subjugate things. It can easily be shown that such a will would, in reality, be impotent, constantly suffering from inadequacy, and affected with endless longing. Alternatively, it might be taken as synonymous with a "superiority complex" (after the fashion of Adler), always wanting to extend itself without seeing any limit to its imperialism. Whatever the psychologizing interpretation might be, power is understood as a concrete and empirical goal, something exterior to the will (riches, political power, glory), a goal pursued or manipulated with presumptuousness. In any case, there would be a distinction between the power and the will, one being the object desired or possessed by the other.

However, in Nietzsche, the Will to Power is something totally different from the psychological relationship between will as subjective and power as objective. Will to Power is indeed the "word for being," but this word is a locution, whose two terms are inseparable, with each term losing its habitual meaning. Although the issue is the affirming of the totality of beings (and in this sense is a "metaphysical" claim), the locution is designed first of all to destroy and eliminate the traditional metaphysical concept of the will. As for the term "power," it receives its own meaning only in the course of the attempt to overcome that concept: it comes to designate the very essence of this newly-thought will. Thus, the Will to Power, a term bursting at the seams, a term that cannot be reduced to an identity, comes to express anything but one variety of volition.

The classical view of the will in effect turns it either into a metaphysical substance or, more commonly, into a faculty of the subject. Moreover, this view sees in the will the cause and source of our actions. Finally, it conceives of the will as a unity, an identity.

In opposition to this classical conception, Nietzsche posits as the guiding theme of his analyses of the will the astonishing affirmation that "there is no such thing as will."[11] Why does he do this? First of all, because the will as a conscious faculty is neither a unity nor a primary term. It is plurality and complexity, and it is derived. What we call "will" is only the symptom and not the cause. On the one hand, "will" in the psychological sense and in everyday language entails the simplification of a complex interplay of causes and effects. On the other hand, the will, posited as a *center* or as a *foundation*, is taken falsely by metaphysics as a unique origin within reality as well as within the individual: for there is no center, and there is no foundation. There is no such thing as will: this means, as against Schopenhauer, that there exists no unique and universal will constituting what things are in themselves, that behind the phenomena there is no substantiality of the will.

No such thing as will: this also means that the individual does not possess an identical and permanent will from which all his actions flow. What the individual calls his "will" is a plurality of instincts and impulses in constant battle with one another to gain the upper hand. An analysis of the individual's "I will" shows that what we call "will" is the result of a reduction following the dictates of practical necessity as well as of linguistic structure, and that it represents merely an imaginary entity, a pure fiction. Volition is composed of distinct emotions and polarities: there is that which wills and that which is willed, and then also, at the very core of the "individual," that which commands and that which obeys, the pleasure of triumphing over a resistance and the different pleasure of feeling oneself as an instrument doing its job. What language designates by the word "will" is in reality only a complex and belated feeling, which *accompanies* the victory of one impulse over others, or the translation into conscious terms of the temporary state of equilibrium that has obtained among the competing impulses.

Indeed, the will, like consciousness itself, is for Nietzsche not a beginning but an end, not the first term but the "last link in a chain." The will (like consciousness and thought in general) is the distant echo of a battle that has already been fought out, the aftermath coming to the surface, or the "code language" for a subterranean struggle of impulses. To will is to feel the triumph of a force that has cleared a way for itself quite apart from our knowing anything about it: the supreme illusion consists in taking this feeling, this sentiment, for a free causality. "There is no will" means that there is no fixed and defined center (the center is always shifting and it cannot be grasped), but rather a plurality of elementary "wills," i.e., unconscious impulses, forever in conflict, alternately imposing themselves and subordinating themselves. "There is no will: there are rather fulgurations of the will that are constantly increasing and diminishing their power."[12] Seen with regard to these impulses, the whole of our conscious motivations comes down to a fiction or, rather, a *symptom*. In psychology we never cease to confound effects and causes. Generally speaking, the realm of the intellect and the sphere of consciousness are but symbols to be decoded, symptoms of impulsive movements, i.e., symptoms of bodily movements. That is why it will always be necessary to philosophize, i.e., to interpret the phenomena, by taking the *body* as the "abiding clue."

Is the Will to Power, then, merely a name designating the realm of the unconscious, the realm of the body? Quite the contrary. On the one hand, the locution applies to every possible kind of force: it does not refer uniquely to the forces that underlie psychic phenomena (i.e., the impulses of the body) but rather to all the phenomena of the world. On the other hand, the locution applies more precisely to the inner dynamism of these forces, to the orientation that qualifies them. In fact, rather than naming these forces themselves (as new metaphysical substances of the sort that Nietzsche rejects as fictitious), the Will to Power names the polarity that orients them, structures them, and defines their *meaning*. It is not an absolute meaning, nor a univocal direction, nor any finality whatsoever, but a multifaceted meaning that takes its shape from the moving diversity of perspectives. In its widest signification, the Will to Power designates a deployment of forces that is non-finalized but always oriented. Every force, every energy, whatever it may be, is Will to Power—in the organic world (impulses, instincts, needs), in the psychological and moral worlds (desires, motivations, ideas), and in the inorganic world itself—inasmuch as "life is just a special case of the Will to Power."[13] Every force participates in this same essence: "It is one and the same force that one expends in artistic creation and in the sex act; there is but one kind of force."[14] However, the concept of a single force diversifying itself does not suffice to account for the Will to Power: "To the concept of force must be attributed an inner will, what I refer to as 'Will to Power,' i.e., as an insatiable demand for the demonstration of power."[15]

It is this "insatiable demand for the demonstration of power" that expresses the meaning of the complementary phrase "to Power," conveying the sense of the "movement toward" contained in the German *Wille "zur" Macht.* What, then, is this Power? It is precisely the intimate law of the will and of all force, the law that to will is to will one's own growth. The will that is Will to Power responds at its origins to its own internal imperative: *to be more.* This imperative brings it before the alternative: it is bound either to augment itself (to surpass itself) or to decline (to degenerate). According to the direction the force takes (progression or regression), and according to the response (positive or negative) one makes to the conditions imposed upon life or imposed on life by life itself (as Zarathustra says: "I am the one who is ever forced to overcome himself"[16]), there appear *right at the origin*, at the very heart of the Will to Power, two types of force, two types of life: the *active* force and the *reactive* force, the *ascending* life and the *decadent* life. If all volition is a volition to be stronger, if all power is overpower, our volition can also try to escape from itself and from its own demand for growth. There is a paradox here, for, strictly speaking, it is impossible to cease to will, because that would mean to cease to be. However, the decadent will that refuses to "admit the fundamental conditions of life" remains nonetheless a will: "Man would rather will *nothingness* than *not* will at all."[17] Only, in this case, the direction of the will is reversed: growth becomes *advance in decadence*. The "intensification" essential to the Will to Power works itself out backwards. For Nietzsche, in the special case of moral decadence, its most extreme creation is the ascetic ideal.

The Will to Power therefore always has to do with itself. It possesses a fundamental reflexivity, it always overcomes itself, through action or reaction. At its origin it presents itself to itself as a chaotic and contradictory diversity of elementary impulses; it is primordial affectivity. What Nietzsche calls "chaos" is this primordial indetermination of the Will to Power. Undetermined as it is, it can assume all forms, for it is just so many masks: it is Proteus. Being without form because of its excess of possibilities, Chaos signifies, on the one hand, not disorder at all, but rather the multiplicity of impulses, the entire horizon of forces, within which knowledge and art are to delineate their differing perspectives. On the other hand, Chaos is to represent equally the moment when, after the collapse of all values, the Will to Power returns to itself, returns to a sort of zero point.

When considered in conjunction with Chaos, the Will to Power appears both as the principle defining a hierarchy for the forces contesting for the upper hand and as the tendency to appropriate an ever larger field of action. That will is strong which can harmonize its own forces, forces in themselves divergent, and can dominate their constant development. That man is powerful "who longs to see chaos," i.e., who agrees to face all impulses (or at least the greatest number possible), and who can master them. This mastery is conveyed in and by such expressions as "great style," "great politics," "great reasoning," "great educator," "great hope," in which the adjective "great" designates a Will to Power attaining, in each case, its fullest affirmation. In contrast, that will is weak which cannot bear this task and seeks out a solution in the elimination or repression of this or that force. When affirmative and strong, the Will to Power takes upon itself variety, difference, and plurality. When negative and weak, it shrinks into reflexes of flight and defense, willing but its own diminution in the shadow of a bloodless ideal, in complete opposition to the grand simplification that perfect mastery can produce.

This initial bipolarity of the Will to Power forms the basis from which the whole enterprise of genealogy receives its definition. The "genealogical" critique of values consists in relating any given value to the originary direction (affirmative or negative) of volition, in unveiling the long lineage issuing from this primordial orientation, and in unraveling the long thread weaving together encounters and inventions that have since frozen into "values."

But what are values? As instruments that the Will to Power grants itself in order to confirm itself in its initial direction, values constitute the conditions of its existence; they are the "points of view" that permit it to maintain itself and to develop itself. Nietzsche defines values as follows: they are "conditions of conservation and increase, namely in regard to complex creatures having a *relative duration* of life within the realm of becoming."[18] The production as well as the "hierarchy" of values (i.e., their situation, constantly in flux, with regard to one another, e.g., as the changing rank of art with respect to knowledge at a given time) makes sense only in relation to the originary direction of the Will to Power; the "position" of values favors, sustains, and propels movement in this direction.

As the origin of values, and the origin also of every hierarchy of values, the Will to Power fixes the value of all values. But this origin cannot be reduced to a primordial unity, to any kind of identity, because it is nothing but a direction to be determined each time. On the other hand, this origin has and gives meaning only in retrospect, namely in and through the genealogical development that issues from it, and by which it is recognized.

## Nihilism

But what does the genealogical view discover when it turns toward the prevailing—the supposedly "highest"—values? It finds them in the throes of that crisis called Nihilism.

In this word, too, we can read a duality (if not a plurality) of meaning. On the one hand, it designates the contemporary situation (probably destined to last for a long time) where the "highest," i.e., the absolute, values are rendered null and void. On the other hand, the word applies to the unfolding as well as to the internal "logic" of all so-called "European" history since Plato. In this second sense, Nihilism has more historical continuity than the "decadence" marking the moments of "weakening" of the Will to Power (the Alexandrian civilization as against ancient Greece; Christianity as against imperial Rome; the Reformation as against the Renaissance). Inasmuch as Nihilism presided over the original institution of those values that are currently tottering, and inasmuch as it directs their evolution and every possible transmutation, Nihilism is in some fashion *always* present, *always* at work—before, during, and after the moment of its violent explosion. Concurring with the very humanity of man, it can rightly be called man's "normal condition" (whereupon the question might be asked whether a race of men who no longer knew nihilism would still be men). But insofar as it is the peculiar disease of contemporary man (one requiring a homeopathic remedy), Nihilism is also a "passing pathological condition."

Indeed, Nihilism is much more than *critical thought* wielded by man and his culture against beliefs, values, and ideals: it assails man and his culture as the experience and sentiment of a *critical condition* that has become brutally current. For, before crashing down with all its weight, Nihilism makes inroads as "the most alarming of all guests"[19] and installs itself insidiously as a sentiment first of gloom, then of terror, in the face of the collapse of all meaning. It is the progressive consumption of everything having signification, the growing predominance of empty significations, drained to the last drop. It is the moment when we feel ourselves flowing or drifting toward ill-defined borderlands where every previous meaning, every previous sense, still subsists, but has been converted into non-sense (as in the onrush of a nightmare or as in a complete disorientation in space and time). "The wasteland is growing," Zarathustra says. All the old meanings (whether moral, religious, or metaphysical) slip away, steal away, refuse their services: "The goals are missing."[20] All sense totters, vacillates, sputtering like the few last rays of a dying sun. Nihilism, the experience of the exhaustion of meaning, amounts to a great weariness, a "great disgust," on the part of man, and directed at him as well. Nothing is worth much anymore, everything comes down to the same thing, everything is equalized. Everything is the same and equivalent: the true and the false, the good and the bad. Everything is outdated, used up, old, dilapidated, dying: an undefined agony of meaning, an unending twilight: not a definite annihilation of significations, but their indefinite collapse.

Precisely because it is *complete* disorientation, this kind of nihilism can abruptly change in *Stimmung* (mood, tone), ceasing to be anxious *inquiétude* and changing to complacent quietude. Here we have the experience of a will satisfied with meaninglessness, with non-sense, a will happy that there is no longer any sense or any meaning to look for, a will that has found a certain comfort in the total absence of meaning and a certain happiness in the certainty that there is no answer to the question "why?" (or even "what?"). Nietzsche describes this stage as that of the "last man."

The remark made by Zarathustra and taken up again in *The Gay Science* (Section 125) that "God is dead" summarizes the collapse of all values. For disaffection in regard to religious faith is only one sign among many indicating the bankruptcy of every ideal: not only of every ideal, but of every intelligibility, *every idea.* With God there disappears the guarantee for an intelligible world, and therewith the guarantee for all stable identities, including that of the ego. Everything returns to chaos. Nietzsche compares this event to a natural catastrophe: to a deluge, to an earthquake, but most often to an *eclipse of the sun.* The Sun of intelligibility has grown dark and the

Earth has lost its orbit, becoming a roving star that suffers the eclipse by growing dark itself. Here we have "complete nihilism," although it is neither its first nor its last form.

Initially, Nihilism is the expression of a decadent will, of impotent Will to Power recoiling from an affirmation of "life" and changing into negation. (That which is negated in and by Nihilism is what Nietzsche calls "life," i.e., the world as plurality, as becoming, as contradiction, as suffering, as illusion, as evil.) This negation of "life" and of the world proclaims that "this world is worth nothing and nothing in it is worth anything." Taking this proclamation as its point of departure, Nihilism invents a "true world," i.e., a world that possesses all the attributes that "life" does not have: unity, stability, identity, happiness, truth, goodness. Thus the division of the two worlds, the feat undertaken by Plato, constitutes the nihilistic act *par excellence*. All metaphysical values and all categories of intelligibility contain, implicitly, a will to negate, to depreciate, and to slander life. But in its first form (the Socratic and Platonic one), Nihilism remains *latent*. Negation does not show itself. Only affirmations are in evidence: the affirmation of great, supersensible values (the True, the Beautiful, the Good), and, later on, the affirmation of the great principles of logic (identity, causality, sufficient reason, etc.).

Between the larval nihilism of triumphant metaphysics and the "complete" nihilism declaring that none of the earlier constructions, nor any value, has any meaning, we encounter various forms of "incomplete nihilism." In these forms, the will for negation comes more and more into the open. Incomplete nihilism is but the decomposition of the "true world," the recurrent attempt to find replacement values to substitute for the Platonic and Christian ideals (Christianity having only "popularized" the concept of a "true world" with its idea of a "world beyond"). One noteworthy substitute, among others, is the Kantian ethic, which can no longer do more than *postulate* the other world: "Fundamentally the same old sun, but now obscured by fog and skepticism; the Idea grown sublime, pale, northerly Koenigsbergian."[21] And, then, there are the "secular" ideals: the faith in progress, the religion of happiness-for-everybody (socialism appearing as the successor of Christianity insofar as it promises happiness on earth), the mystique of Culture or of Man. However, after killing God, i.e., after recognizing the nothingness of the "true world"and placing himself where God once was, Man continues to be haunted by his iconoclastic act. He cannot venerate himself, and soon ends up turning his impiety against himself and smashing this new idol. Among the forms of incomplete nihilism are to be found the characters that Zarathustra calls the "superior men," the "vestiges of God on earth," those who desperately uphold an ideal the fragility of which they know all too well. They are like that "conscientious soul" who, latching onto the ideal of a perfect science, no matter how limited and ridiculous, studies but one thing, albeit very thoroughly: the brain of the leech! For this study he gives his blood and his life, and he grinds himself into the dust.

Although not yet "consummated," Nihilism is "complete" when the will to nothingness has become manifest and patent. Up to that point nothingness (i.e., the condemnation of "life" as non-being) hides behind various representations of the ideal and various fictions of the supersensible. It is on these representations and fictions that Nihilism, their proper counterpart, now expatiates. The distrust that had given rise to the "true world" turns against its own creations. The sensible having been depreciated and the supersensible ceasing to be of value, the essential metaphysical differences (Platonic, Christian, and also Kantian) between being-in-itself and appearance, between truth and illusion, end up rejected. What gets abolished is not only the "true world," whereupon we would have to re-evaluate the "appearance" that would be left over, but also the very distinction between the "simple" appearance and the idea: "With the true world we have also done away with the apparent world."[22]

"Appearances," according to Nietzsche's conception of them, become the "only reality," the All: that is why the whole range of predicates associated with what used to be called appearance, "including contrary predicates," are suited to this reality. This "new" sense of appearance contains both truth and lie, both reality and fiction. It signifies at once "appearance" in the sense of paralogism (a sin against logic) and in the sense of a veracious vision of being as Chaos. Gathering within itself all contraries, it deliberately shatters the logic of identity. Appearance, thought of in this new way and transfigured by the abolition of all opposition, never comes to the point of referring to an ultimate foundation, nor to a central focus of interpretation, nor to anything "in itself": rather, it always refers to a further appearance. Everything is a mask. A mask once uncovered uncovers another mask. "Becoming" is simply the indefinite play of interpretations, an indefinite shifting of masks.

Thus, Nihilism is not overcome simply because the essential metaphysical distinctions cease to be of value. In order to transform "complete" nihilism into "consummated" nihilism (or "ecstatic" nihilism, that which precisely allows us to take leave [*ek-statis*] of the difference), it is necessary that we pass from the mere observation of the dissolution to an active, affirmative dissolution. The new affirmation includes an *act of destruction* whereby all the relations issuing from the difference are destroyed. This unity of creation and destruction at the core of a force supremely affirmative (active nihilism) comprises a perspective that Nietzsche also calls "Dionysian": the perspective of the joyous, pure affirmation of the unity of contraries.

It is in this latter sense—namely, as an invalidation of all metaphysical differences and as a radical abolishment of the "true world," as a negation of the singular God (Christian representative of the world)—that "nihilism might indeed be a divine manner of thinking":[23] delivered from the paralysis effected by the Singular, the instinct creative of Multiple gods would be re-animated. This "divine" form of Nihilism prefigures an essential transition.

## Genealogy and the Former Codes

As a kind of symptomatology or semiology, the genealogical critique interprets values as so many signs (values being but a "cipher-language" to be decoded), signs of subterranean impulses or, more precisely, signs of the originary direction, whether ascendant or decadent, of these impulses. Genealogy shows at once a birth and an affiliation: it allows us to see how the initial direction prevailing in such-and-such evaluation persists through each and every derivation and transformation, no matter how distant from the origin. Like all values, the True and the Good serve as instruments, as conditions for the possibility of a Will to Power maintaining and developing itself thanks to them. Just where and how the line is to be drawn between the true and the false, the good and the bad, depends upon the kind of life that these values uphold. They have no intrinsic value at all; their entire "truth" lies in their adequacy to a particular Will to Power. "You will always have only that ethic which suits your own force,"[24] i.e., which will harmonize with the orientation of this force. Values that advise being prudent or taking risks are dictated by a particular type of force. In exactly the same way, the supposedly immutable principles of logic, as well as the discoveries of science, serve as a support, as a base of operations for a determinate type of humanity. "The force of the various modes of knowledge does not lie in their degrees of truth, but ... in their character as conditions of life."[25]

Thus, Nietzsche strives to demonstrate, by the genealogical method, that science (and knowledge in general), contrary to its own pretensions, is not at all disinterested, but rather is supremely "interested."

There is no "immaculate knowledge," says a chapter of *Thus Spoke Zarathustra* (II, "On Immaculate Perception"). And Nietzsche attacks the myth of a "pure" objective knowledge that could hover over reality without being implicated in it, that could, without prejudice or point of view, be the faithful mirror of reality. The illusion peculiar to knowledge, i.e., the illusion of objectivity, consists in imagining that it is possible to penetrate the essence of things, right down to its innermost recesses, while merely reflecting it. However, knowledge is essentially active even when it takes itself to be passive, it is essentially solar even though it takes itself to be lunar (i.e., revolving around reality and borrowing from it what little cold light it possesses). All knowledge thus comes down to *belief* and *conquest*.

Knowledge is *belief*, inasmuch as truths (including the principles and categories of logic) do not correspond to any "In-itself" of things, are not adequate to "objects" but rather to the Will to Power. We are forced to believe in a logic in order to bring things under our control. To "deduce" logic from the Will to Power means to relate it to needs and desires: the desire for stability introducing simplicity, order, identity; the need for prediction inventing the categories of causality and finality, which in turn make possible various systems of repetition and the consequent foreseeable character of phenomena. Logic rests upon a useful and necessary falsification, born of the vital need to lean upon identities despite the fact that nothing real is reducible either to unity or to identity. Therefore, "truth is that kind of error without which a certain kind of living being cannot live."[26] But truth is, in addition, "*falsification of the False*," for the "In-itself," namely "pure becoming," presents itself to us as Chaos, i.e., as non-(logical)-truth, eternal and infinite.

Knowledge is also *conquest*, inasmuch as it is imperative by nature, inasmuch as it imposes laws upon Chaos, inasmuch as it is an assimilating activity. Knowledge behaves like a despot because it never ceases to suppress, to simplify, to equalize. Like ethics, logic springs from a will to reduce all phenomena to "identical cases." While feigning objectivity, the enterprise of knowing schematizes and creates a fictitious coherence, as it appropriates with inexhaustible voracity everything strange to or other than it, with the sole view of mastering it. But that is not all: the schematizing and assimilating activity of knowledge is not even the work of consciousness. This activity emerges at the level of the body, and from there passes on to the conscious level. Knowing and judging are simply matters of recognizing a particular schema of assimilation that happens to be available because it is already traced out by the body, i.e., by the Will to Power.

The destruction of logic by means of its genealogy brings along with it the ruin of the psychological categories founded upon this logic. All psychological categories (the ego, the individual, the person) derive from the illusion of *substantial identity.* But this illusion goes back basically to a superstition that deceives not only common sense but also philosophers, and is in keeping with the belief in language and, more precisely, in the truth of grammatical categories. It is grammar (the structure of subject and predicate) that inspires Descartes' certainty that "I" is the subject of "think," to which Nietzsche objects that it is thoughts that come to "me": at bottom, faith in grammar simply conveys the will to be the "cause" of one's thoughts. The subject, the self, the individual are just so many false concepts, since they transform fictitious unities that have at the start only a linguistic reality into substances. Moreover, the "self," once brought into relation with the Will to Power, proves to be a simple illusion of perspective insofar as it is posited as an underlying unity, permanent center, source of decision. Rather, the "self" and the individual are fictions concealing a complexity, a plurality of forces in conflict. Conscious and personal identity, aside from being but a "grammatical habit," hides the original and fundamental plurality constituting the Will to Power in bodily form. "We are a plurality that has imagined itself a unity,"[27] a multiplicity of impulses that have provided themselves with an arbitrarily coherent and substantial center. The actual "functioning" of the Will to Power comes into clearest view with regard to the body, originally understood as a multiplicity, yet ascribing a unity to itself. To philosophize by taking the body as the "abiding clue" amounts to revealing the "self" as an instrument, an expression, an interpreter of the body. It also amounts to revealing the body (in opposition to our petty faculty of reasoning, where only surface "causes" make their appearance) as the "great reason," i.e., as the totality of deeply buried causes in their mobile and contradictory diversity. Philosophy has never ceased showing disdain for the body; it has not wished to recognize that it is the body that whispers thoughts to the "soul," and that consciousness is only a superficial and terminal phenomenon. Psychology has always idolized superficial unities for fear of facing the unsettling multiplicity at the depths of being.

Our logical and psychological categories derive their falsehood precisely from this "will to find out the truth," i.e, what is fixed, stable, identical, and noncontradictory. But by devaluing contradiction, we bring into evidence a *moral prejudice* at the very basis of knowledge. This prejudice can be summed up as follows: what is always stable, always identical, is not only True, but also *Good,* and in a twofold way: knowledge claims to bring salvation and is itself haunted by an ideal of ethical honesty. It is as shameful to deceive as it is to be deceived, and the true has more *ethical* value than the false. If the will to know the true is the will to be good and to be saved, this will is, then, a way of negating "life."

Indeed, if the logically true takes shape in the course of searching out identity at all costs and rejecting the contradictory character of life, the will to truth is associated with a nihilistic Will to Power, or, put more bluntly, with a covert will to die, a covert deathwish. All knowledge is motivated by this ascetic will, this will to self-destruction that turns out to be the supreme form of ethics. There is in all knowledge an aspiration to place oneself definitively beyond all contradiction, which Nietzsche construes as placing oneself within nothingness.

Thus, any genealogy, whether it be of logic, science, psychology, or anything else, comes down to a genealogy of morals, since the ethical ideal is the archetype and source of every ideal, and especially of truth. Things are true or false only inasmuch as they are good or evil. The ideal of knowledge turns out to be but a special and derived case of the general ideal: "The need to know what *should* be gave rise to the need to know what is."[28] The genealogy of morals is more radical and poses the question about the *meaning* of the Ideal, i.e., about the originary direction of that Will to Power to which such an invention corresponds and renders service. While at the same time detailing and unveiling the process by which the Ideal is fabricated, genealogy reveals moral consciousness as a formation issuing from a long development and assuming varying degrees.

From a genealogical point of view, it appears that ethical systems can only be defined univocally, in purely negative and pejorative terms: moral consciousness and its ideals are analyzed and unmasked as inventions of "ressentiment." But what does ressentiment mean if not hatred, condemnation, depreciation of "life"? In other words, ethical systems derive from a weak and impotent Will to Power reacting against the most affirmative impulses and favoring negation and destruction. Ressentiment is, as Nietzsche most generally defines it, the instinct of negating life, "the instinct of decadence." Since every value expresses the point of view necessary for the maintenance and growth of certain beings and for a certain period of time, and since every value also serves as a condition of existence, an ethical system, itself a sign of sickness, constitutes at the same time a remedy, or rather an attempted recovery. It serves the purpose of a defensive wall, of a systematic protection against the unrelenting impulses of sex, egoism (every ethic being a disdain for the self, a rejection of the self *(Entselbstung)*), aggression, cruelty, etc. Since these impulses cannot be taken up and expressed as such, they are kept at a distance, or, if at all possible, extirpated (morality playing, for Nietzsche, the role of an instrument of castration) by assigning to them their specific nature: the embodiment of Evil and of immorality. Their "immoral" nature amounts to a projection of the fear they arouse.

But why can't these impulses be expressed? Two obstacles, one internal and the other external, stand in the way. 1. On the one hand, these impulses are *already* weakened, degenerate, and sickly, in such a way that they cannot in any case find a satisfactory outlet (witness the case of Socrates, who distrusts instincts simply because his own are decadent). This internal obstacle is by far the more complex of the two, for it arises from an ambivalence: although the decadent type is characterized by an unprecedented decay as far as his instincts go (Socrates: the "amystical" creature *par excellence*, monstrously insensitive to art and to music), and by a hypertrophy of his reasoning and conscious faculties, he is also one who feels that he is "capable of every evil" and always on the brink of brutally expressing his desires and erupting into all sorts of bestiality. The decadent man feels within himself the terrifying proximity of animality, which is poorly constrained by a frail film of civilization, of civility and good manners, and is on the verge of breaking out. "Instincts want to play the tyrant: it is *necessary* to invent a *counter-tyrant* that is stronger yet."[29] The Socratic ethic (virtue is knowledge, the only sin is ignorance, a virtuous man is a happy man) represents this counter-tyranny; it is the ultimate and obligatory recourse in the face of instincts that are at once weakened and yet also threaten at any moment to boil over into anarchy. 2. On the other hand, the external obstacle consists of the repressive external organization (society, in essence) that prevents these impulses expressing themselves.

The development of man's "interiorizing process" and the birth of his ethical consciousness takes its foothold and beginning from the impotence of the instincts, their powerlessness to find a way of expressing themselves outwardly, and the resultant turn inward. However, precisely in the figure of his adversary Plato (Plato the man rather than Plato the philosopher) Nietzsche envisages still a third possibility to account for the origin of the reactive (ascetic) ethic: there are indeed people in whom the overabundance of life and sensuality is such that asceticism, in them, redoubles their strength by giving them a victory in the face of an obstacle that they set for themselves for the sole pleasure of proving themselves triumphant over it. In this sense, we might say that Plato was an extremely sensuous man who happened to be "enamored with his own contrary." But this explanation holds neither for Platonism nor for Christianity.

Whatever the case may be, the illusion peculiar to any ethic lies in its erecting into a universal rule, into an *imperative*, that which is only a *constraint*, i.e., a need, an imperious condition of existence.

Meanwhile, and at the same time, the genealogical method reveals the ambivalence and the duplicity of the concept of "morality." For even if it is ordinarily a function of a weak and reactive Will to Power, it can also arise from the values willed by a strong and active will. In addition, the *highest* point of view of the affirmative Will to Power necessarily is reached beyond good and evil, since the very distinction of good and evil itself is the work of weakness. To the affirmative Will to Power, the strong and the weak appear equally moral and equally immoral. Immorality finds itself assessed from two different angles. Unilateral morality is thereby dissolved. As Nietzsche says in *The Genealogy of Morals,* the concept "good" has no one meaning.[30] There are neither "virtues" nor "vices" that could not be taken in at least two diametrically opposed ways. Just as there is a lowly and vile prudence of the weak, so there is a noble and proud prudence of the strong; a cowardly and weak cruelty as well as courageous and strong cruelty; a pessimism that is a symptom of exhaustion and decomposition as well as a pessimism that manifests a superabundance of energy, that constitutes a kind of luxury of strength. The need for destruction and change can be the expression just as much of an exuberant and overflowing strength as of a hatred and malcontent in the face of what is. In the same way, the need for stabilizing, fixing, and "eternalizing" can come as much from generosity and happiness as from rancor and a morbid desire to perpetuate suffering and unhappiness. In the same culture, the "good" man can mean "he who is courteous and nice," but also "he who longs for battle and victory." Thus, the genealogical point of view brings to light a *typology of antithetical morals:* the initial fundamental opposition between "strong" and "weak" reappears in the gregarious type (passive, defensive, vulgar) and the solitary type (active, aggressive, noble). The profound insight of Nietzsche is that this antagonism is necessary and *not to be overcome:* "The *moral* instinct consists in constructing types; for that it needs antagonistic values."

Of course, Nietzsche's analysis does not preclude a multiplicity of degrees and intermediary stages, even mixed types. However, the antagonism of the two types must be thought of not as a conflict that brings them into mutual relations and attaches them to each other, but as a mutual separation that detaches and distinguishes them from each other. A caesura, a fault, keeps the two apart. The Hegelian opposition of master and slave is a dialectic, a reciprocity of relations. Nietzsche's opposition is based upon a rupture, a cleavage within humanity. Nietzsche does not want the moat between them to be filled in. He rather wants to underscore what he calls the "pathos of distance." The antagonism must be further aggravated, pushed as far as possible, to bring out the two irreversible propensities leading, on the one hand, to making gregarious, to leveling, to uniformity, and, on the other hand, to the formation of higher men, exceptional men, "great solitary figures."

At first, the antithesis was present not only in the opposition between the "noble" as self-affirmation and the "vile" as self-negation, but also in the opposition between Dionysian tragedy (affirmation, even of suffering) and Christian theory (negation, even of happiness). It was then repeated in the modern opposition between the classical type (capable of mastering all contradictions) and the romantic type (expressing the weakness of instinct). Finally, it is bound to recur in the future (at the other extreme) in the ultimate opposition between the "last man," the complete nihilist, and the Overman.

But, to come to the point, why and how did the weak man, the man of ressentiment, come to be exclusively identified with the moral man? From whence derives this prolonged immobilization of the Good exclusively on one side, this "hemiplegia of virtue," as Nietzsche calls it?

By inventing moral inwardness (from which stem the ideas of doing wrong and being justified, of being in debt and having responsibilities) the weak man has "triumphed" over the strong, happy man who affirms himself in his individuality apart from obligations and without need for approval. Once moral inwardness was discovered, the strong man was bound to doubt the legitimacy of his actions. Ever since Socrates, the Good has not taken care of itself; instinctive action has become suspect; only that action is good which can give answers before the inner court. The logical and disinterested appearance of Socratic dialectic is now unmasked: it is the "weapon" of the weak man who seeks to unsettle whatever is affirmative without daring or being able to engage in mortal combat with it. For the man of ressentiment, the "slave," never enters into a truly reciprocal relationship with the man of strength, the "master"; rather, he receives his only definition as the one who rejects the ethic of the "master." It is clear enough that, for Nietzsche, the "master" (and such are the Overmen, the future "Masters of the Earth") is not the master of the slave, but the master of himself, his acts, and, above all, his "inward chaos." The master is the individual who gives himself his own law, and whose ethic is built on pure self-affirmation. The master is the one who is *different:* "My ethic would be to deprive man more and more of his universal character and to specialize him, to make him to a certain extent unintelligible to others." Here is the ethical principle of the master: "That which is good for me is good in itself." By contrast, the man of ressentiment rejects every form of affirmation, of joy, of happiness. He bears a grudge against life. Nothing is good enough for him.

He posits as evil that which is Other, different or affirmative. He suffers incessantly. He is incapable of either forgetting or assimilating events. He is also plagued by memories, by the past. "He cannot shake anything off, he cannot get rid of it. Everything is an injury. Men and things press about him. Every event leaves its mark. Memory is a purulent wound."[31] Furthermore the underlying meaning of ressentiment, what Nietzsche also calls the "spirit of revenge," becomes in the course of time a certain version of the Will to Power: it is a rebel will, taking revenge on temporality dominated by the dimension of the past and understood Platonically as disappearance and non-being. Meanwhile, this "insane" will does not see that it is its own prisoner.

The impotence of the weak man is so great that he cannot bring his ressentiment to an external expression. He can only turn it against himself, thus suppressing it. This repressed hatred and cruelty, this grudge and accusation (not only against the strong and against affirmation, but also against time itself and the entire world) turns into self-accusation and produces that mutation of ressentiment called *bad conscience*. Whereas at first everything external is accused and found guilty, now it is the ego, the self. Just as the master is the master of himself, so the slave is enslaved to himself. The inwardness, the process of "interiorizing" for man, thereby results in a "regression" of the force that reacts upon itself: aggressiveness and cruelty, whose own impotence, in addition to the repressive social structure, forbids them to manifest themselves in any external fashion, direct themselves inwardly, and find on the inside a vast field of "new and subterranean satisfactions." Suffering thereby assumes, for the first time, an internal signification ("it is my fault") that the Christian religion, the religion of the weak, is well able to nourish, refine, and exploit: "You suffer, therefore you have sinned: suffering is punishment for having done wrong," says the priest, securing for himself infinite powers over those who accept this article of faith. However, we should bear in mind that, if there is a religion of the weak, there is also a religion of the strong, or rather two such religions: the primitive Greek religion of Dionysos, and the future religion of the Eternal Return.

But ressentiment necessarily evolves into its third stage, where the ultimate realization of its peculiar goal is embodied (a goal already present from the beginning): the *suppression of the self.* One's conscience, being its own executioner, ends up not being able to stand itself. It wills its own death, i.e., it becomes necessary for the individual *to live and experience his own death.* The ascetic ideal, with its fiction of an afterlife, of a "true world" possessing all the characteristics contrary to the world of "life," represents the means of achieving this death at the heart of life. The will can live out its own impossible self-destruction, continuing to exercise itself as a will, just by willing nothingness (the nothingness of itself and of the world). Self-accusation changes into self-destruction. At first, man immolates himself to the "beyond" prescribed by religion, undergoing the mortifications of ascetic existence. When the religious ideal has gone bankrupt and finds itself replaced by the scientific ideal, the sacrifice is still determined by the ascetic ideal. Whether life is sacrificed to God or to truth makes no difference with regard to the principle of the ideal. Finally, even the suppression of the ideal (not just of the ideal of God, but of each and every ideal) appears as the mere extension and application of the very principle of negation already present in the ascetic ideal. Atheism and nihilism result from the application, from the unconditional practice, of the ideal "truth at all costs!," which is the ideal born of the ascetic ethic. Indeed, as Nietzsche shows, atheism has its source in nothing but the ideal of scrupulous sincerity, the ideal of rigorous intellectual honesty as developed under the influence of Christianity itself and the refinement of conscience. Thus atheism is, in the genealogical sense, "the awe-inspiring *catastrophe* of a two-thousand-year training in truth, a training which in the end forbids itself that *lie which is faith in God*."[32] Atheists, and above all the scientists, are the most pious of men. Religion and morality thus die from their own exigencies: they commit suicide. "God has killed God." Everything great can only perish by "an act of self-suppression": thus wills the Will to Power.

Nihilism proves that, until now, only pain, sacrifice, destruction of the self have given meaning to life, that there has never been any other ideal. But this Ideal is no longer: "Goals are missing." The Will to Power demands of humanity that it surpass itself. But how are we to define this *new goal*, the Overhuman, by contrast to all those that are strictly human in type?

## The Overman and the Transmutation

As the ultimate "goal," the Overman obviously cannot be identified with any type or level of humanity actually existing. In this sense, the philosophy of the Overman presents itself as a philosophy of the Future while being something altogether different than a philosophy of Progress.

Insofar as the strong type of man has disappeared at the present period of nihilism (complete or incomplete, but not yet ecstatic), and insofar as there are no longer any "masters," it seems that the Overman can be taken to mean some strong type in the future, i.e., the man who has vanquished nihilism. But this is not at all the case.

To be sure, we have already under our eyes the absolute "opposite" of the Overman. This opposite is the "last man," the extreme representative of weakness, a man frozen at the level of passive nihilism, totally reduced to a "herd animal," rendered uniform, equal, and level (he is a man who has found happiness). But, as an ultimate horizon, isn't the Overman radically different from any *human* type we might be able to describe? One thing is certain: he is not incarnated by the "higher man" *(der höhere Mensch)*, who is still the prisoner of an ideal (as in the case of the scientific ideal held by some scrupulous specialist on leeches) and thereby of Nihilism. Even Zarathustra himself is not the Overman, but rather his "spokesman," his prophet. Might not the Overman, then, be the "total" man who has become once again affirmative, the "highest man" *(der höchste Mensch)* undertaking and completing the task of transmuting all values? But this does not seem to be be the case, because the Overhuman is what stands already as the goal toward which the "strong men of the future" surge; these men have to prepare the way for the Overman. What Zarathustra does is to announce the coming of a new type of man: he calls himself "the herald who summons numerous legislators." But it is in the midst of these higher men, beyond and above them, that there will tear, in sparse solitude, the "lightning flash" of the Overhuman.

The metaphor of lightning underscores the absoluteness of the emergence. The idea of the Overman seems to correspond to the possibility of an ecstatic break away from humanity. Isn't the appearance of the Overhuman foreseen precisely as a break with humanity, as a series of breaking faults destroying the very concept of humanity considered as an identity, a unity, and a totality universally embracing all thinking beings? The Overman will thus bring it about that the identity of humanity will, by itself, "burst at the seams" understood as it is as the highest form of life and a universal.

One question is of utmost importance: are we to interpret the Overman as some sort of highest type of man, the perfect embodiment of the essence of man (who actualizes what was, in the past, only a potentiality), or are we to interpret the Overman in a much different way, as a species higher than man (perhaps a god) and, in any case, as *some living being* other than man? The question is of decisive importance because the point is not simply to quarrel over a difference of degree or of nature. The point is to determine whether Nihilism is so coextensive with the essence of man that it will prove possible to overcome it only by overcoming humanity itself.

Nietzsche's answer to the question is clear enough: against the humanism of progress (implying an accumulation of gains for the entire species, i.e., the distribution to each and every man of "attributes" they have picked up together), he opposes a non-egalitarian and anti-universalistic vision of the future, where hierarchy and selection increasingly come into power and evidence. On the one hand, to be sure, there will be a humanity made "gregarious," subsisting and prospering precisely by stabilizing itself at the nihilistic level of the search for happiness: here the nihilism of the last man will settle and spread out. On the other hand, though, the new "masters," turning toward the ultimate goal, will create the primer for the *counter-movement* that will allow the Overhuman to thunder forth at some undetermined time in the future: this they will achieve by destroying the old values with a "stroke of the hammer"—a stroke that must both smash and liberate—and by instituting new codes. It is this operation, in which certain men are separated off and isolated from the others, which constitutes the condition for obtaining individuals surpassing man. The total man, the synthetic man, therefore represents only a stage of transition (a type no doubt allowing of various degrees) on the way toward the Overman. The "highest" man, the "legislator of the future" (i.e., the man who lays down the law, submitting himself to it as well), amounts merely to an "attempt" on the part of the Will to Power to attain the Overman—a bold and dangerous experiment.

In any event, the Overman is "an attempt at something which is *no longer* man."[33] Once again the logic of identity breaks down, not because the Overman contains an ambiguity (he is not, after all, both the fulfillment of man and the surpassing of man), but because he stands in opposition to the identification of man with himself as the highest living being. Man can no longer idolize himself. The "will for justice" ("justice" meaning, for Nietzsche, at once a respect for distance, and separation from, as well as an adequacy to, the Will to Power) commands Zarathustra to "smash, according to the image of the Overman, *all your images of man*."[34] Having irrevocably sold itself into slavery, humanity ceases to be the goal: "The Overman is now the goal." The Overman stands out as that type of living being who finally cuts himself loose from all the ties that even an affirmative humanity keeps with Nihilism. For Nietzsche, this "detachment" constitutes the future of the future, its promise. It presupposes as already accomplished the immense task of the transmutation, a task itself belonging to the future.

The Overman, who is as different from man as man is from the animals, is not a myth, but rather an "economical" exigency of the Will to Power. In fact, he represents the necessary compensation for the degradation and the loss of energy, evidenced by the present species that has been leveled down. The Will to Power must be able to retrieve itself wholly in the figure of the Overman, because in the figure of man there is only degeneration. Thus, the Overman does not fulfill humanity but rather that which, in humanity, is more originary than humanity, namely, the Will to Power. The Overman is the fulfillment not of the essence of man, but of the essence of life.

It might seem utopian that two such different species of thinking beings, which Nietzsche deems "as far apart as possible," would ever subsist " side by side" in the distant future. But that is only because we find it difficult to think of the opposition between master and slave in terms other than domination or dialectical reciprocity. Yet, the opposition between the Overman and man simply continues to push the fundamental antinomy governing any type of moral construction to the very limit, where it culminates in the opposition between gregarious/passive/vulgar and solitary/affirmative/noble. These two fundamental determinations of the Will to Power end up existing in absolute separation. In addition, Nietzsche can conceive of a *reign* that is not a *domination:* "Beyond those who dominate, live the highest men who are freed from all ties: and these make use of the men who dominate as of instruments."[35] The future "Masters of the Earth" will possess neither political power, nor wealth, nor any effective governing force. Those who actually govern and dominate will themselves originate in the slave class. The Overman will not govern or dominate the leveled-down humanity. Nietzsche describes him as soft, austere, isolated, sober, powerful, resembling a "god of Epicurus," not concerning himself with men. His reign will therefore be a secret reign. But how will he reign if he places himself beyond all political action and finds himself exposed to the disdain for the slaves? He will reign in the sense that he will exercise an indirect influence over humanity and this influence is what Nietzsche calls "great politics": being the only one to have preserved the power of creating, he will steer the world toward a goal that necessarily remains unknown to men. He will reign inasmuch as he will incarnate precisely the possibility of a future. The Caesarism of the Overman—nonviolent Caesarism ("Caesar with the soul of Christ")—must be understood as a *tyranny of artists.* The "Masters of the Earth" will, as artists do, mold and fashion the masses of humanity to the extent to which, unknown to these masses, they can serve the "masters" as an instrument. Indeed, only masters will be conscious of a higher goal. Moreover, this "artistic" side of the Overman not only requires that he gather into himself all the characteristics of various creators of the past (scholars, heroes, poets), but also really points to something quite different from artistic talents or gifts, even prodigious ones: it points to the fact that art is henceforth to be acknowledged as the highest value and that the principle of evaluation has been fundamentally overturned.

The Overman is only possible once the transmutation of values is accomplished. By its very nature, this transmutation presupposes a radical transformation at the core of the Will to Power, a transformation in which weakness and negation are once and for all eliminated. Everything will be transfigured, because all creation will find itself liberated at long last from every fetter. In its final form, the transmutation will no longer retain anything but affirmation: at the summit of the hierarchy it will place *Art* with the value of pure affirmation, a value that with all its infinite differences will provide the highest differentiation for the Will to Power. Thus, the Platonic domination of science over art is abolished or, rather, overturned. No longer the artist, but rather the scholar, is placed several removes from the truth (thought of as adequacy to the Will to Power).

Why does art have "more value" than truth? In Nietzsche no aestheticism of any sort can be found. Art is not a refuge, although certain statements might suggest a withdrawal in the face of truth (thought of, however, as knowledge): "We have art so that we will not perish from truth."[36] But the (future) primacy of art rests on a twofold necessity governing the very relation between art and knowledge, once these are envisaged in genealogical fashion. First, knowledge is always derived: it comes from a primordial and forgotten artistic creation that is none other than the very creation of language as "an artistic formation of metaphors" (these being later mummified into concepts). Science retrieves, in the form of icy, bloodless, and discolored concepts, the images and the schemas that language had primordially superimposed on the world. But it is art that, first of all, made the Chaos over into anthropomorphic form. The man of knowledge, the conquering and faithful one, is an artist who does not know himself as such. To know means merely to rediscover schemas that the artistic instinct has already cast over things. Second, if art is to become the highest value, it is because art corresponds best to, is most adequate to, the essence of the Will to Power as permanent growth of the self, as unfathomable depth of beneficent and exalting illusion, and as reinforced affirmation. Since *The Birth of Tragedy* Nietzsche has called art "the highest task and the authentically metaphysical activity" (see the end of the book's preface) because art is the "great stimulant for life": art drives the creator on to overcome himself, art enlarges the world by reinvoking its originally explosive and chaotic character. Art is drunkenness, celebration, orgy, break with identity, whereas science contents itself with ordering that which is basically already acquired. Art intensifies the feeling of power because art reaffirms all reality: it reaffirms it by using the power of establishing appearance within appearance and by continually confirming it as such. Appearances are selected, corrected, and magnified; but this procedure entails an adherence to what has always been regarded merely as illusory: it entails a glorification of illusion as illusion.

Finally, the transmutation gives birth to the ideal of a species of knowledge that needs no longer be the enemy of art but that, in submitting to art, is to submit directly to the Will to Power. Such is the ideal of a "Gay Science," a science that is also *tragic* (for Nietzsche's "tragic" is not at all sad or pessimistic: it is the state in which, thanks to an affirmation of the highest degree, we are able to include within ourselves, and to vindicate, even the deepest suffering). In *The Birth of Tragedy,* Dionysian tragedy finds its most original representation in the phenomenon of musical dissonance, i.e., in the pleasure felt in pain itself. Suffering thereby ceases to be an argument against life. Up to the present, the enterprise of knowing has been connected to seriousness, pain, and labor (all previous judgments of value being dominated by the idea of work): knowing, so far, has been funereal, deathly, a desire to be over with life, a will to die, individual and moralizing asceticism. By contrast, an artistic manner of knowing tends to break the narrow limits of individual identity, something that the Dionysian wisdom of the first Greeks, the Greeks before Plato, was able to do. *The Gay Science* teaches the loftiest teaching of Nietzsche (we can just as well say "of Dionysos," since this teaching ultimately destroys even the identity of the proper name of one who proffers it), it teaches the "innocence of becoming," which is the same as the "Eternal Return of the Same."

## The Eternal Return

The doctrine of the Eternal Return is encountered first and foremost as an experience. But this experience is *multifaceted* as it contains a pure effort of thought, a test, a particular moment of lived experience, and, finally, an endeavor having an ethical import.

In *Thus Spoke Zarathustra* ("On Redemption") the doctrine is introduced in the form of a question: how can the Will to Power liberate itself from ressentiment, specifically the ressentiment that is turned into hatred of time? How can it apprehend time differently than as passing, disappearance, non-being, wherein it encounters only its own passing, its own disappearance, its own non-being? How can the Will to Power liberate itself from the entire weight of the negative, which at the bottom resides in its core, which is but its own will to disappear, its will to nothingness?

How can the Eternal Return bring an end to the condemnation, the "vengeance" that is brought to bear upon Becoming? How are we to escape the idea that everything that passes deserves to pass, that it is therefore without value, and the idea that, by disappearing, it simply undergoes just punishment for the sin of having existed? This idea of the Eternal Return is very old: Nietzsche finds it even at the origin of Greek philosophy, in Anaximander's thought, according to which Becoming is guilty and the death of beings represents punishment for their erring into existence. In the face of this long tradition, how are we to recover "the innocence of Becoming"?

For the Will, "redemption" must be something quite different from "reconciliation," which, by virtue of a dialectical operation, would consist in maintianing the negative at the core of the positive. The redeemed Will must cut itself off, absolutely and radically, from the Will's saying "No!" in order to refashion itself into pure saying "Yes!" But what does this "Yes" affirm? It affirms time in absolute opposition to the malignant will that revolted against it (and viewed it merely as the past that has already passed, as passing away). The Will to Power must learn to "will backwards" *(zurückwollen)*—i.e., so deeply to will the past and the passage itself that the passage vanishes of its own accord as mere passage, changing thereby into incessant passage, or into a passage that is always present, into Eternal Return. In this way, not only will human time be "saved" from death, but the Becoming of the entire world will find redemption. However, this enigmatic metamorphosis of Becoming into Re-coming, into coming back, is only announced as a possibility: it depends on the will's being able to "will backwards"—i.e., being able, on the one hand, to affirm in all truth both the past and the passage itself, and, on the other hand, to turn back into itself in order to affirm itself as willing the passage. What we face here, then, is the possibility of a conversion of the will.

In the section entitled "On the Vision and the Riddle," this possibility, still *purely hypothetical,* reappears, this time no longer as a new relationship of the will to the past, but as a possibility of a new relationship between the present taken in itself and the past taken in *itself.* Nietzsche does not set out to prove that the Return is actually inscribed in the course of things; instead, he introduces a simple fiction or a hypothesis, like a free play of the imagination, which comes out in the form of a question: "And what if everything that *is* has *been* already?" This fiction assumes an intrinsic value because a double necessity immediately confers value upon a thing: if the present is a repetition of the past, then every moment must find itself multiplied to infinity, both forward and backward, and enlarged by its own repetition until it is equal to eternity. Then, too, every future must already be past, and the possible must be defined in terms of what has been completed. Finally, if everything comes back, no cause exterior to Becoming is thinkable, and Becoming determines itself simply because it is *already* determined the moment it is past. Everything is equally necessary.

This consequence appears first as rather sinister and dismal. But then, the idea of the Eternal Return is itself a *test:* it represents "the heaviest burden" weighing us down.[37] In fact, it comes uncomfortably close to complete nihilism. If everything has already been, if everything is bound to come back, not just in similar but identical fashion, isn't everything indifferent? What goal could such a repetition have? Hence, it is the ghastly gnome named "spirit of heaviness" ("On the Vision and the Riddle," Section 2) who for the first time makes the affirmation bound to inspire disgust for one's own existence and to drive one into despair: "Time itself is a circle." In his mouth the formula "everything returns" resonates as an eternal "in vain!" If everything comes back, everything is eternal: but if one thing is worth as much as the next, everything is equally useful and useless, and the best and the worst are worth the same. Thus, the idea of the Eternal Return first resembles as a caricature the most extreme form of Nihilism (although it was supposed to be the opposite). "Let us think this thought in its most terrifying form: present existence, just as it is, without either meaning or goal, but unavoidably returning, without coming to an end in nothingness: 'the Eternal Return.'"[38] He places quotation marks around the expression because this thought is a *test,* i.e., an instrument of discrimination: who would want to start his life all over again under absolutely identical conditions? Only those who are strong, only those who consider their existence as worth being infinitely repeated, will be able to bear such a thought.

If this doctrine ever takes hold, it will accentuate the cleavage between the strong and the weak, it will reinforce the strong by driving them to affirm themselves even more, and by contrast it will crush the weak by driving them to want to negate themselves even more. It will thereby contribute to the great task of selection. But how will this doctrine take hold? In the same way a religion does. The elect are those who have faith in their own lives as lives worthy of being repeated innumerable times. It is a religion diametrically opposed to all those religions that only promise a better life, happiness in a world beyond: this doctrine offers happiness *on earth* to all those who are capable of this faith. It is a religion that, Nietzsche says, will be "easy" on unbelievers, for although it has a paradise, it has no hell: "He who does not believe will be conscious of life as fugitive."[39] It is a religion without sin and without error; for everything that repeats itself infinitely is neither good nor bad, is innocent, simply *is*. As the only religion devoid of longing, eliminating every desire to flee the world and every devaluation of the "here and now" made in view of some transcendence, this doctrine establishes a connection with the divine understood as the totality and unity of self and world. But, as we shall see, Nietzsche's sense of "divinity" is not synonymous with perfection; it is rather synonymous with absolute affirmation embracing imperfection itself. Ultimately, the Eternal Return must be understood as a religion of pure possibility: just as the simple thought of eternal damnation was able to modify the actions of men, so the faith that each moment of life is worthy of returning should raise humanity far above itself. Just as the religion of the Return represents a test at the level of the individual, the Return of everything constitutes a test for the Will to Power in general, inasmuch as it implies the return of all forms of Nihilism, the return of weakness and the return of decadence. For the Return signifies that even if the Will to Power liberates itself and attains to the Overman, the nihilistic and reactionary man will nonetheless eternally return. Here lies the greatest obstacle for the Will to Power. It can only triumph over this obstacle by adhering to a new kind of "necessity," one that includes the negative but does not elevate it.

The Eternal Return is *experience* both in the sense of a possibility and a test, and in the sense of the privileged time saying "yes" to the moment. An affirmation truly full and complete, it is also contagious and bursts into a chain of affirmations that know no limits. "If we say *yes* to a single moment we say *yes* to all existence." However, this moment is a privileged one: only a moment of joy can be affirmed in this way. Only joy possesses the power to will itself, and thereby to will the totality of things, including pain: "Have you ever said *yes* to a joy? Oh, my friends, then you have also said *yes* to all pain. All things are tied to one another, wrapped up in one another, bound together by love."[40] In a single moment felt as necessary—necessary down to its most extreme contingency—a necessity reveals itself to us that ties this moment to all others. Such a moment cannot exist without implying all others. Once its own contingency is eliminated, all contingencies are eliminated. Any experience of joy that is supremely affirmative is also, is both an experience that multiplies the moment and the experience of the necessity of eternal and universal ties: "If you have ever, just once, willed that one time come a second time, ... then you have willed the return of everything!"[41] This experience represents the exact *reverse* of the fundamental experience of Nihilism conferring value and meaning as a function of pain and of the will not willing itself (or willing to be rid of itself). The experience of joy is so intense that it can will pain itself, death, and going to the grave as tied with the eternal. "All joy wills the eternity of *all* things, *wants a deep, a profound eternity.*"[42] The idea of the Return is begotten and sustained by joy.

Finally, considered as applicable to action, the doctrine of the Return has an ethical import. At every moment we are to act as though each of our acts were destined to be repeated an infinite number of times in exactly the same way: in my own life, I am to try to modify my relationship with the moment, to will each act as intensely as if it were *not* destined to pass, but rather to remain eternally. I will the idea that what I do involves my eternal being. However, this ethic opposes every categorical imperative (every "I should") with an imperative of necessity ("I am constrained to"). As Nietzsche says: "My doctrine teaches to live in such a way that you *are forced* to wish to relive everything all over again." The law of the Eternal Return cannot be formulated in the indicative mood: the mood is imperative and at the same time implies a necessity. "Let us impress upon our life the image of eternity."[43] This life is your eternal life: *Non alia, sed haec vita sempiterna.* I am to act in such a way as to be forced to will the repetition of my acts, and, conversely, I am to will whatever it is I am constrained to do. This ethic—namely, being forced to will a necessity that is the necessity of willing itself—is circular. The significance of this circle is: the will, which wills the Eternal Return, is the will that wills itself and *in itself* finds the necessity to will itself.

But just what is the "necessity" of which we speak here? Nietzsche declares that he has set himself to the task of "liquidating the concept of necessity." Indeed, the formula *"Amor Fati,"* which sums up the wisdom of the Eternal Return, is meant to shatter the traditional concept of necessity. Fate, in Nietzsche's sense of *fatum,* revolves around a necessity that is neither the causal necessity of the laws of nature (mechanism), nor that of a blind fatalism "in the Turkish sense," nor that of self-determining freedom. In his sense of the term, "necessity" is no longer a category; rather, it encompasses logical contraries such as Chaos and Form, chance and law. " I want to learn more and more to see what is necessary in things and what is beautiful in them: in this way I will be one of those who make things beautiful. *Amor fati,* may this be my love from now on!"[44] Inasmuch as it claims everything necessary, *amor fati* is a contradiction for conceptual logic. Yet, it has eliminated something: the opposition between love, as an activity of the will, and destiny, as a purely passive determination of what has already been settled. No longer qualified by desire, aspiration, or want, the will has been transfigured: it no longer searches for what is not yet. Rather, *amor fati* is the fullness and perfection of a will turned toward what is. This volition is love, where loving is to will what is as such and not otherwise and that it be an infinite number of times. In the willing that loves necessity, the initial difference between the Will to Power as "being more" and the Eternal Return as "completed being" is reduced. "Necessity" embraces all at once the *fatum,* the will and the tie uniting the two (a tie that is also the "ring" uniting all things). For a willing that loves necessity as though it were *its own* necessity *(ego fatum),* there is no longer any contradiction between determinism, freedom, and contingency. That is why "the most extreme fatalism is identical with chance and creativity."[45] There is no longer chance for a will that affirms itself indissolubly as its own destiny and that of the world. This will is absolute freedom within absolute necessity, since it wills so strongly, and affirms so invariably, whatever happens to itself or to the world, whether or not it has chosen it. "Every 'it was' is a fragment, an enigma, terrifying chance until the creative will adds: 'But I wanted it so!'"[46] Yet, does not the *ego,* by unifying itself thus with the fatalism of the Return, lose its own unity and identity?

Indeed, the idea of the Return, once it is *experienced* in all its varying forms, shatters the time-honored distinctions (the principles of identity and contradiction , which traditionally defined the modalities of existence). Just as individuality cannot be the same as totality of the world, things cannot belong at the same time to the categories of possibility, contingency, and necessity, any more than they can refer both to time and to eternity. Traditional logic *prevents* us from confounding the order of freedom, the order of chance, and the order of destiny. Even Hegel's speculative logic treats these conflicting categories as "moments" within the reconciled totality of Absolute Knowledge. But Nietzsche attacks the very idea of metaphysical contradiction and antinomy.

The thought of the Eternal Return is the "lightest" thought because it melts the ice of metaphysical antitheses and causes logical contraries to vanish. Indeed, the Eternal Return is neither real nor ideal, but something like a fatal possibility. It is a way for the Will to Power to be supremely affirmative, to give rise to a new connection, to a new necessity, out of the dissolution of the old oppositions. This new "necessity" has harmonized with its old "contrary" (namely, chance, disorder, and dispersion), just as "appearance" has harmonized with the "true world," which it contains ultimately. In other words, the complete circle of the Return (the coherence of everything) *includes* Chaos (the incoherence of everything). The divine ring of eternity is a broken ring. The theory of the Eternal Return, as the theory of the "vicious circle," consists precisely in according the most positive value, or perfection, to the circle's break. The break signifies that the circle is a form without goal, a form that contains in itself chaos. "Universal chaos, which rules out the efficiency of finality, *does not contradict* the idea of circular movement: this movement is nothing more than a *nonrational necessity."* Thus the inclusion of Chaos in the necessity of the circle does not constitute a synthesis or a reconciliation in the manner of Hegel: chance and disorder are not "surpassed" by, but rather gathered into, the perfect circle, such a circle being defective in its very essence. The totality of the Return is a shattered totality. Its necessity has for its symbol the coherence uniting the scattered stars of a single constellation: "Supreme constellation of being! ... Emblem of necessity." Produced by a pure affirmation, "which no wish attains, which no negation sullies" and emancipated from desire and want, this necessity within, and of, disorder surpasses every thinkable antithesis: it is "the celestial necessity that forces even chance events to dance in stellar formation."[47]

It is clear that Nietzsche was never able to offer a scientific demonstration for his doctrine as a theory of nature or to defend the Eternal Return in realistic terms: in his argumentation he would have had to subscribe to the logical principles that science obeys but that his own doctrine repudiates.

Thus, while canceling the major opposition of metaphysics, namely the one between being and becoming, the thought of the Eternal Return still validates each term as a possible "point of view." The circle is the permanent within Becoming. As the law of Becoming, the circle is not something that has become. Although Becoming is in itself the unstable, namely Chaos, the circle is the highest stabilization possible for this instability. As a consequence, the Eternal Return appears to be just one more interpretation, an interpretation of Becoming *according to the perspective of Being;* but it is also the *highest* perspective to which the Will to Power can raise itself, for this interpretation secures the greatest of triumphs, eternal triumph for the Will to Power. By willing the circle, the will secures itself for itself in its constant mastery over Chaos, it contains the certainty of always being able to overcome even the Return of the negative. We encounter what Nietzsche calls the "summit of contemplation" and "recapitulation" or summation of his abyssal thought: "To impress upon Becoming the character of Being—*this* is the highest form of the Will to Power ... That everything returns—here a world of Becoming comes closest to the world of Being."[48] Thus the Eternal Return appears as that perspective of the Will to Power which confers upon the world (fundamentally interpreted as a world of Becoming) the highest possible value. This perspective eternalizes the world of Becoming from the very point of view that, throughout all history, has devalued it, namely, the *fictitious* point of view of a world of Being. Thus values are overturned in a twofold way.

In the end, by effacing all the differences on which language and history are built (especially the opposition between remembering and forgetting), the thought of the Return leaves us face to face with the highest *aporia*. Paradoxically, the affirmation of the Return of the Same destroys all partial identities, especially the firm identity of the self contrasting with the identity of the world, because the "total" identity of self and world does away with the particular identity of the individual self. What is, then, the "new history" Nietzsche proclaims will begin after the idea of the Return takes hold? The "logic" that eliminates personal identity from the *ego fatum* allows Nietzsche to say: "At bottom I am all the names of history."[49] Every identity, including that of the self and of proper names, amounts to an interchangeable mask in keeping with the universal Game, which is merely the indefinite inventing and shifting of masks.

What does this loss of the "proper" names mean? Is this ultimate explosion merely the leap into madness of Nietzsche the man, the lived moment when the abolition of the antitheses sustaining metaphysical language reduces philosophy to science? The language that the self uses in order to gain a fictitious center, the language of fixed and arbitrary identities, appears to be so bound up with this system of contradistinctions that denying it exposes one to the dissociated and inexpressible forces of Chaos. At the moment when the self of Nietzsche the individual coincides with the totality of history, the coinciding deprives him of both speech and writing. Like Dionysos, his last "identity," Nietzsche the individual is torn apart, and the pieces scattered, all in accordance with the perspective of the dispersed totality that he will henceforth incarnate. The final silence of madness is, as he put it shortly before ceasing to write, "the mask that hides a knowledge which is fatal and *too certain.*" But what kind of knowledge is this? Perhaps it is the knowledge that language cannot shatter the principle of identity without shattering itself, and yet cannot submit to this principle without renouncing the effort to bring the depths of Being to words. Thus, for Nietzsche the destruction of metaphysical language can be looked upon as an experiment that went so far as to destroy the destroyer *qua* speaker. This attempt at subversion was one that both succeeded and misfired because it forced to the forefront the essential impasse of Western metaphysical discourse. This made Nietzsche into the greatest "tempter" for us who have no other language.

If "every word is a prejudice"[50] and grammar always reestablishes an indefinite multitude of substitutes for the dead God, what more precious legacy does Nietzsche bequeath us than (beyond his "great distrust," beyond showing the disconcerting syntax of destroyed words and the surprising distribution of terms, or limits, of the discredited language) an infinite concern for leading language back into its own?

# Chapter 2

## The Initial Rupture with Schopenhauer

The conceptual system of the early Nietzsche, especially in *The Birth of Tragedy* (1872), is generally interpreted as by and large dependent upon schemas borrowed from Schopenhauer. Thus Dionysos and Apollo allegedly transpose the relation between will and representation, a relation itself derived from the Kantian distinction between the thing-in-itself and the phenomenon. It is only around 1875-76 that Nietzsche is alleged to have detached himself both from Wagner and from Schopenhauer, the man he called his "great educator," and to have started criticizing the latter's doctrine with obstinacy, in every work of the later period in which he deplores his youthful mistakes. The "Essay of Self-critique," added in 1886 as an addendum to his first work, confirms this reading, in that Nietzsche can be seen reproaching himself, among other things, with having "obscured and wasted Dionysian anticipations by using Schopenhauerian and Kantian formulas."[1] But to what extent do these formulas and this language correspond to a true and deep *endorsement?*

Upon closer inspection, it might well be that Nietzsche's distancing himself from Schopenhauer is a much older affair, one that had been operative even before *The Birth of Tragedy,* and was an initial, rather than a belated, occurrence. Also it could very well be that a *very different* thought was making its way through a Schopenhauerian terminology and was being shaped. And, conversely, in spite of the rupture, we may witness a sort of faithfulness, on another plane than that of ideas, to the one he called to the end "my great master,"[2] in spite of the vehemence with which he condemns him.

Two formulas, whose blatant contradiction, however, is merely superficial, summarize this double, but unambiguous, position:

1. "My confidence in him was immediate, it is now still the same as nine years ago" *(Schopenhauer Educator,* 1874).[3]
2. "My distrust with respect to his system was there *since the very beginning*" *(Posthumous Fragments,* 1878).[4]

In the latter fragment, Nietzsche explains that he admired and respected Schopenhauer's character as the "philosopher type," but that he was fooled and "paralyzed by the superstition concerning the *genius.*" The context of the former statement also shows that the "confidence" was directed at the man who was exemplary in his "heroism of truthfulness."[5] Rising above the virtues and vices of his epoch, Schopenhauer educated himself *against* it, alone, without the least amount of concession to either the dominating philosophy or the powers-that-be, especially the University! The respect goes to the philosopher, to his freedom, to his courage, to his strength of character. Already, indeed, the third "Consideration Out-of-Season," whose goal is in principle to pay tribute to a great thinker, remains strangely silent on the *ideas* of this thinking hero and contains merely scant allusions to his doctrine! At the very end of his writings, Nietzsche claims that in that particular "Consideration Out-of-Season," in focusing on the obstacles his master had successfully dealt with, he had in fact really described himself and the truth he was seeking. "In *Schopenhauer Educator* is inscribed my most intimate history."[6] From the beginning, confidence in the man in no way amounts to approval of his system.

## Increased Divergencies and Lasting Affinities

Of his initial *distrust* he dares not utter a word for a long time to his closest friends, E. Rohde and Overbeck, or to Wagner naturally. To the young Baron von Gersdorff, his oldest friend (one he addresses as *"Du"* since Pforta and who is a true aristocrat for whom Schopenhauer is, as he is for many others, a veritable cult), Nietzsche does not hesitate to write with some truth, but little frankness at the end of September 1869: "I find myself at the center of a true cobweb stretched with Schopenhauerian threads woven throughout the world. For my part, I feel that this conception of the world has the greatest closeness to my inner personality and penetrates my thinking ever more, even in the scientific domain." And he adds that to understand his future Basel lectures,[7] "one must have already entered under the skin of Schopenhauer so as to notice all the shifts influenced by the decisive spell of his thought." Nietzsche claims further that Wagner, who came especially from Tribschen to hear the lecture, "constitutes the living illustration of what Schopenhauer called *genius*."[8]

However, at the time (the fall of 1869 and winter of 1870) when he makes this public profession of faith, the drafts and the first notes for his book on tragedy already announce theses that contradict *radically* the very principles of the Schopenhauerian system. Consider for example the statement that "art as festival and jubilation of the originary will is the most powerful seducer in favor of life."[9] It is precisely the contrary of the negation of the will-to-live! Also consider the idea that the originary will is *not pure suffering,* but "pleasure *and* suffering,"[10] or (several months later, at the end of 1870) "alternation of pain and pleasure,"[11] or "mutual penetration of suffering and pleasure in the essence of the world,"[12] or else "*inconceivable suffering* that endlessly produces a strong sensation of pleasure at every moment,"[13] or finally "*at the same time,* supreme suffering and supreme pleasure."[14] We shall come back to the even more troubling and important fact that the Will, or the In-itself of the very early drafts, is defined as originally multiple, fragmented, pluralized. Appearances and the phenomenal realm, Nietzsche repeats constantly, are "already in the originary One: for example, plurality is already in the will."[15]

True, two years before the publication of *The Birth of Tragedy,* Nietzsche was far from having overcome *all* borrowings from Schopenhauer in his vocabulary, to which major doctrinal residues are attached, in his Wagnerianism, and in his admiration for Schopenhauer's theory of music (with its primacy of music over concept, a primacy which Nietzsche transformed since, for Schopenhauer, music was not "the essence of the world").[16] Yet it remains beyond dispute that even then Nietzsche was entirely *free* from a doctrine that he used as a springboard and took apart without hesitation. He was himself already!

To be sure, he was still going to stand as a defender of Schopenhauer! He would side with him tactically against mediocre opponents such as David Strauss[17] with his vapid optimism, scorn for the unhappiness of humankind, and insipid and superficial neo-Hegelianism; against E. Dühring,[18] in 1875, who in *The Value of Life* (1865) had rejected Schopenhauer with an impure mixture of Feuerbach's materialism and neo-Kantian idealism (it is "absolutely false and ignominious, Herr Dühring, to claim that Schopenhauer brings the noblest aspects of nature in the gutter").[19]

Soon thereafter, however, the critique of Schopenhauer became more substantial, was broadened, and became increasingly argumentative, harsh, even brutal. As early as 1872, Nietzsche stated that "since Kant, philosophy has been dead; Schopenhauer: a simplifier who clears scholasticism out of the way"[20] and thus indicated a return to Kant that would no longer be denied: no "intellectual intuition" is to be had, no intuition of the body, no direct apprehension of the will or of the unconscious. Of the "In-itself," which is chaos, we only know symptoms. The "will to live" and the anxiety of death cannot belong to pure *animal* nature because man's relationship to death is not "natural" but the outcome of education and training in a long process through religions and philosophies. Against Schopenhauer's theory of life and pessimism, Nietzsche turns the weapons of a minimalist Hegelianism, of a genealogy of culture, and of a thought of artistic creation as anti-nihilistic impulse. It is with regard to the last point that Nietzsche's condemnation reaches the highest pitch of vehemence: he denounces in Schopenhauer not only "a scandalous misunderstanding of art"[21] (his replacing an aesthetics of creators with a passive and feminine aesthetics of spectators), but also, and most of all, a profound misunderstanding of tragedy. In no way is tragedy a lesson in "resignation"[22] and an instrument of negation of the will; rather, it is the highest affirmation including the most terrifying aspects of existence. Doesn't *The Birth of Tragedy* say about *Oedipus Rex* that the mere progressive revelation of the fall and ruin of a noble character (awash in his or her measureless will to fathom the secret—the In-itself—of nature) produces so great "a pleasure as to suffuse a superior serenity into the work as a whole"?[23] Nothing is more powerful than this artistic pleasure, a pleasure deeper than any suffering, "an *original* pleasure felt even within *suffering,*" "the common matrix of music and tragic myth."[24] Tragic art, in the dramatic play, i.e., in the musicality of voice and singing, as well as in the plastic character of the stage, is able to convince us of "the eternal pleasure of existence." If we find in *The Birth of Tragedy* brief glances of the "In-itself," of "original being," and even the mention of a possibility of quasi-mystical, ephemeral fusion with it, this is due to the "metaphysical joy that arises from the tragic," to an "indestructible and eternal" pleasure, which is that of life itself when it gives itself away for propagation. "For short moments we are really the original being itself, we feel its irresistible desire and pleasure to be alive."[25] And in this text, Nietzsche does not compare, but identifies, this voluptuousness with the "orgasm" *(Zeugungslust)* of a *"unique* living one,"[26] a voluptuousness that penetrates us because this living one, Dionysos, encompasses us and dwells within us.

Consider the numerous accusations that the later Nietzsche aims at Schopenhauer: a Buddhist, a nihilist, a fanatic of morals, a hypochondriac negater of the world. His "bad taste," his being heavy-handed in seeking out animality in the human being, his instinct for "decadence," his "religion of piety," his covert teleology, his hatred of pleasure and his old bachelor's aversion for the flesh, his romanticism of weakness: all these "spoil" even his pessimism, making it something quite lacking in masculine and tragic vigor.

Yet in spite of the violence of extreme formulas—such as "one must begin by rejecting Schopenhauer,"[27] or, "he had it wrong on everything"[28]—there still remains in Nietzsche a deep-seated attachment, with a mixture of gratitude and admiration prior to any doctrinal content. I see at least three reasons for this:

1. Schopenhauer always remained for Nietzsche the one who had revealed to him his vocation. The true master is the one whom the student encounters again after taking leave of him, as Zarathustra teaches us, because the master is the one who frees the student to be himself. That is why in many posthumous fragments of the *later* years Nietzsche calls Schopenhauer "my revered master," "my great educator,"[29] my precursor,"[30] although he finds himself "a hundred times more radical than he was." Nietzsche remains the disciple of a master who was a "destroyer-liberator."[31]
2. He is the one who allowed him to discover the non-historical power of life, to which are linked forgetfulness as an "active faculty" and the body as the true basis for culture–one that precedes society, the state, even the family:

> Schopenhauer reminded us of something we had almost forgotten and in any case wanted to forget: that the life of the individual cannot have any meaning by being historical, by disappearing in whatever species and in the great and changing configurations of the State, society, or in the smaller formations of the community and the family. The one who is only historical has not understood the lesson of life and will have to be taught the lesson agaåin. [32]

The second *Consideration Out-of-Season* shows how much it is necessary for the life of a culture to sink its roots into the *non-historical* soil and to cultivate, along with its models, a creative forgetfulness, although this forgetfulness may reveal itself as unfair to the past.

3. "Schopenhauer was as a philosopher the *first* self acknowledged and inexorable atheist .... In this lies his honesty" Nietzsche wrote in *The Gay Science* (Section 357).

> Yet, Nietzsche did not espouse this "absolute atheism" *(ibid.)* at all, because in the Eternal Return existence is invested with divine features, and because, following Heidegger, one may claim there is even a "negative theology" of the *circulus vitiosus deus*. But Schopenhauer must be credited for having raised, "almost as a problem in itself, the fearful question mark of the crisis and the awakening of religion."[33] Such a nihilist brought us to a corner from which no escape is possible. Nietzsche, however, did not realize that eternity, immutability, and the circularity of the will-to-live merely repeat the oldest onto-theological structures of metaphysics.

## The Metaphysical Overturning Prior to *The Birth of Tragedy*

It is undeniable that the fundamental inspiration[34] of Nietzschean thought in *The Birth of Tragedy,* as well as its conceptual departure point, is the impressive metaphysical construction of *The World as Will and Representation.* It is also undeniable that the distinction between the Dionysian and the Apollonian clearly and from the outset demarcates itself from the opposition between will-to-live and representation, and this with respect to at least two essential issues. First, in *The Birth of Tragedy* there is no longer any radical separation between the absolute truth "in itself" of the will and the fallacious phenomenal appearances (both are, so to speak, accomplices from the beginning). Second, there is no longer any absolute separation between suffering and pleasure, or between suffering and the absence of suffering (a separation that Schopenhauer associates with the previous opposition). To be sure, there are still many similarities of structure.[35] Dionysos, who holds the place of the will, is named "the original being" or the "originary one" *(das Ur-Eine),* or the "great living one," which seems to refer to a cosmic principle similar to the natural will-to-live. Likewise, Apollo, who is identified with the principle of individuation, the principle of beautiful appearances and of plastic forms, designates the law of phenomenality as well, and the Apollonian plays the role of the "principle of reason." As in Schopenhauer, deliverance from the fetters of individuation—the deliverance presented by tragedy as a "promise" of "restored unity,"[36] the abolition of the individual and its return within the One-and-All—seems to be the ultimate aim of every art and every wisdom.

Nonetheless, Nietzsche takes a double step away from the Schopenhauerian dichotomy.

*First,* the "appearance" in which the entire world consists, as well as Apollonian art itself, is not illusion pure and simple, or a "veil of Maya,"[37] but rather the "projection" *(das Projicieren)*[38] of the Dionysian foundation itself, i.e., its manifestation and its exaltation. The appearance is trans-figuration. It is not the loss of meaning from the degradation of the absolute in its figures, but the *presentation* of Dionysos himself. The god is present in the tragic mask; he eclipses the choragus, he surpasses the hero. Those figures do not represent an absolute essence, true in itself, by means of a fallacious and illusory externalization. The presentation is the god himself. The god himself is his presentation. The appearance is an appearing, not an illusion. Nothing happens here that was not within the realm of original possibility. That is why Nietzsche maintains (against Schopenhauer) that appearances must already be included in the "will." "The *will* is already a *form of phenomenon" (Erscheinung),* or, as stated earlier in the same fragment, "the will belongs to appearances" *(Schein)*[39]. Appearing appearance is therefore the most general concept of which each will becomes a particular case. In this fashion, the foundational difference of *Schopenhauer's metaphysics* is canceled. Moreover, this reversal—present in many other formulas—entails the identification between *appearance* and *phenomenon* in the sense of any being whatever. "The will is nothing but the appearing itself" *(Schein)*[40]. In other words, Nietzsche uses terms such as *Schein* (appearing) and *Erscheinung* (phenomenon) indifferently. Everything that is—either in the case of metaphysical will or the empirical artistic will—comes to appearance, i.e., is a phenomenon. However, the distinction between the originary "being true" and being a merely superficial and illusory appearance is preserved, but now as an intra-phenomenal, thus relative, distinction. The "will," the "originary one," is itself a "phenomenon": *"There is no path toward the originary one.* [The will] is in its entirety a phenomenon."[41]

This new identification of *opposite* terms, whereby the very distinction between the One unsurpassable and its dispersion amidst multiplicity is abolished, constitutes nothing less than the birth act of Nietzsche's philosophy. As early as 1870, thus before writing *The Birth of Tragedy,* he claims: "Plurality is already in the will."[42] Thus, art is not to be as in Schopenhauer, "the imitation" of ideas, those first and eternal objectifications of the will, but rather the originary (essential) production of *appearances,* or a particular case of universal phenomenalization.

Second—and this explains the first point—Nietzsche inverts the Schopenhauerian relation between pleasure and suffering. If he allows both affects to communicate, it is *against the backdrop of joy.*

The metaphysical unity promised by tragic art, is a joyful unity. In art we are no longer seeking the path of negation and extinction of the will-to-live, which as such suffers and is unhappy. On the contrary, tragic art feels and communicates "the incommensurable and original pleasure of existence,"[43] a Dionysian joy stronger than any death and every suffering, "an originary joy in the midst of the originary One."[44] Such a joy is both "aesthetic joy" and vital joy, identified with sexual pleasure of a non-individual but cosmic kind.[45] This fundamental metaphysical position remains unchanged from 1870 until the last writings.

To be sure, the abolishing of individuation, and consequently of the world, is an appearance in the sense of an illusion, of a "mirage," but it is also the "supreme mirage of pleasure."[46] Yet artistic pleasure does not correspond, as in Schopenhauer, to a complete illusion, to a fallacy, to a deceiving representation that, so to speak, suspends the unending torment of the originary suffering of willing. There is illusion only with respect to the Apollonian separation that isolates and blinds individuals. The artistic pleasure is a *true illusion* inasmuch as it opens us to the originary, extra-individual pleasure of which it is the privileged revelation. Such an originary pleasure itself is *proto-artistic* (ontologically prior to human art); it is the pleasure of being in existence. "It is necessary that artistic pleasure should exist independently of human beings." Being experiences ecstasy in order "to produce the world as a work of art."[47]

The pre-individual, joyful *unity,* the Dionysian unity presented in the tragic work of art, and, most of all, the reciprocal ontological dependency that Schopenhauer's duality between will and representation presupposes, provide the condition for the possibility of the Nietzschean reversal—or shall I say, effacement—of the absolute difference between essence and appearance, between originary suffering and the absence of suffering. The reasoning through which Nietzsche overcomes Schopenhauer is the following: If the will *needs* representation, the representation is already in the will or is *originarily* associated with it. Isn't such an association or such a primitive link the Dionysian itself? Hence the reading that Nietzsche makes of Schopenhauer in the fragments contemporary with *The Birth of Tragedy* is ruled on the whole by the following schema (where Nietzsche borrows exclusively from Schopenhauer's language to overcome him): it is not we alone who need redemption in the appearances, the originary One does too. The One is originally divided. It does not suffer from this division, but finds its highest joy in it. In other words, if the originary One needs appearances, appearances are not a loss, a fall, or a phenomenalization that is secondary with respect to the One; rather, the essence of the will is appearance. Hence the heterodox formula that we have already quoted, *"The will is nothing but the appearing itself."* In the language of *The Birth of Tragedy,* the suffering one (Dionysos) and his representative (the originary actor, the first of the celebrants, the prototype of the hero) are identical. Such an identity is accepted by Schopenhauer only on the level of the individuals of the world: "The executioner and the patient are one."[48] The Nietzschean reading consists in transporting this unity into the In-itself, which as a consequence ceases being the In-itself so as to become the *unique plane of appearances.* For the young Nietzsche, the suffering will and the representation free of suffering are the same, for it is the will itself that sees itself without suffering, that aspires to contemplate itself without suffering. Such are the two "sides" of "our one reality." "Our reality is on one side the originary One that suffers; on the other, it is reality as representation of this originary One. This self-suppression of the will, this rebirth, is only possible because the will is nothing but appearance itself."[49] Once more, appearance designates here the most general essence of Being.

Yet let us note in passing that although from now on appearance is a single plane, its former Platonic connotation of "lesser being" is not suppressed, but made relative. First, the work of art is not the absolute synthesis, the completed identity. The apparent death of the hero on the theater stage provides the representation of an illusory reconciliation with Oneness. The truth of art (beautiful, serene forms; the pleasure of feeling oneself in harmony with other individuals) goes hand in hand with the illusion of a reconciliation with Oneness. Second, the illusion is not evil—it is good, healing, and a condition for life. "Life is possible only through artistic hallucinations."[50]

One of the most unexpected consequences of the reversal of Schopenhauer is that, besides the pluralization and the scattering of the One into phenomena, it also very logically entails the *eternalization of the realm of the phenomenon.* For, because it is originally the unique and eternal will (as Being and One) that contemplates itself, it must do so from the perspective of its eternal appearance. "When the will intuits itself, it must always see the same thing, i.e., the appearance must *be* unchanged and eternal, just like Being itself."[51] Such anti-Schopenhauerian propositions are frequent in the first drafts and notes for *The Birth of Tragedy.*

All the fragments concerning the "originary one" show that, contrary to Schopenhauer, its ultimate simplicity has always been twofold: the originary One is at the same time will and appearances, supreme suffering and supreme pleasure, and this originary dissonance is the melody of its internal ecstasy.

We are now in a position to recognize that Nietzsche's distance from Schopenhauer, and his effort to reverse him, were much greater *before The Birth of Tragedy* than in the later work. Did Nietzsche try to avoid irritating the touchy feelings of Wagner or some of his other friends, who were diehard supporters of the Master? This interpretation is probable, but merely psychological.

Metaphysically speaking, Nietzsche's doctrine of *generalized appearance* is pushed further in the texts of his youth concerning the overturning of Plato and Schopenhauer than in the final philosophy of the "will to power as knowledge." Indeed, knowledge—albeit fictitious—is not the *illusory* representation of a *true* In-itself, but the "schematization of a *chaos* for practical ends." *Chaos,* an infinite multiplicity of forces through which the Will to Power offers itself to itself, to its self-organization, escapes any direct intuition. For all that, Schopenhauer's other world is not restored. No way leads to this originary gaping openness. Cognition is pure phenomenal character *[phénoménalité],* the symptom of symptoms *ad infinitum,* Never is the bottom revealed, except as a cave of caves *as far as the eye can see.* Nietzsche says it quite literally: "Behind every cave there is another one that opens up, deeper yet, and below each surface a vaster, more strange, richer subterranean world, and under every bottom, every foundation, there is an even deeper subsoil."[52] The latent grounding of the world is not negated, but plunged dizzily into the abyss and hidden from sight *[dérobée].*

From the very beginning, Nietzsche played the inaccessibility of the Kantian In-itself off against Schopenhauer, that is, an In-itself radically stripped of the moral determinations of the noumenon but not, for all that, de-divinized, since it would continue to be called *Dionysos* until the end! Should this be construed as the final procession toward the nihilism of completed metaphysics or as the first step toward phenomenology?

# Chapter 3

## The Overturning of Platonism and the New Meaning of Appearance

"My philosophy, *Platonism overturned [umgedrehter Platonismus]*: the further one moves away from true being, the purer, the more beautiful, the better it is. Life in the midst of appearance as goal."[1] This famous fragment from his youth is the birth act of Nietzsche's philosophy. But is it not also the circle within which it encloses itself? Appearance, i.e., beauty, the body, the sensuous, beautiful forms without content, illusion: these are exalted, absolutized, even divinized; they take the place of "true being," of truth conceived of as pure self-identity, the purely logical "being," the A = A closed to becoming and to history. Do they not, then, become a new totality, a new absolute, an aesthetic absolute that sustains itself by abasing the former absolute, knowledge? Consider the new motto: "art against science;" "We have art not to perish from the truth." At the outset science is treated as a form of subordinate, inferior, dangerous illusion—dangerous because it fails to recognize itself as illusion. The motto derived from the "metaphysics of the artist" that closes the fragment "Life Amidst Appearance As Goal" therefore requires the lucid acceptance of illusion, a trust in the beneficent character of appearances. Yet, has not the idea of *goal* become obscure, even obsolete? To be sure, the logic of reversal implies the idealization of appearances, especially as artistic transfiguration, but how is it possible to posit as ideal, as goal, that which constitutes what Nietzsche later calls "the true and unique reality of things"?[2] Doesn't this amount to the circular positing (perhaps even without realizing it in a speculative structure) of the real as ideal and of the ideal as real? Finally, why is this difference to be maintained? If there is no other "reality" than appearance, why is it even necessary to keep the word "appearance" whose traditionally restrictive connotation reappears inevitably, and why reintroduce the idea of goal that entails a separation and distance to fill, an ideal to implement? Wouldn't it then be necessary to do without the word "appearance," since it surreptitiously brings back not only the Platonic opposition between truth and illusion, between the same and the other, but also the Kantian and Schopenhauerian opposition between the thing-in-itself and the phenomenon?

As early as *The Birth of Tragedy,* Nietzsche confronts these issues through his critique of Schopenhauer: "The will is part of appearances."[3] Or elsewhere: "the will is nothing but appearances themselves,"[4] or yet elsewhere: "plurality is already in the will."[5]

Even following Schopenhauer's reasoning, how can we understand, he asks, that the nocturnal, blind, and unlimited In-itself casts itself forward into the light of a world, and subjects itself to individuation, to norm, figure, measure, unless it is inhabited by an "originary desire for appearance",[6] unless it is permeated by primordial diversification (the plurality of archetypes or ideas)? Nietzsche applies to Schopenhauer the Hegelian critique of the *otherworldly.* Everything here in appearances is as it is in the "beyond," entailed by the fantastic interior of willing, i.e., everything is already pluralized, already fragmented, already diffracted into innumerable facets. The will for parousia, or manifestation of the absolute, as Hegel calls it, implies for Nietzsche its originary pluralization and fragmentation. In short, "appearances" could not be conceived as a fall, or as illusory exteriorization, or as the loss and degradation of the absolute in its figures. "Appearances" is the name for a universal process of transfiguration.

Furthermore, the Apollonian appearance should not be conceived as the contrary of the Dionysian essence, of which it would be the degraded image. The Dionysian is not the essence of things, which would stand apart like the Schopenhauerian will; on the contrary, its manifestation belongs to its essence. For how would it be possible to understand the Dionysian if not as the unbounded power of producing appearances, as the power of phenomenalization, which is always in excess of any positive phenomenality?

In the texts of Nietzsche's youth, as well as in some later texts from the 1880s, the term "appearance" is devoid of a contrary. Being is being apparent, which, at the end of Nietzsche's itinerary, is self-offering from a perspective, self-manifestation from a point of view, appearing in just such a way, at just such a force according to just this degree. In spite of Nietzsche's evolution, from one end to the other of his philosophy, "appearance" is all that comes to daylight.

Thus, from the outset, is not Platonism, as conception of the hierarchy and separation between a higher being and a degraded one, between two "worlds"—the first, the eternal model, and the second, its changing copy—more overcome than merely overturned? Rather than being merely overturned, Platonic duality seems to have been dismissed altogether.

Yet the strange and stubborn persistence of the concept of "appearance" (no matter how much modified) in Nietzsche's problematic and vocabulary no doubt poses an obstacle to this definitive dismissal or elimination. A late, equally famous, passage from *The Twilight of Idols* is the counterpart to the famous fragment concerning the overturning of Platonism. It seems to solve definitively the problem of Platonic duality: "We have rid ourselves of the true world: what world are we left with? Perhaps that of appearances? ... But no! *Along with the true world, we have also rid ourselves of the apparent world.*"[7] Now, isn't the opposition between truth and appearance *maintained,* be it only as contrast, with such a negation? For what are we left with? The former "apparent" world and the "false" other world! Put differently, the world and "nothing"; that is to say, "nothing else" than the world. "The antinomy between the apparent and the true world is reducible to the antinomy between being and nothingness",[8] he writes. Isn't it still necessary to rely on an opposition, on an antinomy, in this case the one between the world and nothingness, in order to make a metaphysical claim? Nietzsche had caught a glimpse here of the ultimate, i.e., insurmountable, difficulty. Doesn't claiming the absolute value and universality of appearances implicitly amount to claiming the relative value of what would pretend not to be a *mere* appearance? Can one do without any antithesis between the "apparent" and the "true," an antithesis that is reborn at the very core of generalized appearance as soon as one establishes the least difference or hierarchy? Hence he writes, "To unlearn our antinomies, such is the task."[9] But how is it possible to *unlearn* them if not thanks to another experience and by dint of another, more joyful, knowledge? Is not the thought of the Eternal Return the only one by which we can escape the entire network of antinomies articulated around the cardinal opposition between being and becoming? Is not the Eternal Return in one of its major formulations, "To impress the mark of being upon becoming,"[10] aiming to cancel the Platonic antinomy?

Nietzsche seems resigned to the coupling of metaphysical categories as a "constraint of repetition" that forces him to maintain the traditional antinomies while denying them (e.g., "truth is this sort of error"), to continue using the term "appearance" even in the latest fragments, while claiming it is fundamentally inadequate, improper, and dangerous, thus giving us the impression that between 1870 and 1888 he was merely running on the spot.

How could Nietzsche simultaneously denounce and give way to this constraint, which seems to come from metaphysical structures ingrained in language? Isn't it proof, as Heidegger claimed, that Nietzsche "remains entirely closed in metaphysics"?[11] Isn't it proof that he got himself entangled in it, caught in its traps? The Nietzschean rehabilitation of the sensuous and of the living body may well attempt to raise itself far above the mere positivism of the nineteenth century; yet does it not constitute a "definitive intertwining in metaphysics"?[12] Such is the Heideggerian suspicion.

Yet on one side, the lucidity evident in the early works concerning the traps of language,[13] the metaphysical and even theological charge of words, and especially of grammar, and on the other side, the work of displacement, of transmutation operated on certain words (such as the word "appearance," when it extends so far as designating *every* manifestation in the world)—do all these factors leave the old antinomies, upon which metaphysics rests, untouched? Does Heidegger mean that Nietzsche does not escape metaphysics as the thought that forgets Being for the sake of beings as such (while seeking a reason for being in an ontic foundation, such a foundation being allegedly the Will to Power as the synergy of all forces). Or does he mean that Nietzsche does not escape metaphysics *as Platonism,* i.e., as the thought of a dichotomy between sensible and supra-sensible worlds?

It could very well be that Nietzsche escapes metaphysics as understood in the second sense. For isn't the *Umdrehung,* the reversal—in which the sensible and the apparent become the true, and the supra-sensible becomes the illusory—really a *Herausdrehung,* an "extrication," i.e., a way of tearing oneself away by a sort of turning motion *(drehen)* from this intertwining? The question of the *Überwindung,* i.e., of the "overcoming" of Platonism, or more modestly of a passage beyond it, remains open at the end of the first chapter of Heidegger's *Nietzsche:* "How far the overturning of Platonism extends with Nietzsche, how far it can go, to what extent it comes to an overcoming and to what extent not—those are necessary critical questions. But they should be posed only when we have reflected in accordance with the thought that Nietzsche most intrinsically willed—beyond everything captious, ambiguous, and deficient which we might very easily ascribe to him here."[14]

Thus, Heidegger refers us to a reading of Nietzsche's subsequent and lengthy production (over the next fifteen years, he says) if we want to resolve the issue, and yet his own commentary has already moved away from the topic! Let us read once more the initial injunction: "Life Amidst Appearance As Goal." This motto is quite ambiguous. For it can assume a perfectly affirmative, ontological, even ethical sense: one must be like the Greeks, "superficial by dint of profundity" (having fathomed the fearsome abyss upon which the world rests and being capable of being content with the skin depth of things); one must think without being ponderous, without weighing things down with gravity or multiple hidden strata; one must not cultivate the illusion of absolute knowledge, or of any knowledge, but rather immerse oneself both in "gay science" and "tragic knowledge" (which teach that illusion is necessary to thought, just as sleep and forgetfulness are necessary to human beings; and that science at its sharpest point turns into art). But this motto can be interpreted, mostly in the light of the Heideggerian reading, as the expression of a nihilism both manifest and latent. To live in the midst of appearances amounts to claiming that life is the flickering of the surfaces, an infinite game of masks and fantasies, and that it rests upon fables. It means *to want to err,* to prefer making mistakes *oneself,* rather than *being led* into mistakes. The position of such a "goal," necessarily indeterminate, can only force the will that projects appearances to come back upon itself endlessly, as the true goal, in order to force itself to will *itself* unconditionally. "Life amidst appearance as goal" might therefore be the first implicit formulation of the will as will! Once more the question arises, why should we take as *goal* the necessary and unavoidable condition of life? And the response comes forth: in order to defend life from the destruction that threatens it when it loses itself in a pseudo "true world," one of the fixed items or ideal stabilizations that we find in logic, science, or reactive morals. But since, *stricto sensu,* this true world is appearance *par excellence,* isn't the affirmation of "truth" as stability, the arbitrary "identification" that negates becoming (which is thus an "error")? Isn't this affirmation *also* the projection of a series of appearances? Now, if in the choice between two major "appearances," science and art, one chooses the second in preference to the first, i.e., the one that requires and produces the highest degree of appearance, illusion, fiction, isn't this requirement still made in the name of some concern for truth, i.e., in order to remain *faithful* to life, to *conform* to its most fundamental essence, the projecting of an illusion? In this case, Nietzsche would appear to remain always subjected to the traditional ideal of truth as correctness, rectitude, *adaequatio.* Hence Heidegger's probing: Nietzsche does not seem to have been able to question this traditional definition of truth. Yet, although by and large he remained prisoner to it, didn't he at the same time discover something else, i.e., the universal and pure phenomenality, i.e., the radical immanence and the unique plane of the phenomena?

The invocation of a goal, however, is paradoxical. *Das Leben im Schein als Ziel. Als Ziel:* as early as *The Birth of Tragedy,* Nietzsche rejects any position of a goal for life, or nature in general, any teleology immanent in the totality. Every individual goal, and, even more, a universal one, imposes an ideal external to becoming, an ideal that looks down upon the latter and inevitably ends up abasing it. The obsession with goals causes fissions, dualisms, and fabricates other worlds. Metaphysically speaking, this refusal of a goal brings Nietzsche closer to Schopenhauer, or more exactly connects him to a Schopenhauerian context from which, at that time, he had not freed himself. "For the will there is no question of a goal."[15] The will is blind, all it does is will, it does not know why or even what. In the eyes of the Nietzsche of *The Birth of Tragedy* or of the *Fragments* contemporary with it, goals are mere "phantasms" (*Wahnvorstellungen,* i.e., literally "crazy representations," fixed or delirious ideas (*Wahn* means "delirium"), or even "hallucinations" (*Wahngebilde*)). The Socratic *Wahnvorstellung,* that of science, is the delirious illusion that it is possible to know the essence of things in their depths and better still to correct them. But every idea is such a phantasm. The entire universe of representations from logic, science, morals, metaphysics falls under the concept of phantasm. "Phantasms: the one that sees through them has nothing but art for his consolation."[16] Art itself is a particular form of phantasm. "The artistic appearance makes us see the world according to the phantasm of its necessity."[17] It is surprising that Nietzsche should speak here of goal when he rejects the very notion of goal even more than he does later in *Thus Spoke Zarathustra* ("It is high time that man should assign a goal to himself: it is not man, but the Overman, that is the goal"). Art is a spontaneous production of nature through the artist. It is therefore necessary to conceive the expression "as goal" as the affirmation of the primacy of the value of art, but also to concede that it reintroduces an opposition between a more illusory phantasm (science) and a lesser one (art). To what extent does Nietzschean philosophy succeed in extracting itself from the Platonic-Schopenhauerian opposition between the true In-itself and the illusory phenomenon? Does the reign of generalized appearance anticipate phenomenology, or does it fall prey to the illusion of nihilism and the triumph of illusions?

"Life amidst appearance" for the young Nietzsche already means total life, full, if not absolute, being. What is the meaning of the expression he uses, *Sein als Schein* (Being as appearing)? *Der Schein* means *semblance*, erroneous appearance, a false look, but also it has the non-restrictive connotation of simple luminous radiation, from the verb *scheinen* (to shine, to glisten): it is what is *appearing, what appears in its radiance, what truly shines forth.* Should *Schein* be understood first and foremost as *phenomenon, Erscheinung,* i.e., as the luminous manifestation and the transparency of what shows itself, or, on the contrary, should it be understood as a superficial and false image, a mere inconsistent reflection and illusion? Deleuze claims that appearance in Nietzsche is a *simulacrum*, a simulation of the same, a simulated resemblance, an effect of what he calls the "Dionysian machine." By contrast, Heidegger's interpretation of *Schein* in the first lecture of *Nietzsche I* takes it to be a self-showing with something phenomenological about it. Artistic appearance presents life in the clarity of its being, that is to say, in its highest clarity. But, then, how are we to understand that this supreme clarity should only be a perspective, an illusion? Nietzsche described the philosopher as caught in the nets of language. Isn't this evidence of his own entanglement within the word Schein? "There are some *disastrous [verhängnisvolle]* words, that seem to express some knowledge, while in fact they represent *an obstacle* against it; among these are the words *Schein* [appearance] and *Erscheinung* [phenomenon]."[18] Concerning Kant, Nietzsche said later that the most "fatal" word of all is the word *"Erscheinung,"* the phenomenon that still preserves the In-itself, the other worldly. The word *Schein* produces *Scheinbarkeit,* semblance, logical appearance, transcendental illusion. How, we may ask again, are we to understand the ultimate, twilit formula, "Along with the true world we have rid ourselves *[abgeschafft]* of the apparent world"? Does the "appearance" that still *remains present* in the Nietzschean vocabulary, although it is often surrounded by quotation marks or is written as a *word to exclude*(!),[19] entail the defeat or the dissolution of Plato's metaphysical difference, or merely its displacement? If appearance becomes the "unique reality," the sole level of Being, one must concede that something else happens besides the reversal pure and simple—in the sense of a maintained upside-down position—of the Platonic schema. There is still a metaphysics since there is a name for beings as such, namely the living flux of the appearances produced by the Will to Power. But isn't this a self-canceling metaphysics, one that slides toward the "everything equal," toward the leveling and indifferentiation in meaning?

The generalization of appearance, however, does not result from some hatred for or indifference to truth. On the contrary, it results from a rejection of a genealogy of truth, conceivably originating in hatred and in "the secret will to die." If the issue is the task of loving truth in the way of an artist, that is "with its veils," by revering and admiring what remains hidden after each appearing, then the nihilistic leveling seems to be excluded. Indeed, if appearances as phenomenal amount originarily to appearance or showing, then doesn't the doctrine of generalized appearance itself designate a form of unveiling, of non-latency?

Yet the suspicion remains: Can the doctrine of generalized appearances retain something of a *secret reserve* in the appearing? Is it not destined to lead to the infinite platitude of a bottomless surface game, a despairing one-dimensionality? If in the later, as well as earlier, Nietzsche we find nothing but *one single plane,* that of "appearance," i.e., an infinity of perspectives[20] and points of view, are we not condemned to a strict *phenomenalism,* to some phantasmagoria, or to dreaming awake, where the world is reduced to an endless round of mirages? Isn't the belief in the Eternal Return then merely necessary to bring back some consistency to this dream, to this mirage? If every "goal" is an appearance, in the sense of a point of view, life amidst appearances is its own "goal." The place for the ideal, final, and transcendental goal is obviously empty. The world is an appearance, and outside it there is nothing.

Nietzsche is alleged to have rung in the reign of the uniformity of all points of view, the triumph of the "total absence of meaning," and of "completed absurdity." Such an interpretation, which is Heidegger's, actually goes against the explicit meaning of Nietzsche's analyses, since he intends to overcome nihilism by positing a new hierarchy, hence the contrary of leveling. Indeed, the reversal of values means that art is to be preferred over science and placed above it so as to legislate over it: "Consider science from the perspective of the artist, but art from the perspective of life!"[21] Must one admit with Heidegger that such an overturning presupposes the cynicism of calculation and leads to the equalization of all values from the perspective that dominates from now on, the artistic Will to Power? For Heidegger, valuation as such, i.e., thought functioning in terms of values, is calculating, since all values are "calculated" to support such and such forces and to promote their self-intensification; valuation announces the unconditional reckoning of goals in general in the era of technological planning. Scientific values, but mostly the artistic ones, are, according to Heidegger, "circuitous terms"[22] for "technology," of which they are the unthought anticipation. Art is art only because it continuously stimulates and reinforces power. The Heideggerian interpretation demands that we take sides: Is Nietzsche's philosophy "merely" the overturning of Platonism? Or does it go beyond such an overturning and is it, by way of the "completed metaphysics" that it prepares, the adumbration of the unleashing of power for power's sake? But why should the unleashing of technological domination present itself as the reign of art?

If in the context of *The Birth of Tragedy* appearance means both something pejorative, echoing Plato's *phantasma*[23] (i.e., the erroneous image or deceitful semblance that is later translated in modern terms as phantasmagoric representation and as "delirious idea") and something non-pejorative and radically innovative (namely the manifestation, phenomenalization, or projection of the Dionysian power), what then is the ultimate meaning of appearance in Nietzsche's early philosophy? Isn't the phenomenological sense of appearance eliminated, and doesn't appearance regain its traditional sense of illusion, even though it is assimilated to phenomenality and to appearing in general? Doesn't Nietzsche remain, in spite of what Deleuze[24] claims, prisoner to a mere *anti-Platonism,* i.e., to the "anti-metaphysical" affirmation of the *truth of illusion?*

For Deleuze, appearance amounts to a *simulacrum,* that is to say, an image whose resemblance with the original would be feigned, *simulated.* For him, phantasm-appearance defined in terms of *simulacrum* (as copy without a model, or an image *without any resemblance* to an original) escapes the opposition between true and illusory worlds, between the same (model) and the semblance (copy).

> By rising to the surface, the simulacrum causes the Same and the Similar, the model and the copy to sink under the power of the false [phantasm]. The simulacrum renders impossible the following: the order of participations, the fixity of the distribution, and the determination of the hierarchy. It inaugurates the world of nomadic distributions and of crowned anarchies. [25]

Although Deleuze is not wrong in detecting in the overturning of Platonism more than a mere reversal of the hierarchy and the leveling of meaning, in my view, his interpretation raises a twofold objection. First, what corresponds in Nietzsche's text to the notion of *simulacrum?* Doesn't Deleuze introduce this notion inappropriately? For what Nietzsche calls "phantasm" is in keeping with the admittedly restrictive and pejorative concept of "delirious representation" *(Wahnvorstellung).* Consider the obsession with science dating back to Socrates, truth at any price, at the price of fanaticism (death is preferable to error); such an illusion—that truth is the greatest good—amounts to an *idée fixe.* Such a fixed idea does not "simulate" anything. It erroneously believes in the saving power of truth, understood as identity and fixedness pure and simple–free of stain, evil, error, both immutable and unmarred by becoming. The notion of "phantasm" taken in Nietzsche's sense has absolutely nothing to do with an imitation or a simulation. As an *idée fixe,* or obsessive idea, it has no connection whatsoever with a false idea, much less with objective *simulacra* such as false pearls, or those gun or aircraft decoys used to *fool the enemy* as to the nature of the real weapons at one's disposal. To be sure, we find in Nietzsche the idea of *fiction* (the Will to Power constantly produces fictitious identities, such as the logical identities and the laws of nature). But we never find the idea of *simulation* and especially not the idea of a "demonic image,"[26] which for Deleuze amounts to pure dissimilitude or pure otherness, without any resemblance with anything. The "high power of the false" that rules over art according to Nietzsche is not diabolical because it only presents the "false" with respect to "truth," defined in Platonic fashion as self-equality or as the sameness of the same. The diabolical character of appearances would presuppose some hypostasis of the other, an inversion that would make the other into the model of infinite dissemblances. A sort of black mass or witches' Sabbath, this is what the Nietzschean play of appearances becomes in Deleuze's interpretation.

The second objection concerns the notion of a suppression of the original. The fact that for Nietzsche there is no model for appearances in general does not mean that there is no *origin*, and most of all it does not mean that the presence of the origin can only be alleged or simulated. Appearance refers to an originary productive power without correlation to an *original.* The Dionysian is the origin*ary,* or, if one prefers the origin*ating,* as the creative force, without however being the origin*al* of which there can be copies. Inasmuch as they *represent* Dionysian forces the Apollonian forces do not copy them, nor make manifest "an absence of origin," as is claimed by Blanchot (see the beautiful text quoted in a note by Deleuze, which seemingly is the source of his inspiration)[27]. Instead, these forces represent an original and latent presence, precisely that of the Dionysian. Is such a presence-absence "metaphysical" or not? It is metaphysical inasmuch as it functions as the *Grund,* i.e., both an ontological basis and a productive source, and is analogous to the Schopenhauerian will and hence, in the end, to *ultima ratio?* It is less so, however, if one considers that it does not contain, as in Schopenhauer, items such as archetypes and Ideas of things. It is even less metaphysical inasmuch as it is not substantial but "abyssal," a non-localized, non-determinable "location" of irruption and of the tension of forces within themselves, the principle of exchange and mutual transition between original pleasure and suffering. The originary productive power is undoubtedly a *matrix,* since it gives birth to a world, to art, and it seems impossible to interpret it either as absence of origin or as originary absence, or as empty location for the fallen origin, or even as the originary absence of meaning.

Indeed, if the artistic Will to Power is itself named "the highest power of the false," surely this is not with respect to a truth that might be superior to it, but rather because it is this very power that finds itself settled *in the full position of origin,* and recognized as such. Or should we say that tragedy and the work of art in general are born out of nothing, from the "absence of origin"? By what sleight of hand are the "natural artistic impulses," their vitality, their character as forces, identified with a fundamental absence?! Through the various formulations describing Dionysos and the Will to Power, in spite of his criticisms of substance and subject, Nietzsche always recognizes and maintains the necessity that the world should have an overall structure and a "background." The reason is not that the world derives from a unique source or point of origin, but that it participates in an immanent power that has a meaning. This meaning is "being-ever-more," the originarily active or reactive direction of forces always involved in a process of self-overcoming. One of the most frequently quoted texts bears witness: "Do you want a name for this universe, a solution for all its enigmas? ... This world is the world of the Will to Power, nothing else."[28] Even if the Will to Power may not be reduced to traditional *essentia*—as Heidegger would have it[29]—it still does designate the unique and privileged name, the Being of all beings: the most radical "identity" common to the world in its entirety, to the individual living beings and to ourselves.

But the power that produces phenomena does not hold itself "behind" the phenomena. It circulates—transpires—entirely *in them,* and that is why the word "appearance" is to be preferred to the word "phenomenon," which one is inevitably tempted to understand as the appearance of something that, in part, remains hidden. "Appearances" give themselves as "reality" fully and exclusively.

In fact, Nietzsche identifies in striking fashion "appearance" *(Schein),* "the true and unique reality of things," and "Will to Power." Let us consider the following text "Against the Word 'Phenomenon' *[Erscheinung].*"[30]

> N.B. Appearance, in the sense I take it, is the true and unique reality of things—that only to which all existing predicates are applied and that which, to a certain extent, could not be better defined as by the totality of those predicates, i.e., also by contradictory predicates. Now this word expresses nothing but the fact of being inaccessible to logical procedures and distinctions: it is

> appearance, then, if compared to logical truth, the latter itself being possible only in an imaginary world. I do not posit therefore "appearance" in opposition to "reality;" on the contrary, I consider that appearance is reality, the one that resists any transformation into an imaginary "true world." A precise name for such a reality might be the "Will to Power," thus designated for its internal structure and not from its all-pervasive, elusive, and fluid nature.

"Appearance" is not a subject among others, but the one *subject* to which all thinkable attributes are adequate; it is the unique structure, and the unique content, of every being—whether manifest or hidden, true or deceitful, inessential or essential. It designates the totality of everything in existence and that is why all "positive" or "negative" predicates can be applied to it. There is nothing like non-appearance, except pure nothingness. Every being—real, possible, imaginary, logical or illogical—belongs to "appearance."

By rejecting the phenomenon in Kant's restricted sense (the phenomenon that leaves behind a residue of the thing-in-itself) for the benefit of generalized "appearance," doesn't Nietzsche anticipate phenomenology, i.e., the idea that every being shows itself from within itself and that appearing is equivalent with being? In the last subdivision of the *Nietzsche I* ("The New Interpretation of Sensibility"), Heidegger suggests that the Nietzschean concept of *Schein* necessarily entails the notion of the *original monstration* of beings from within themselves. There can be *semblance* only against the backdrop of some appearing, of an emerging apparition. Appearing presupposes emerging: "Every appearance and every semblance are possible only if something is able merely to show itself."[31] The condition for the possibility of appearing is the unfolding of life, or of the Will to Power, in its intimate structure, namely of those forces containing points of view capable of preservation and intensification. There are "appearances" only because the Will to Power comes to "appearance," manifests itself as a plurality of endlessly evolving perspectives.

Nietzsche attempted to surmount what he called the dangerous or "disastrous," "fatal" *(Verhängnisvoll)* character of traditional words, *Erscheinung* and *Schein,* phenomenon and appearance. For even if one crosses out the first term from the lexicon and defines the second as the single type of appearing by crossing out, so to speak, the idea of originary productive ground, the mere word *Schein* irresistibly restores the caesura between manifest and hidden. The word never ceased irritating Nietzsche, who was never able to dismiss it entirely. It seemed to him, however, that he should have. Such a word has no more meaning, no more "reason for being"! "There is not even left here a shadow of reason to speak of *appearance.*"[32] Why, in applying such a principle and after dismissing both the true world and the *apparent* one, doesn't he also dismiss the *word* "appearance"? He *almost* does so at times, in order to speak only of the "world," or of the Will to Power, or Dionysos. Thus, for example, when he writes, "The antinomy of the apparent world and the true one is reducible to the antinomy between the *world* and *nothingness,*" it is all too evident that the reference to appearance still serves to define the *single world*. Thus also in Section 568 of the old edition of *The Will to Power,* which bears the title "Critique of the Concept 'True and Apparent World,'" he writes: "Appearance itself belongs to reality ... In a world where there is no being, a certain calculable world of identical cases must first be created through appearance."[33] Or elsewhere: "The 'real world,' however one has hitherto conceived it, has always been the apparent world *once again.*"[34] "Fundamentally, Plato, as the artist he was, *preferred appearance* to being lie and poetic invention *[Erdichtung]* to truth, the unreal to the present-at-hand *[Vorhandenen]!* But he was so convinced of the full value of appearance that he gave it the attributes 'being,' 'causality' and 'goodness,' and 'truth,' in short everything men value."[35] Positing appearances as does the man of knowledge, or the philosopher who arbitrarily "fixates" identities, or the artist who is more faithful to becoming, amounts only to suggesting interpretations of the unique force productive of appearances.

If Nietzsche "lost" the sense of the "appearing" that he found implicitly operative in appearances, the reason is that he had no sooner caught sight of it than he reverted to the old structure of truth as *adaequatio.* Such a definition of truth can be found indeed throughout the questioning of the value of appearances, or more radically the value of values. To say that art has more value than truth, amounts to saying that art is "truer," i.e., as Heidegger shows it, "more in agreement with becoming" or with the Being of beings as Will to Power, than "truth," defined as the fixation of logical and scientific truths. Nietzsche does not question the principle according to which the true is more adequate to what appears. Artistic appearance is more true than truth as permanence, stability, non-contradiction, because it displays a greater concordance with the infinite flux of life, which is also called "chaos." The equation appearance = living reality is a simple overturning of Platonism. This does not mean that the Nietzschean path does not take him beyond such an overturning.

Indeed, paradoxically this path requires both *maintaining a hierarchy* (art above science, reversing the previous one that had science above art) and *abolishing every hierarchy,* since in such an inversion of values every value derives its origin from the sole principle of appearance.

Which of these two consequences of the overturning—one being the new scale of values that derives from the primacy of the artistic Will to Power, which is the source of knowledge through the production of fictions, and the other being the equalization of every value in the generalization of appearance—which consequence, the hierarchy or the leveling-off, ends up winning in Nietzsche's later philosophy? Might not the later Nietzsche have stepped back from the advance he had made beyond Schopenhauer at the time of *The Birth of Tragedy,* canceling the thing-in-itself, but keeping the idea of reserve, of privacy, or of a withdrawal from being immersed amidst phenomenalization? "Each time truth unveils herself, the artist can only remain with his gaze fixed on what is still hidden in the unveiling."[36] "To love truth *with* its veils," and not without veils nor under veils, such seems to be Nietzsche's both first and last position: the impossibility of a total, complete unveiling, as required by science, the necessity of an unveiling acknowledging privacy, one never completed, and harboring a secret reserve. Now, the idea of generalized appearances deriving their origins from a single principle could lead us to believe that Nietzsche is returning to some phenomenalist version of Schopenhauer according to which there would be appearances only with respect to the veil of Maya. One of the most striking texts in this respect is Section 54 of *The Gay Science,* precisely with the title, "The Consciousness of Appearance," in which knowledge turns out to be nothing more than a dream, a dream built upon the oldest past in one's life, a dream that is necessary, impossible to overcome:

> I suddenly woke up in the midst of this dream, but only to the consciousness that I am dreaming and that I must go on dreaming lest I perish—as a somnambulist must go on dreaming lest he fall. What is "appearance" for me now? Certainly not the opposite of some essence: what could I say about any essence except to name the attributes of its appearance? Certainly not a dead mask that one could place on an unknown X or remove from it! Appearance is for me that which lives and is effective and goes so far in its self-mockery that it makes me feel that this is appearance and will-o'-the-wisp and a dance of spirits and nothing more—that among all these dreamers, I, too, who "know," am dancing my dance; that the knower is a means for prolonging the earthly dance and thus belongs to the masters of ceremony of existence; and that the sublime consistency and

> interrelatedness of all knowledge perhaps is and will be the highest means to *preserve* the universality of dreaming and the mutual understanding of all dreamers and thus also the *continuation of the dream.*[37]

Here knowledge is not seen from the point of view of art, but in the perspective of a force of "fiction-making" that is more elementary than art itself, a force that produces appearances conceived as universal living inventiveness. Maya's veil no longer covers anything, has neither an origin nor an end, but forms as coherent a fabric as the world does in Schopenhauer's view. Dionysos regulated by the principle of reason, Apollo meets Dionysos. There is coincidence between the regulative principle of forms and the lucid dispensation of forces. Such a paradoxical world, firm and fluid at the same time, both substantial and dreamlike, nevertheless excludes a *pure Apollonism* and a *pure Dionysm*. For pure Apollonism would require that the illusion of appearances (pertaining to knowledge as much as art) never be destroyed or revealed (indeed, science never escapes its phantasm of truth, never acknowledges that it is dreaming, while art shows dream as such, namely as fiction); and pure Dionysm, even more impossibly, would require the immediate embrace of life,[38] an obscure immanence of the Will to Power that would dwell among its own chaos without ever projecting any "value," in order to interpret itself and register an increase. Absolute disillusionment in the midst of knowledge and absolute illusion in the midst of life would be untenable *border situations,* which would be reversed to their contraries and, paradoxically, fused and identified. There is no absolute illusion, and therefore no dance, that does not know that it is dancing, that is not "ironic toward itself."

*Illusion* ("dream") *recognized as such* is illusion that has been shattered and stripped, not some illusion caught in the midst of its own confusion. The fact that the Will to Power can, and must, *want* illusion means that *it is not mistaken itself,* that it recognizes itself as the source of all perspectives, that it is "in the true."

Is it the case or not, that this point of view encompassing all points of view corresponds to an unconditional, to an *anhypotheton,* to a metaphysical essence of things in the traditional sense? Heidegger is ready to acknowledge that there probably is in the Nietzschean originary unfolding of perspectives the idea of an openness accompanied by a withdrawal, and something akin to the echo of the Greek *aletheia.* "Adequation and disclosedness, *adaequatio* and *aletheia* rule over the Nietzschean concept of truth as the prolonged and nevertheless unheeded echo of the metaphysical essence of truth."[39] What is the strange withdrawal that rules over the unfolding of illusion? Such a withdrawal is twofold: the illusion reveals itself, is being disclosed and thus negates itself, but recreates itself and weaves its veil again as soon as tearing occurs. In other words, the illusion is being abolished when it gains knowledge of itself as such, but the power that produces either useful fictions (the true) or stimulating ones (art), remains intact, restores itself indefatigably. Thus, the metaphysical essence of truth as adequation, which states that every value is reducible to "art" because art alone is in concordance with life as power of illusion, *is being doubled with the secret reserve of the artistic force* that animates the entire universe and, in the renewed upsurge of its primordial simplicity, *causes one to forget endlessly its essence by returning to and within itself.*

The reserve of the "artistic force" that is being creative throughout every living being, but mostly throughout the artist, such a force that "we see at work within ourselves,"[40] is radically different from an In-itself such as the will in Schopenhauer. Such a reserve is not another realm. It only means that the unique plane of appearances, which allows no other world, is not devoid of a backdrop. Its self-envelopment entails that the world is not reduced to the scattering of dispersed surfaces, *partes extra partes*, but that the bodies maintain themselves, correspond to each other, and articulate themselves amidst the thrust of the forces, and that the reserve, or latency, of the world refers to the ever-unbridgeable difference between forms and forces.

The metaphysics of appearance operates in a double way, or leads to a double conclusion. By bestowing upon appearance the dignity of the essence, *it keeps sustaining Platonism while abolishing it.* It sustains it especially by insisting upon the difference between the originary and the derived, between the affirmation of appearance and its negation, between becoming and "being," between the artistic Will to Power and the "logical" fixations of the truth such as the true, the same, the non-contradictory. It abolishes Platonism by affirming that "everything is appearance,"[41] that there is only a single world and a "single level" of life, or that the Eternal Return "impresses upon becoming the mark of being,"[42] i.e., brings to coincidence Plato's opposed terms. In such a fashion, the metaphysical difference between existence and essence is implicitly suppressed. Appearance does not refer to any other realm of beings than itself. The generalization of appearances thus opens the way to a leveling of beings that for Heidegger amounts to the prelude of the forgetfulness not only of Being, but also of metaphysics as such. This double forgetfulness allegedly constitutes the unthought of the post-Nietzschean era, that of technology. Nietzsche's metaphysics remains just short of its completion: it merely constitutes the "penultimate step"[43] before the final one of the "will-to-will." In "completed metaphysics,"[44] no longer is there any stated or explicit metaphysics: every meaning of Being has become "evident," beyond questioning. The abolition of Platonism would thus lead to frantic nihilism, to a "perfect absence of meaning" *(vollendete Sinnlosigkeit)*[45] of the artificial world where the "destitution of the absence of destitution"[46] rules.

Nietzsche's metaphysics of appearance confirms for Heidegger the traditional essence of metaphysics and yet opens the way to its complete disappearance. How does such a double-edged theory, turned on one side toward the past and on the other toward the future, get to be articulated to form a single position? In other words, how can Heidegger justify the simultaneity of the sustaining and the eliminating of Platonism? Is there a link between the eliminating of metaphysics and the unleashing of the technological will-to-will? Is it possible to retrace the logic of the transition from the penultimate to the ultimate step? Let us try to answer these questions briefly.

The *sustaining of Platonism* is manifest by way of a double structure in Nietzsche's thought. On the one hand, there is *adaequatio, homoiosis* (the adequation of the sensible realm to "chaos"): *art* is *the most adequate* response made by the Will to Power to its own foundation, the changing and illusory flux of the forces and perspectives. Yet, it must be stressed that the secret reserve of the artistic force *of the world* (whether or not it originates beyond any artistic production) seems to escape any sort of adequation. On the other hand, we witness the *separation,* the *chorismos,* the determination of a difference between a foundational reality and a derived one: science, logic are mere fictions—which do not know, do not recognize, themselves as such—derived from some originary "fiction-producing."

*Adequation:*

"The sensible world is false, contradictory, deceitful. Art alone is *in agreement* with the essential characters of our world."[47]

"As an aesthetic phenomenon, existence is still *bearable* for us" and art gives us the means "to be able to turn ourselves into such a phenomenon."[48]

*Hierarchy* between the originary and the derived, the foundational and the founded:

"The will-to-know is founded on another much more powerful will, the will-not-to-know."[49]

"The world of the spirit, this world of signs is nothing but appearance and illusion."[50] "It is the greatest artists in abstractions that created the categories."[51] The logical forms, the world of science and "identical cases" derive from the artistic Will to Power, which is thus the common source of all "truth" (as fiction of identity and stability) and of appearance. There is indeed a new inverted hierarchy of the true and false:

"The respect for truth is the consequence of an illusion. One must rank the plastic, simplifying, constructive, inventive force *higher*."[52]

*The neutralization or the dismissal of Platonism* is linked to positing appearance on a single plane, but also to the essentialization of existence that the Eternal Return produces. Indeed, after thinking the *quid*, the *essentia*, as Will to Power and the *quod*, the *existentia*, as Eternal Return, Nietzsche claims that there is *identity* of the highest Will-to Power and the Eternal Return. The traditional metaphysical difference is, in Heidegger's view, both retrieved and lost. It reemerges in its highest acuteness and, at the same time, it evacuates and empties itself of all meaning. The characters of constant presence (or consistency, or essence) can be exchanged against, and confused with, those of factuality (or contingency, or existence). This "elimination of the difference between *quiddity* and *quoddity*,"[53] which ensures that theWill to Power and the Eternal Return mutually find each other, and that both signify permanence as well as change, this elimination remains *unthought*. The pure identity of the fundamental terms of Nietzsche's philosophy, far from restoring the unity of the originary essence of the *phusis*, opens up an area of confusion in which, because no difference between the apparent and the essential is valid, what matters alone is the power to "set-up-in-front," in the sense of representing and fabricating.

But what is the unthought link that connects metaphysics and appearance in the age of modern technology? What relation of similitude—which makes possible, in spite of the inevitable leap from one epoch to another, such a transition as, say, from the Aristotelian *energeia* to the Medievals' *actualitas*—can be established between the generalization of fiction on the one hand and the reign of "machination" *(Machenschaft)* or universally imposed reckoning on the other?[54]

Heidegger discovers this unthought link in what might be called the hidden rationalism of the most affirmative Will to Power, i.e., in the artistic Will to Power. Art is not a game without goal, since it is precisely its goal to establish values that allow the will to ensure itself of itself absolutely, to be unequivocally certain of itself. "Values are everywhere *reducible* to numerical and mensural scales of force,"[55] Nietzsche wrote. In other words, values are instruments, points of anchor that have been moored consciously and correspond to specific levels in the forces down to the least degree. In addition, Nietzsche describes the artistic Will to Power as a capacity for schematization and organization *superior to any logical will,* but of the same nature. What he calls "great style" in art consists in ordering, dominating a "chaos" from above, i.e., an originally non-unified plurality of forces. Art brings the multiple to reason. "To compel one's chaos to become form: to become logical, simple, unambiguous, mathematics, *law*—that is the great ambition here."[56] The "classical" artist knows how to choose the paradigmatic appearance, how to exclude the exception, how to repeat what is necessary—how to simplify, to concentrate, to obtain more effects with less means (according to a rational principle extremely consonant with Leibniz). The artistic will, which calculates its effects in total sovereignty, would be a foreshadowing of the will-to-dominate set to work in planetary technology, able to integrate all things in its organized planning.

But by thus granting a priority to the "rational," i.e., "effective" structure of the art-value, doesn't Heidegger forget what for Nietzsche amounts to the essential of the artistic phenomenon, namely, on the one hand *appearance* (i.e., the *fictitious* and radically irrational, *ineffective* character of artistic forms), and on the other hand the phenomenon of the artist, his body, his "physiology"? The artist is one who experiences as "content," as "the thing itself," that which non-artists call "form," including his own life.[57] Nothing is more foreign to the artist than transforming the real world, since, as Nietzsche says in the same fragment, he feels that he belongs to an "inverted world." And yet what Nietzsche describes as "the aesthetic creative state," *inebriation*, may indeed be interpreted just as well as cold, *"logical"* hyperlucidity, which is detached from every subjective passion. Such a state, however, remains the peak of subjectivity, an individual "state" that the work will have to reawaken and bring to life again in the subjectivity of the "spectator." It must therefore be granted that there is a rupture, an *absolute leap,* between, on the one hand, the game-oriented character (as well as the subjectivism) of art and on the other hand, the desperately serious efficiency (as well as the perspective-free, neutral, and world-wide realism) of the technological "Enframing."

The young Nietzsche had already called his philosophy a "metaphysics for artists."[58] Beyond a "metaphysics of art" in the fashion of the Romantics and a physiology of the artist, this philosophy constitutes what could be called, in a Heideggerian perspective, an "aesthetic onto-theology." For the issue is not only to consider, i.e., to rank all things, the entire world, from the perspective of art, but in fact to claim that all phenomena are, in conformity with the essence of life, *in themselves* aesthetic phenomena. Aesthetics, claimed the young Nietzsche, is to be thought of as "a science of nature," i.e., as a doctrine of beings as such. Let us quote once more:

> As an aesthetic phenomenon existence is still bearable for us, and art furnishes us with eyes and hands and above all the good conscience to be *able* to turn ourselves into such a phenomenon.[59]

He claims more clearly in the 1886 Fragments: "The world in itself is nothing else but art," "the universe is a self-creating work of art."[60]

The artistic Will to Power is not only the diffuse essence of all things, but their divine essence, *Dionysos*. Nietzsche even sometimes sketches out a theodicy that justifies the absolute creative power of every indictment of evil: "I think that the existence of evil and suffering proves nothing against the artistic genius of God. Perhaps only against his 'goodness.'"[61]

The relationship that, for a while,[62] Heidegger wanted to establish between the artistic Will to Power and the technological will-to-will rests on the sole notion of "calculus" being common to both. For each, the will would "calculate" the values needed in order to support and promote the various forces in the process of maturation or various groups of such forces in activity. Yet the artist's hand does not "calculate" its moves as the C.E.O. of a company calculates investments, gains, and expenses. The aimless calculus of the creator has nothing to do with the Leibnizian calculation of the planner. The competition between fictions, which in any case cannot rule in isolation and are forced to compose, to play, within themselves, has nothing to do with the technological, economic, and political competition that has to take account of the constraining laws of the market that reach throughout the planet. In his latest texts *(What is Called Thinking?),* Heidegger renounces turning Nietzsche into the involuntary prophet of the technological Enframing: he sees in him the thinker who liberates us from metaphysics' fundamental will for ressentiment, i.e., from the hatred for everything temporal and temporary, the hatred for everything that is mere transition, for anything no sooner appearing than doomed to disappear.

Appearances appear and disappear continuously. Doesn't saying that they return eternally amount to speaking in images, with symbols, according to appearances? The answer, indeed, is positive. But doesn't this aesthetic transfiguration of appearance, its "eternalization," simply raise it to the level of the former truth. Appearance does not function as some new absolute. It only reveals the generic name of all interpretations. The "metaphysics of appearance" signifies that there are only interpretations, that there is no longer a *metaphysical* difference. Isn't the leveling, or the removal, of metaphysical distinctions, itself a metaphysics? Such is the debate opened up by the Heideggerian interpretation. But is this not, first and foremost, a debate over the essence of metaphysics, rather than one over Nietzsche's thought?

# Chapter 4

## The Native Malady of Language

*The word is of delicate health,*
*Now sick, now convalescent.*
"The Word," *Gedichte* (Kröner Edition, p. 513).

Nietzsche's explicit discussions of language seem merely to prolong a debate that is as old as metaphysics. They champion the nominalist point of view, which makes language the simple result of convention, and oppose the Cratylian point of view, which derives language from the nature of things. Thus, posing in his turn the question of the origin of language, Nietzsche appears merely to repeat the ancient alternative: Are words an *adequation* to *nomos,* to man in society, or to *phusis,* to Being? Are they *signs,* chosen arbitrarily and perhaps ultimately nothing more than *flatus vocis,* or are they *symbols* that stand in natural and essential relations to things?

Nietzsche's answer seems unambiguous: There is no bridge leading to some "In itself" of things. Words and concepts result from man-made "metaphors;" not from faithful images but from "arbitrary transpositions," forgotten originary experiences that are now forever lost. Yet, paradoxically, this rigid conventionalism immediately reverses itself. For if language is the product of the artistic activity of the human subject—the sole author of those metaphors—then it necessarily conceals a "natural" element. Words, expressing through their sounds and rhythms the movements of the *psyche,* manifest some type of Will to Power and thus reflect not only the essence of things, but also the essence of subjectivity. In this way, Nietzsche is, as Heidegger would have it, the thinker of the completion of metaphysics, the thinker who interpreted "Cratylianism" in terms of modern metaphysics to mean that language is *adequate* to the true "nature" of things, that is, to the human subject.

This Cratylianism, however, is in its turn put in question. The adequation of word and subject is blurred and rendered opaque, in that Nietzsche describes their relation as one of oblivion. The objectivity of language rests upon the subject's forgetfulness of the fictive process that produces language, and is thus illusory. The "artistic" element of language constantly masks its transpositions of the world under the guise of a purportedly stable and objective truth designed to serve communication: the concept. Linguistic fictions disguise their fictive character; language consists of dead fictions become independent of their author through amnesia. Hence, any return to the "origin" of language, to the metaphoric activity of the artistic Will to Power, is impossible—at least within the ordinary use of the linguistic code. Confronted by this "facticity" of ordinary language, the language of the herd, Nietzsche's first diagnosis is flatly pessimistic. When he observes the everyday function of language as a machine for fabricating illusory identities, for reducing all experience to "identical cases," for transmitting only banalities, superficialities, herd meanings, Nietzsche is led to a pejorative conception of the very essence of language. Not only is language intrinsically ill, it is also the carrier of the universal illness: nihilism, the triumph of the reactive forces.

Is this illness curable? How can the "singular case," the body, the most affirmative experiences be introduced into a language designed for repression? "Of all that is written, I love only what a man has written with his blood."[1] By what alchemy can words and concepts, which analysis has dissolved into bloodless and mummified things, into veritable "tombs of intuition," be transmuted into body and blood? To be sure, this inner metamorphosis of language, which runs against the tendency of its herd and metaphysical purpose, would be the advent of a *new writing*. But how could this new writing overcome the herd essence of language? Its ruses and resources (parodies, aphorisms) seem rather mere surface disturbances of a code that they indirectly confirm, perhaps reinforce. Is language as such incurable?

## Language as Symbol and Symptom

Although the majority of Nietzsche's thoughts about the origin of language are concentrated in the years 1870–1873, they are not limited to the well-known interpretation in *The Birth of Tragedy*. In fact, Nietzsche formulated nearly simultaneously *two* hypotheses, deriving language on the one hand from music and on the other from metaphor. Only later will he discover the unity and convergence of these apparently separate sources, but without ever denying or modifying his initial position. Nietzsche's unique and constant insight remains that language derives from a pre-linguistic element that controls it and is essentially "aesthetic." The apparent divergence between music and metaphor resolves itself within the core of the artistic Will to Power, the origin of every fiction. For Nietzsche, contrary to Plato *and* to Heidegger, *logos* is subject to art. *Logos* is a form of art, and not art a form of *logos*.

In *The Birth of Tragedy* and the fragments from that period, language is described as an Apollonian manifestation that reflects "symbolically" Dionysian "music."[2] The term "Dionysian music" refers to a phenomenon prior to musical art proper, whether instrumental or vocal. It designates "the original melody of the affects" (emotions, sensations, feelings), the rhythms and pulsations corresponding to shifts in intensity of the universal will. This melody of the affects, forming the "tonal background"[3] of language, does not constitute an absolute foundation; it is merely the "echo" of the sensations of pleasure and pain that constitute the primitive will.

But in what sense is language a "symbol"? It is a symbol in that it is a radically unfaithful replica. Admittedly, the relation between the melody of the affects and its different degrees of objectification (music *qua* art, epic and lyric poetry, literary and scientific prose) is regulated by a model that remains Platonic and Schopenhauerian: a relation of *reproduction,* of copying. But it is also a relation of *analogy,* from which all exact imitation is excluded. To describe this relation between "music" and language, Nietzsche uses the word *"Abbild"* ("musical mirror of the word,"[4] "Dionysian mirror of the world),"[5] but often also the word *"Gleichniss."* To symbolize, then, means to reproduce analogically, with increasing loss of the original. If the music of musicians is, like language, a *code,* a "cipher language of the affects," it is also an analogy of the original melody, Dionysian and nocturnal; language on the other hand is an Apollonian analogy, formal and luminous. Language suffers from a fundamental powerlessness to reveal what it claims to reveal: "Language, as an organ and symbol of manifestation (i.e., as a symbol of symbol) can never bring forth the most intimate basis of music."[6] At the same time, all language possesses its own musicality, a vocal aspect which refers to its origin and which also constitutes its universality, for the "tonal background" is the "same in all men" and represents "a general and comprehensible basis beyond the diversity of languages."[7] Language is divided into an arbitrary and superficial sign-aspect, linked to certain movements of the mouth, to the predominance of certain vowels and consonants; and into a symbol-aspect, an echo of the pre-linguistic melody, a vaguely proportional translation through rhythm and sound of the melody of the affects. Thus, the analogical derivation is produced by a degradation, a descent degree by degree, obedient to a pseudo-imitation, without any true continuity of emotion to sound, and of sound to sign. Poetry searches, therefore, in vain to reconstitute the affective music that has been lost since the leap from inarticulate to articulate sound. According to this pattern, all language is founded upon entropy, upon a dissipation of force that alone makes possible the fictive constitution of abstract meaning and universality.

The same structure of entropy is revealed in *Truth and Lying in the Extra-Moral Sense,* although this essay concerns neither music nor the affects. The point of departure here is perception. All perceptual experience is "metaphor," that is, transposition. The images of perception constitute transpositions of a sensuous contact immediately involved with the world, the nerve excitations. A second type of transposition is produced by words and concepts, which are entirely abstract and arbitrary metaphors of those primal metaphors of sensation. Each degree of transposition is equivalent to "a complete leap from one sphere to another."[8] By emphasizing the absolutely gratuitous character of this leap, Nietzsche rejects the "naturalness" of language only on one side—that of reality—in order to reaffirm it on the other side–that of the subject. The artistic activity of the human subject is indeed the origin of language; but unless the human subject forgets his activity of creation, of fiction, he can never confer upon words generality and objectivity. "It is only the amnesia of this original world of metaphors, it is only the fact that man forgets that he is a subject" that permits him the peace and security of a logic. Amnesia of self and forgetfulness of infinite sensory differences, such an obliteration is the first condition of language. Language is the self-dissimulation of the creative state, of which it is at the same time the product. But it is only by means of the repetition of social, collective needs that this amnesia inserts and imposes itself irrevocably. Language is founded not only upon the oblivion of metaphors (of their fictive as of their individual and discrete character), but also upon social constraints, which impose the use of only the most conventional and worn-out metaphors. In order for the herd to communicate, its language must transmit only those metaphors whose metaphoric meaning has been blunted and is lost. Only a certain type of "lying," that of totally defused fiction, is socially permitted. Language is gregarious deceit.

Yet if language is not an imitation—since it is not a real transition between the sphere of the image and that of words—it is even less a mere convention. A metaphor conserves a power of symbolization, insofar as words sustain a relation of allusion to the forgotten originary world. The original metaphoric fictions are not entirely forgotten, for words are the *"residue* of metaphor"[9] and the heterogenous spheres of image and word are linked by an aesthetic relation. Concepts are the remains of this work of fiction begun at the level of perception. As in the relation of music to language, so in the transition from image to word there is a kind of *emanation.* In words, which are the derivatives of effaced images, a trace of experience survives.

Language is preserved from arbitrariness by being a *symptom* of a force that dissipates itself (whether this be a Dionysian dissipation, or a dissipation of the uniqueness of perception) and that dissolves itself into a herd surrogate. More generally, language is a symptom of Will to Power, be it active or reactive. For although language belongs in some sense *de jure* to the artistic, therefore affirmative and active Will to Power, in fact it is constantly claimed by reactive forces. Thus, the first to arrogate to himself the "sovereign right to confer names"[10] is the affirmative, aristocratic individual. Such individuals are the strong, the happy, the well-born, and they determine according to their own natures the meaning of the word "good." This myth (and it is a myth, for the inaugural event occurred in an irretrievable past) reflects the ideal of adequation between words and the force of affirmation. To create, assuming that this is still possible, is to be innovative within language. "All those who create, are in search of a new language." But today, a time when the noble values have lost sway, the ancient words are revamped and repeated to serve the opposite values. For the man of *ressentiment,* the herd man, the words "good" and "evil" are not his own creations; they are words of a noble language whose meaning he has reversed. The "good" for the reactive man "is *precisely* the good of the other morality reinterpreted and deformed."[11] In this way, the herd instinct ends up being creative ("and also discovers its *words*)"[12] by, for example, reactively inventing a bond between "good" and "non-egoistic." As the weak triumph over the strong, so the debased and weakened meanings of words triumph over the strong meanings. This is why Nietzsche's genealogy is an historical philology for tracking down the provenance of words, for revealing the deformations of meaning that lie behind the current meanings, for exposing associated and collusive words. The symptomatic analysis of language is a phenomenology of decay.

## The Herd Code: Logic, Grammar, and Metaphysics

Dissipation of force defines language more *essentially* than affirmation of force. It would be easy to cite numerous Nietzschean aphorisms in which language itself appears as a power of deceit that levels, deforms, makes shallow, produces monstrous and absurd generalizations, aggravates the hypertrophy of consciousness, establishes the vacuous circulation of clichés. "The word flattens and makes stupid."[13] "Every word is a prejudice."[14] "Every word is a mask."[15] And yet, neither the amnesia consubstantial to language, nor the intrinsic nature of the concept which produces belief in imaginary and hidden influences, is enough to justify such a condemnation.

The essence of Nietzsche's distrust is rather that language tends inevitably to vulgarize, to make herd-like. The dominant language is always reactive—simultaneously reducer and castrater as well as protector of the weak against "dangerous" impulses and the emergence of explosive differences. Language becomes the means to this end thanks to the invention of logical, grammatical, and metaphysical categories that effect the triumph of reactive forces. Like all values, categories are fictions that support a certain type of Will to Power in order to ensure the "conservation and increase" of certain beings. The reactive will invents logic, the reduction of all phenomena to "identical cases," in order to preserve itself. The schematizations of logic, its imaginary expropriation of the real, allow the reactive will to flee its disconcerting contradictions and to shelter itself in a make-believe world of stable and reassuring identities. Thus, logical language answers to both psychological and social needs. Psychological needs: categories such as cause and effect, classifications, laws, and equivalences defend the herd against the fear of "the unformed and unformulable chaos of impulses."[16] The very principle of causality succumbs to this critique: it is necessary that causality be true only because we could not do without it; causality is a "condition of existence." Social needs: the necessity of communication demands that we posit fixed, uniform, interchangeable units of meaning—always "identical cases." The logical *will* to discover the identical and the non-contradictory is stronger the more it is reinforced by moral prejudice (identity for the herd-man is not only the True, but also the Good) and by metaphysical prejudice (those substantial identities become "subject," "substance," "being"). As defenses against impulses and differences, logic and herd-language in general are products of the repressed body: languages forever a shadow of a lost body.

Logical and metaphysical categories easily escape even radical criticisms, thanks to the subterfuge of grammar through which they insinuate themselves into the core of language. Thus, well-known theories of knowledge neglect to criticize the simple grammatical "habit" that imposes, as the basis of every proposition, an unshakeable belief in the trinity of subject-verb-predicate.[17] A reciprocal mechanism engenders and reinforces metaphysics and grammar. Every onto-theology is secretly and intransigently rooted in the elementary structures of language, which every school-age child and every reasonable person obeys. "Our oldest metaphysical foundation is the one that we rid ourselves of last—assuming we do rid ourselves of it—that foundation which is incorporated in language and in grammatical categories and makes itself indispensable just at the point where it seems that we must cease to think if we are to renounce this metaphysics."[18] Grammar induces belief in the existence of real equivalents to grammatical rules; thus, it makes us believe that the grammatical subject is the effective cause of action expressed by the verb. That the "I" determines the verb "to think" is the grammatical superstition from which Descartes, despite his resolve to doubt everything, could not escape.[19] The Cartesian *cogito* is only one among many examples of the power of grammatical prejudice. It is also responsible for the very notion of substance. The simple function of the verb creates the illusion of a substance behind the verb. When one says "the light shines," one arbitrarily isolates a cause, "the light," as an entity separate from its effect, the act of shining. Similarly, morality falsely separates the force from its effects.[20] From the point of view of the subject, this grammatical structure reflects a metaphysical desire: the desire to be the cause of oneself, the desire that expresses itself every time I say "I think that..." Thus, metaphysical categories derive not from the metaphysical subject but from that more imperceptible form of subjectivity: the grammatical subject. "The concept of substance is a consequence of the concept of the subject, not the reverse."[21] Whence the category of Being. Following this reasoning, one immediately infers acts from an underlying, permanent cause. The plurality of phenomena is propped up by a single, simple substance: Being. "From the concept 'me' directly follows, as from a deduction, the concept 'Being.'"[22]

The concept of God, too, belongs to the implicit metaphysics of language. "God is only another hypostasis of various concepts of cause, subject, substance, being, converging in the same word, their imaginary focus. Only allow language to behave spontaneously and it will produce a 'natural' theology. Whence the celebrated remark: "I fear that we will never rid ourselves of God so long as we still believe in grammar."[23] Atheism is thus as difficult to conceive of as the categories of grammar are to refute—it seems not only illogical, illegitimate, and illicit, but even inexpressible. To say "There is no God" is a slip of logic and grammar known since the time of St. Anselm and well before him. That is why Nietzsche resorts to a linguistic subterfuge: "God is dead," or "He has committed suicide," "God has killed God." But it is easier to rid ourselves of God than grammar. By rote, grammar constantly reintroduces cause and substance, ideals, absolutes, all sorts of surrogates for the dead God.

What is to be done amidst the triumph of herd language? New words are lacking: "We find ourselves in the painful situation of no longer having at our disposal any formula for our concepts and everywhere being obliged to introduce the old categories."[24] What hopes can we place in a new syntax?

## Writing and the Limits of Its Therapy

The degradation in which we find language actually stimulates the search for new resources of "style." Rejection of herd communication and its metaphysical presuppositions compels a revival of the devices and effects of writing. The "new language" needs the "dead language" of the old categories as a contrast, like a material become inert and in need of regeneration, revivification.[25] Nietzsche does not doubt that his writings have the quasi-miraculous power to remedy this inertia: "I have ... words that will restore sight to the blind."[26] Using the conceptual web of the herd in order to overturn, to outflank, to parody it, Nietzsche's writings thrive to a great extent—but to what degree exactly?—on the destruction of the old order. This explains the recourse to parody, the necessity of which is constantly reiterated (and put into action): from *Truth and Lying,* where Nietzsche proposes to challenge herd-language with "derision and the destruction of old conceptual barriers;"[27] through the penultimate paragraph of the *Gay Science,* where the ideal of "great health" implies "the most concrete and involuntary parody" of grandiose words and attitudes; to the *Incipit parodia* and the anti-Hegelian programs sketched in *Beyond Good and Evil* Section (223). All of these are "parodies of universal history." But parody is only one among many stylistic and syntactic ruses designed to pervert the metaphysical code and to thwart the perpetual tendency of language to reduce the singular to the identical. Another weapon in Nietzsche's strategy (and one from which he expects still more) is the aphorism.

Parody and aphorism are modes of de-structuring, as are all plays upon words such as reversals, forbidden comparisons, or simply quotation marks (for there is aggression in wrapping quotation marks around a word!). Aphoristic and parodistic destruction signals a higher intensity of writing than the discursive style of critical analysis that dominates Nietzsche's early works (though there are, of course, aphorisms in *Considerations Out-of-Season* and *Human, All Too Human).* At this higher intensity, the struggle against herd-communication is transcended, aggression is forgotten, approbation is freed and reigns supreme in lyricism, dithyramb, prophetic flashes, divinatory lucidity. This intensity is produced like a fusion in verbal material heated to incandescence, the affirmation emerging from the destructuring. The phenomenon of fusion illuminates the doubleness of style in *Thus Spoke Zarathustra:* on the one hand maxims, sallies ("flying arrows," as Nietzsche says), exuberant wickedness, and the hardness of the hammer that smashes idols; on the other hand, the intoxication of morning and midnight songs, hymns, benedictions, tenderness, ecstasy. These two aspects—destruction and affirmation, nihilism and transmutation, language for everyone and language for no one—are further merged, fused to produce that mixture of malice and joyfulness, perhaps the hallmark of Nietzschean "innocence." It seems that as Nietzsche's writing develops, it overcomes increasingly the servile character of critical analysis and becomes pure affirmative activity, sufficient unto itself, like the world, or like the living body of which this writing becomes symptomatic.

The *intensity* of this writing is best displayed in aphorisms. Aphorisms sunder the temporal sequence of discourse and the linear and deductive logic of succession. "The aphorism, the maxim ... are forms of 'eternity.'"[28] (Note the significance of the quotation marks, which seem to say, "Look out, don't be taken in by the traditional meaning of the word," and which pervert the concept in a still undetermined way, to be defined by the new syntax.) The "eternity" revealed by the aphorism is not some motionless transcendent Being, but the upsurge—so sudden that it happens in "no time"—of an absolute moment, absolute inasmuch as the aphorism dispenses with a context; or rather inasmuch as it draws, with the suddenness of lightning, its own separate horizon. As etymology indicates, the aphorism presupposes horizon or limit *(horismos),* but one that is apart *(apo);* it presupposes a plurality of horizons and perspectives, an indefinite number of other aphorisms whose multiplicity can never be subordinated to a single dominant horizon. It is independent without being isolated. Aphoristic writing thus deranges all order, logical, chronological and metaphysical, making nonsense of the rule that would have a principle enunciated prior to its consequences and thus creating its own time and situation. Every aphorism radiates from its own center. Its sovereignty flows from its own "overhuman" concentration of Will to Power. "This mosaic of words, in which every word—as sound, as place, as meaning—pours out its strength right and left and over the whole, this *minimum* of signs and this *maximum* of energy—all this is Roman and, if you believe me, *noble* par excellence."[29] This quasi-organic coalescence of words possesses that power to regenerate worn-out signs which Mallarmé accorded only to poetry, "which from several words, i.e., worn-out words, again makes a whole word—new and like a stranger to language" (i.e., to herd language).[30]

Such a recharging of the word is noble because synonymous with singularity, with the pure affirmation that laughs away herd models and stereotypes. The intensity of this language is its *density,* its *Dichtung,* compactness; as Zarathustra says of his poetry, his *Dichten und Trachten,* "To connect into unity that which is only fragment, enigma, terrifying change."[31] The words of the herd are scattered scraps, hardened residues, into which the poet-philosopher will breathe new force through the unity of his unexampled style. Note the alliance of *Dichtung* and rationality: this writing submits itself to a calculus that permits it to obtain a maximum of meaning with a minimum of signs. The aphorism thus fulfills the requirements of artistic Will to Power that Nietzsche calls "Great Style": "To act in a logical, simple, categorical, mathematical manner, making itself *law*—in this lies the great ambition."[32] To mathematicize the chaos of words—is a rationalism of the will to writing, which reproduces exactly the Leibnizian theory of "determination"[33] (minimum and maximum as the principle of divine creation)—and illuminates in a deceptively familiar light the meaning of the aphorism. The aphorism still belongs to the light of Being and its logic. Like the Idea, the aphorism sets up a *horismos.* But in the aphoristic universe, the supreme horizon, the Idea of the Good, is missing. Although now pluralized, this logic of Being makes possible a systematic coherence, yet one for which only the reader is responsible. Several possible series of aphorisms, more or less dissimilar, connect the diverse horizons. "In aphoristic books like mine, there are all sorts of forbidden things and long chains of thought hiding themselves behind and between short aphorisms: there are also many questions that might be of interest to Oedipus and his Sphinx. I do not write treatises. They are for asses and readers of newspapers."[34]

Thus the aphoristic text requires, or intends to educate, a new type of reader: neither receptive nor reactive, nor a better listener, but an agent and creator, inquisitive and bold enough to go searching in the hidden background and in the interstices of the text for enigmas and *possible* systems. Whereas the traditional metaphysical text forcibly subordinates to a single and dominant point of view, a text made of aphorisms incorporates no directions or constraining orders. In this way, the fragmentary text diverges still further from the traditional metaphysical aim of furnishing a horizon. Fragments free us from the obsession with absolute correctness, exclude all possibility of imposing a single order upon the fragmented and dispensed meanings, deliver us from the obsession with an ultimate ground. But it is not the case—as Blanchot seems to think in *The Infinite Dialogue*—that the mere discontinuity of the text is liberating, as if by magic, for both the writer and the reader.

If non-linear writing inspires and provokes thought, this is not only because it gives the reader the free choice of a point of view, but also because it communicates "moods" of affective tonalities, *Stimmungen*. "To communicate through signs—this includes the tempo of the signs—a mood, or the internal tension of a passion—such is the meaning of all style."[35] The mood that achieves this communication is the aesthetic mood, the musical mood, the "Dionysian" mood of the body (the mood that is the "source of languages,"[36] as a 1888 fragment says). A more frequent metaphor for this creative mood is the dance, or the mood of the dancer, levity. "The goal: to give to the reader a *Stimmung* that makes him light, that puts him on his toes."[37] In diametrical contrast to the edification of morality, this sort of text aims at arousing the body toward the aesthetic mood. Rather than the communication of a content, this womb of ideas is a corporeal mood and such writing is communication of the body's matrix.[38] "The better style," writes Nietzsche, "consists in creating a more desirable *Stimmung* in the reader."[39] As for the better reader, he will have to learn to perceive and to feel all the elements of writing—rhythm, punctuation, choice of words, length of sentences, etc.—"as gestures of meaning."[40]

This more intense and affirmative writing does not develop from herd affirmations, from categorical propositions (each and every one of which *must* be obeyed), but from suggestions and insinuations. The greater the force of language, the greater its reserve and modesty. Nietzsche admittedly hesitates to communicate his "abyssal" thought: too great a communicability makes language suspect of vulgarity. Therefore, one does not find in the works that Nietzsche himself published the thesis-like, "theoretical," absolutely positive formulation of the Eternal Return. It suffices to read the first announcement of the Return in the *Gay Science* ("What would you say if one day ...", Section 341) to perceive that it is a pure play of virtualities, entirely in the conditional, that it calls out to a "you" in a style that is intimate, strange, mysterious. Similarly with the Overman. The least herd-like thought can be expressed only in a language that contradicts the logical codes. Because the term "Overman" is a contradictory synthesis of "Caesar" and "Christ," of "scholar" and "poet," it mocks the code from which it borrows the ill-assorted fragments out of which its "concept" is fabricated. This is no longer parody; it is the active forgetting of the code. Making the conditional the mode of supreme affirmation (for *might not* the most crushing possibility for the herd be the most exalted vision?),making the fusion of irreconcilables a sign not of weakness and incoherence, but of sublime perfection—this amounts to a new language that no longer worries about the old one but instead exploits it creatively.

At this intensity, lyrical, hymnic, dithyrambic writing celebrates the "Yes" while no longer being preoccupied with the "No." In Zarathustra's "The Song of the Seven Seals," anger, sarcasm, wickedness (all allied with the destruction of old values) are evoked as attitudes of the past (II), malice becomes laughing malice "that dwells in the valleys full of roses and rows of lilies" (hence innocent malice) (VI), while at the summit of the affirmation, discursivity—language itself—is transcended, giving place to "the wisdom of the bird," epitomized by the disconcerting counsel, repeated twice, "Sing! No more talk! Are not all words made for the heavy and dull-witted? Do not words lie to those who are light? Sing! No more talk!" (VII). Here, the chronically reappearing opposition between the herd, heavy and verbalizing, and the solitary, light and musical, reaches its breaking point. Here also are the limits of language's cure. Although not incurable, language is destined finally to fall into decadence, into heaviness and dullness. Yet it does possess some recuperative powers. Through the recourse to song evoked by Zarathustra, the circle closes, leading language back to the beyond of its origin: the original melody, the song without words. A "spoken song" would be a poor compromise and another impasse. The writing that aims above all to communicate a *Stimmung* must, at a certain intensity, eclipse itself, either because it reaches its goal or because its goal is too noble for its divided powers. Beyond language is that which always precedes it—not pure silence, but a musical "thought," without words.

How can Nietzsche affirm that there is a "thought" where there are no longer, or not yet, words? "Thought that becomes *conscious* is only a very little part of thought ... only this conscious thought is *produced in words*."[41] There is more thought than language because there is more unconscious than consciousness. Insofar as thought is formulable thought *(Gedanken)*, it corresponds perfectly with the words that we always use, but it is narrower than thought as *Denken*, which is connected to organic impulses. "Thought [*Denken*] is only a certain relation between the impulses."[42] The body thinks, but does not speak. Verbalization is a phenomenon as superficial as consciousness. Language, reactive in essence, abstracts from the thought of the body, protects itself against it, represses it out of fear. "The whole organism thinks, all organic structures are part of thought, of feeling, of will ."[43] The aesthetic mood—musical, imaging—is, like the inexpressible melody of the affects, the body's thinking, which the process of symbolization simultaneously reflects and falsifies. Hence, learning to *let be* the musical silence (instead of yielding to herd conceptualization or exhausting oneself trying to cure the incurable vulgarization of words) may be the secret and the final *word* of Dionysian wisdom. "Sing! No more talk!"

If this seems an odd interpretation of the affirmative Will to Power, too "Heideggerian," consider the way Nietzsche defines learning how to *see,* how to *think,* and also how to *read* and *write*: "To habituate the eye to repose, to patience, to letting things come to it ... the essential ... is precisely not 'to will,' but rather to *enable* the suspension of judgment."[44]

# Chapter 5

# THE CRITIQUE AND SUBVERSION OF SUBJECTIVITY

Consciousness of self is a fiction.[1]

The "ego" subjugates and kills.[2]

Supreme love for the ego goes hand in hand
with pleasure taken at the loss of self.[3]

The theme that the "ego" (by which is meant individual consciousness) is neither the center or nucleus of the subject, nor the principle that determines thought, the theme that the "ego" cannot serve as the foundation for a system of knowledge but, on the contrary, is always found inextricably intertwined within things, within the world, within other egos, the theme, finally, that the ego of reflection, which aims at universality, independence, mastery, and self-certainty, is no more than a fragile and illusory construction of metaphysics—such themes coming after Freud, Heidegger, or Merleau-Ponty are familiar and somewhat "evident" to our modernity. In the wake of psychoanalysis, we no longer believe in the autonomy of the ego (a "pitiful thing" in the words of Freud, sandwiched between the contradictory requirements of the Id and the Superego). Among other things, Heidegger taught us that the "ownmost" first addresses us only under the abstract guise of an impersonal "mineness" *(Jemeinigkeit)*, and is never acquired with the first words or the first gestures, which are all prisoners of the stereotypes and usages in force within the "they." With respect to Being-in-the-world and care—wherein the bite of temporality is experienced—the ego is not a fundamental structure of Being-human. The ego can be understood, for example, as a linguistic effect of care. "With the I,' care expresses itself, though proximally and for the most part in the 'fugitive' way in which the 'I' talks when it concerns itself with something."[4] Merleau-Ponty rehabilitated the anonymous openness of perception, the silent land where no subject has yet settled, but in which every ego sinks pre-individual roots and intertwines an affinity with others that goes deeper than any "struggle of consciousnesses," such a struggle coming to pass only in a future phase.

Now, in his analyses of subjectivity, it seems evident that Nietzsche not only belongs to such a modernity, but even *takes its lead* in many respects. More fascinated by the ontological aspect of the Will to Power than by its psychological one, and by Nietzsche's dependency on the Cartesian metaphysics of the subject, Heidegger does not say a word about the *critical* dimension of the Nietzschean theory of the subject and fails to recognize the ruptures that such a theory introduces into the tradition wherein it inscribes itself. After injecting a sometimes rigid continuity, Heidegger recognizes Nietzsche merely as one who prolongs such a tradition. He thinks of him as "the last metaphysician," one who systematically led post-Cartesian metaphysics to its absolute completion. In this view, Nietzsche supplies the Hegelian subject, which is still "incomplete," with the necessary complement that raises it to "finally completed subjectivity,"[5] which is an absolute in terms of both animality and rationality. This interpretation *obscures* all the objections, as well as all the mutations, that Nietzsche brought into the classical concept of the subject.

Heidegger, however, is not mistaken in his view that it is as metaphysician that Nietzsche thinks both psychology and morals.[6] The latter's claim to be a "psychologist" before all else somewhat confuses the issue. For aphorisms such as "there are no monads,"[7] "man: a plurality of Wills to Power,"[8] "we are a multiplicity *that built an imaginary unity for itself,*"[9] are unarguably metaphysical propositions that directly raise the issue of the transcendental unity of the subject or the relation between the one and the many within subjectivity.

The very point regarding which Nietzsche mounts an attack on, and attempts to dislodge, the traditional doctrine of the subject is precisely the idea of the *logical essence* of the ego. This idea is at the basis of the metaphysical theses of Descartes and Kant on the "*ego,*" and it is against these theses that Nietzsche explicitly mounts his attacks. For rationalism, which above all is concerned with the foundation of knowledge, the ego can only be defined as necessary and universal if it is identified with the *logical power* of the subject. In Descartes, the ego is restricted to, and identified with, understanding or reason. "I am therefore precisely only a thing that thinks; that is, a mind, or soul, or intellect, or reason."[10] In Kant, "the principle of the synthetic unity of apperception," or in less technical terms, the unifying power of consciousness, "is the highest principle of every use of the understanding."[11] This amounts to saying that the unity of the ego is the first condition for the very functioning of our logical faculty. The unity of the ego makes possible the unity of the concepts, the very operation of conceptualization. The ego is the primordial, archetypal unity: "through the ego, no manifold is given."[12] On the contrary, "the originary synthetic unity of apperception," i.e., transcendental consciousness, not only is "the highest point" to which the entire logic is to be connected, but "this power [of unity] is the understanding itself" *(ja dieses Vermögen ist der Verstand selbst)*. One should therefore not say that the pure ego conditions the understanding, but rather that it *is* the understanding. Concerning this identity of the ego and understanding, Kant supplies no other proof than a negative one, or a reduction to an absurd consequence: "Without the latter, my ego would be as diverse and of as many colors as there are representations of which I have a consciousness."[13] The essence of the ego is to be one, identical with itself, non-contradictory—in a word, "logical." "I" am logic itself!

Yet the Nietzschean critique of the ego first involves a critique of *logic* upon which the rationalist doctrines of the ego rest. "The belief in the ego endures and dissolves exactly as the belief in logic."[14] What these two beliefs have in common is the belief in the existence of stable *identities,* i.e., for Nietzsche, the Platonic belief in Being as equal to itself. Why a belief? Because experience supplies no data that are strictly *identical,* strictly *one.* Nothing in the world, in the real, is one. The one, therefore, is imaginary, non-real, fictitious. "Logic is connected with this hypothesis: *on the assumption that there are identical cases.*"[15] That the identity is fictitious does not mean that it is vain or illegitimate. Logic does not regulate itself on facts, but imposes upon them the "schema" of a regulative fiction that allows us to respond to practical necessities (the forecasting, calculation, planning of action) and to dominate reality. Logic is imposed upon by a will that *requires* that something like identity and unity should exist for its own security. The ego is such a unity, both useful and fictitious. The importance of the belief in the ego is fundamental for logic inasmuch as the concepts of "substance," "thing," "cause and effect," and finally those of "reality" and "Being" are deduced from our concept of "subject." We only believe in identity because we have "within ourselves" the model of every identity: it is the ego. So much so that the critique of the concept of "subject" and of its "faculties" should bring about the collapse of the metaphysical system of the categories, which in its entirety is derived from properties attributed to the subject. In other words, the logical beliefs, namely that substance persists *as the ego,* that the cause produces its effect *as the ego produces its actions,* will collapse if one demonstrates that the ego does not persist, that it is not the unique cause of its actions.

But, since they are useful, why destroy these logical fictions? Nietzsche wants to reduce logic to a simple, instrumental, and operational function. The justification of his critique is the confusion that pervades logical "identities" and the principles of reality itself. The transcendental illusion of logic consists in always projecting Being or the In-itself upon logical unities. Thus, the critique of the unity of the ego, its scattering and pluralization have as their ultimate acknowledged final goal to rediscover the *plurality of Being, the "degrees of Being",* as is claimed by the following fragment (among many others): "The concept of *substance* is a consequence of the concept of *subject,* and not the reverse! If we renounce the soul, the 'subject,' the prior condition for substance disappears totally. One gains *degrees of Being,* one loses *Being."*[16]

To renounce the soul, the "subject," means renouncing first of all the abstract universality of these concepts and asserting the individuality of the ego. There is only the individual ego. As Descartes acknowledges implicitly (more cautiously than Kant in this respect), "I am *one* understanding, *one* reason; and not understanding, reason *in general.*" But second, to renounce the subject means that the individual is not one, that the individual unity is fictitious. It means rediscovering inter-individual plurality. At issue is not so much the possibility of thinking this plurality anew, but of *experiencing* it. Once the logical unity of the subject, as well as its moral unity (the "person," the other mask that will have to be stripped off), has been shattered, it will be necessary to let the multiple powers of the ego take the lead with all their roles and their various states of body and soul. Here the ideal of the philosopher as *Versucher,* experimenter and risk-taker, insinuates itself gradually into the quasi-phenomenological description of the multiple ego. The goal is to experience the plenitude of subjectivity ever more, and to recreate it in the process of this experiencing, and not so much to inquire into its true essence. The most human of men will be capable of espousing several ideals, to live inside different characters or roles, to "see through the eyes of a hundred various persons."[17]

The question that can be asked at this point, taking into account the Heideggerian interpretation, is to know whether Nietzsche has reached the stage of the "completion of subjectivity." It is still too early to risk a response. All we can say is that the plenitude of the individual subject aimed at by Nietzsche, a transitional plenitude, has nothing to do with a totalization that conserves its overcome moments (which characterizes the universal subject in Hegel). Nietzschean "authenticity," as we may attempt to call it, is the opposite of Heideggerian authenticity. Whereas for Heidegger any diversity is necessarily "bad" or at least alienating—with the everyday preoccupations and the established interpretations of the "they" threatening the *Dasein* with fallenness in "curiosity" or "business," while the human being, in order to be human, must correspond with the simple givenness of Being—for Nietzsche the ego is found only by forgetting itself as a pseudo-unity, by immersing itself in the round of roles and perspectives. The most authentic movement—in Nietzschean terms, the most affirmative and the most daring one—requires the highest differentiating powers of the ego, not its greatest simplification. A "free spirit" is defined as one who knows to avoid the fixation of beliefs and certainties "by constant variations," so as to resemble a "thinking snowball!"[18] In order to implement the ideal of the traveler in *Human, All Too Human,* one would have to proceed by "going through the variety of choices as noble *traitors* in all things."[19] *Noble* is what matters foremost. For isn't a great deal of *nobility*, as the capacity for generous and vigorous affirmation, necessary in order to encounter this variety without dissolving the ego in inconsistency and frivolity?

Experimentation with "the variance of the ego,"[20] to use Paul Valéry's expression, does not close individuality back upon itself, but takes it outside, transports it beyond itself into the world. The ego that is capable of seizing upon, and living through, the diversity of conditions and philosophies is also the most apt at feeling "the cosmic link," i.e., not only at experiencing itself in its inseparable connection with the chain of all living beings and with all historical ascendancy, but also at understanding that it is part of the universal fatum, that it is this fatum. *Ego fatum.* "Every individual collaborates with the totality of the cosmic being—consciously or not, willingly or unwillingly."[21] "The individual considered from whatever angle is never anything but a fragment of fatum."[22] Must the cosmic ego be understood as the preparatory step to *amor fati*, to the affirmation of the Eternal Return? Isn't subjectivity abolished in this extreme, perhaps unthinkable, form of fatalism? Doesn't the entire critique of subjectivity have as its ultimate goal the leap into this affirmation of the One-and-All that eclipses every ego?

To shatter the logical identity of the subject, to rediscover intra-individual plurality, to develop the cosmic dimension of the ego: such tasks are unquestionably free from the speculative preoccupation of the "consciousness of self," but are characterized by a practical preoccupation, one surprisingly ambitious: changing the very essence of subjectivity.

## Shattering the Logical Identity of the Subject.

"'Consciousness of self' is a fiction."[23] "There is neither 'spirit,' nor reason, or thought, or consciousness, or soul, or will, or truth: all these are unusable fictions."[24] What does *fiction* mean precisely? Undoubtedly, it means illusion, but also "poetic invention," the "poet's creative craft," since Nietzsche often uses the terms *Erdichtetheit* and *Erdichtung,* or simply *Dichtung* instead of the term *Fiktion*. Without questioning the Nietzschean position that views logical categories as illusory units projected upon the multiplicity of the real, an objection presents itself naturally. How can Nietzsche grant a pejorative meaning to logical fiction and at the same time endow poetic illusion, and art in general, with the highest value? This apparent contradiction is solved by considering what is said of *poetry,* especially in the chapter "Some Poets" from *Thus Spoke Zarathustra*. "Poets lie *too much*." The italics are mine, because everything depends upon this "too much." Poetic lies have value only inasmuch as they do not claim in turn to be a substitute for truth. Poets lie *too much* when they forget that they lie, when they claim to utter truth in itself, by direct revelation. Only the fiction that knows itself to be such is beneficent. Otherwise, it is self-mystification. "Only the poet who knows how to lie in full knowledge of what this entails, intentionally, is one who can speak the truth."[25] In Nietzsche, there is a defense of the honest lie, as the one he detects in art. By contrast, philosophers and logicians are far from thinking that they produce fictions. They are mystifying liars, the mystification consisting in wanting to believe that their categories, their "poetic discoveries," express the very essence of things.

Because Nietzsche always keeps to the Platonic definition of truth as being-*one,* as identical and non-contradictory, he can, as part of his overturning of Platonism, merely insert his own definition of truth (a non-dissimulated lie, one recognized as such) within quotation marks! Because for him "true" represents the side of the multiple and contradiction, and "appearance" or "illusion" represents the one and identity, his own "truth" is not one that man can acknowledge, even inadequately, since knowing consists in transposing the multiple into the one and thus in negating the multiple.

Thus it is not so much the fictitious character of the subject that Nietzsche criticizes, as the forgetfulness, or the lack of acknowledgment, of this fictitious character. Believing in its own unity, the subject has a mutilated, shrunken image of itself. "The subject is multiplicity *that built an imaginary unity for itself.*"[26] The danger does not lie in this unity as such, but in the veiling, and hindering, of the free expression of internal multiplicity that such a unity produces.

What becomes important now is to show what these masking effects are, and what relations of dependence obtain between logical unity, consciousness, and the "total" or at least non-logical, subject. Faithful or unfaithful to the metaphysical tradition on this point, Nietzsche can no longer grant consciousness any of the characteristics of the subject, inasmuch as the *sub-jectum* (that which holds itself underneath) must be able to provide a basis and a foundation, or must be capable of receiving the most numerous attributes. Consciousness cannot sustain subjectivity and hold it up! "We have reached the phase where *the conscious becomes modest.*"[27] Consciousness will be called back to modesty by means of its confrontation with more complex and more powerful "forces": the body, non-conceptualizing thought, feelings, the external world, language, and social communication.

Among these, the body is what matters essentially. Why is it necessary to philosophize by "taking the body as one's leading thread?"[28] Because it is the one that deserves to be termed "subject," or that would deserve it if this unifying concept did not risk dissimulating the plurality that belongs to it: it is called "an amazing collection of living beings,"[29] the concurrence of "numerous intelligences,"[30] "a collective edifice of several souls."[31] The unity of innate and living integration of the human body is "the miracle of miracles."[32] With respect to it, "consciousness is nothing but an 'instrument,' nothing more, exactly as the stomach is an instrument of the same miracle."[33] Coordination, cohesion, wisdom, selection, critique, prudence, etc. must be first counted as qualities of the body, not of consciousness. The identity that is conscious of the ego is nothing but a transposition, a weak imitation, perhaps a symptom of physiological and solid unity and cohesion. Although "the body is our ego,"[34] such an organic ego is not a simple conceptual unity but has a real unity, that is to say, a multiple one that is compared to that of a group, "group of leaders at the head of a collectivity,"[35] an "aristocracy" of forces that are used to giving orders and to ruling together, a "directing committee." There is no point in looking for the logical reason in the coordination of the "cells" and the various organic functions, because consciousness would be able to propose only a slanted interpretation of it.

Indeed, consciousness must not remain privy to what takes place in the body. It is compared—and this is yet another political metaphor—to a constitutional monarch who reigns but does not rule. Consciousness must be held apart, protected from the conflicts that brew within the "society" of impulses; if it had to be informed of every sensation and every event in the world that nevertheless affect it, it would be submerged and annihilated; in short, it must be protected from the multiple and capable only of great simplifications, which maintain the order and the policing of the realm. "A certain *ignorance* in which the monarch is kept concerning the detail of operations and even the problems of the collectivity, is part of the conditions that allow him to reign."[36] These problems, which result from the incessant redistribution and internal equilibrium of forces, constitute the hidden (to consciousness) side of the dynamism of the psyche. As a superficial, terminal, derived, and even "superfluous"[37] phenomenon, consciousness is sometimes dangerously capable of erring, especially when it emancipates itself radically from the instincts, when it ignores the origin and the very meaning of *activity* ("the great and principal activity is unconscious").[38] As the faculty of inhibiting action, consciousness must continuously invert "as a mirror"[39] the unfolding of psychic life. Although it thinks of itself as giving orders, in fact it does nothing but register and execute. It attributes the different states of the psyche to a unique cause, itself. It prejudges the continuity of this cause through time. It even believes—supreme illusion—that it is a substratum "controlling" the totality of the subject, determining and guiding events, including the proper functioning of bodily operations. The metaphysical substantialization of the ego would thus result from the vanity and the endless blindness of consciousness that claims to "overlook" and regulate everything and in the end even believes that it orders its own thoughts.

Since consciousness produces neither the unity of the body nor its own unity, it is very far from being a master of thoughts *(Gedanken)*. Nietzsche removes the privilege of thinking *(Denken)* from consciousness. Not only does the body think, but also "conscious thought is a crude and simplified form of this sort of thinking that is necessary to our organism."[40] The ego is posited, constructed by such an unconscious thought;[41] it is not the *autho*r of the thought since thinking goes beyond it. The Cartesian evidence of the conscious ego as consubstantial and "equal" with thought and cause of its thoughts is overcome from a double point of view. On the one hand, this evidence contradicts the experience that teaches me that thoughts come to me when "they" so choose, not when "I" choose.[42] "I" am not the master of the unfolding of my thoughts. A thought imposes itself upon me. On the other hand, the idea that the ego is a permanent substratum identical with thought implies several non-verifiable presuppositions, such as that "I *know* what it means to think,"[43] or that there is a relationship of cause and effect between the ego and the thinking activity. In fact this latter belief, according to which the ego "produces" thought, is nothing but an effect of the "grammatical routine" that identifies the grammatical subject of a verb with the author of the action. It is the same illusion as that which occurs when the sentence "the lightning flashes" leads one to confer upon lightning a substantial reality independent of any flashing.

Far from thinking that thought might be identified with the ego, we must say that it is of a multiple nature, just as the body is. On the most superficial level, we are dealing with conscious, logical, simplifying thought, yet thought unaware of its falsifications. It is tautological thought, a thought of identity, closed upon itself, imagining itself moving amidst the pure freedom of its self-production, in pure self-transparency. At the other extreme, the thought of the body remains directly inaccessible to us, we can only perceive symptoms of it, and we are limited to making mere conjectures on its topic. For example, in the unconscious there is probably a simultaneity of ideas that is incomprehensible to us because we can only think in temporal succession.[44] Only by positing interpretation as an intermediate ground can we correspond with this idea. Interpretation gets hold of such thoughts as present themselves to us not only by being attentive to their symptomatic link with feelings and instincts,[45] but also by being aware that every interpretation is conscious, and thus reductive and falsifying. None of the three degrees of thought (consciousness, the unconscious, and interpretation) leaves the initiative to the ego. The amazing description that Nietzsche makes of the birth of a thought in the subject emphasizes mostly the passivity of the ego, which is "more the spectator than the author of the process."

> Thought *[Gedanke]*, in the form it takes when it occurs, is a plurivocal sign that requires an interpretation, more precisely an arbitrary shrinking and limitation until finally it becomes univocal. It occurs independently of my will, usually surrounded and obscured by a cohort of feelings, desires, or refusals, also of other thoughts; often enough it can hardly be distinguished from a "will" and "feeling." It is extracted from this cohort, it is cleansed, set on its feet, examined to see how it stands, how it walks, all of this amazingly *presto* and yet without the feeling of swiftness: *who* operates all this? I do not know and in the process I am more the spectator than the author of it all.[46]

The interpretation to which thinking *(Denken)* is subjected does not require the presence of an interpreter "behind" the interpretation. This, too, would be a fiction.[47] The interpretation does very well without an ego. It is "automatic." All that can be said is that the interpretation interprets.

The dependency of consciousness on the "external world" is difficult to evaluate, especially from the perspective of consciousness. For the illusion specific to consciousness causes it to recognize in this "external world" nothing but a construction (the fact, for example, that the world is conceived as a *totality)*, an arrangement made with respect to its own needs, one where, consequently, it is incapable of measuring the extent of the influences to which it is subjected. Nonetheless, it is certain that the logical categories do not belong to an autonomous structure of subjectivity, but are responses to threats issuing from the world. The invention of "identical cases," the reduction of the known to the unknown, causality, etc. are as many instruments of forecasting, security, and domination that translate within consciousness the power of the felt danger, i.e., the power of domination of the world over it. Outside of its logical inventiveness, consciousness is nothing but an "instrument of transmission" of the action of the outside world and of our actions on the outside world; "it is not this transmission," stresses Nietzsche, "but an organ of this transmission."[48] As for the succession and the linking of phenomena in the world and of thoughts in ourselves, they are as perfectly hidden to us as is the Kantian thing-in-itself, and consciousness never offers more than "imaginary" explanations. "All of our so-called consciousness is nothing but a more or less loose commentary of an unknown text."[49] The world is unknown to us. We invent all "causes" "after the fact." "The fragment of the outside world of which we become conscious is posterior to the effect that was produced in us, it is projected after the fact as being its cause."[50] Thus, consciousness, far from providing us with information on the world as such, is nothing but the sum of what is *useful* for us to know about it. But this narrow and distorting aim proves the extent to which consciousness is determined by its position in the world and by the world.

By taking consciousness also as an instrument and a product of social communication and by linking the superficiality and the abstraction of language to the phenomenon of consciousness, Nietzsche removes consciousness even further away from its link with the ego, with individuality. "Consciousness does not belong to the ground of the individual existence of man."[51] This proposition is nothing more than the consequence of the thesis that "the body is our ego." Consciousness and language transpose this ego in non-individual terms, because, on the one hand, it is not in "my" interest to let out in front of the collectivity the impulsive and non-logical originality of this individuality of mine, and because, on the other hand, this individuality as such could not possibly be useful to the collectivity. It needs to be "retranslated into the perspective of the herd." That is why Nietzsche can claim, in an apparently biologizing reversal concerning consciousness, that the latter is not the highest form of ideality, but rather the "genius of the species." To be conscious, to express oneself in terms of consciousness, to speak, to write, this amounts to work not in one's own interest, but—by dint of some biologizing reversal—for the benefit of the human species. One must naturally except from this common involvement of speech and writing those forms that upset precisely the conventional essence of language, namely aphoristic and fragmentary writing. But this exception confirms the rule that requires that, thanks to language, consciousness still and always pursue its task of dissimulation.

## Rediscovering Intra-Subjective Plurality

If the logical unity of the subject has a masking effect, as the "faculties" of the subject (will, reason, imagination, feeling) do, it is mostly inasmuch as each of those unities dissimulates the plurality (of forces, of goals) contributing to any action and any thought. It would, however, be equally illusory to claim that such a plurality is accounted for as such because it belongs to the domain of the unconscious and because the simple fact of transposing it into language amounts to transposing it into unity. The actual unfolding of the phenomena of the psyche forever remains impenetrable, unknown to us. "We have no organ subtle enough for this internal world, so that we feel *the most multiform complexity* as a unity and we introduce an imaginary causality into a domain where all the ends of movement and change remain invisible to us."[52] Two paths, however, remain open for analysis. On the one hand, the regressive approach consists in showing the psychological unity (consciousness or the faculties), as a superficial, derived unity, as an "ultimate term," a conclusion. This approach reverts to the prior conditions, to the events that are "behind" the psychological unity, without, however, claiming to restore the "real" and original causal connection. It will suffice that what was considered a cause should clearly appear as an effect. On the other hand, the analysis will show a diversity of latent motivations as concurrent, intertwined, and concomitant. It will suffice to show the intricacy, the absolute solidarity of these motivations, so that the gaps between the former faculties might be made relative. Thus, it will appear that there is no affect-ability without intellect, no emotions nor even sensations that do not contain judgments,[53] no rational will without emotion.

It is precisely the concept of "will" that is the privileged object of the Nietzschean deconstruction. In no way is the "will" a coherent principle, a simple force, a cause determined, focalized and generating effects. The analysis reveals this "purely verbal unity"[54] to be the conscious result of the convergence of a plurality containing feelings or sensations, ideas or reasonings, and quasi internal individualities. For one to come up with an act of willing and issue an order to himself, or herself, he or she must duplicate himself or herself into a master and an executor. And, of course, this act of ordering does not take place in an atmosphere of serenity, but in an emotional climate. However, the "passion to order," along with the feelings that accompany it—the pleasure of imposing a constraint upon oneself, the pleasure of defeating a resistance within oneself—is not the cause of voluntary acts, but only a correlative symptom. The "I want" appears to consciousness when "hesitation" (the conflict between several tendencies) has been surmounted at the unconscious level, i.e., when a certain provisional hierarchy of impulses has been established. "Will" is invoked only when we expect success, the effective possibility of action, imminent or in progress, in other words, when we have the feeling that we are going to be obeyed by ourselves. It is impossible to dissociate the feeling of the *transition* from a given state to another, accompanied sometimes by muscular sensations, *from* a reasoned and pondered project of change. But this project can be the rationalization of an explosion of force or of a change *preceding* the project. Because our body has changed, we "want" to change.

Nietzsche calls *"under-wills"* or *"under-souls"*[55] the different protagonists of this internal struggle (which is only a feeble debate, involving "the one who orders," "the one who obeys," "the one feeling satisfaction") in the midst of the willing subject. These are, in fact, the parts of the unconscious or of the body, an "edifice of multiple souls."[56] Why does he talk about "souls"? The usurpation or the reversal, which attributes the "noble" name "soul" to what tradition considers inferior, is aimed at designating the true "acting principles," the impulses, the instincts.[57]

Yet the sub-ego plurality is not reducible simply to the forces of the bodily unconscious, any more than it can be assimilated to the diversity of feelings and ideas. The logical identity of the ego or the moral identity of the person takes hold at the expense of the presence of multiple "persons," i.e., roles that follow each other or coexist in the apparatus of the individual psyche. Nietzsche does not tire of stressing that the "person" is nothing but some special underscoring, a product of circumstances, within the multiple "persons," i.e., characters or personalities that we carry inside us in a state of greater or lesser virtuality. Most often a *persona,* i.e., a dramatic character, a more or less "arbitrary" mask, sticks to us, occupying the center stage of consciousness alone at the expense of those masks that we carry "inside the body."

> One is richer than one thinks, each one carries in one's body the stuff of several characters, one takes to be the 'personality' what only belongs to the 'acting character,' to *one* of our masks. Most of our actions do not come from the depths of our being, but are as superficial as most volcanic eruptions; we must not be led astray by the noise.[58]
>
> We contain within ourselves the *sketch* of *several* persons: the poet betrays himself in his characters. Circumstances extract from us a certain figure *[Gestalt]*; when circumstances change a great deal, one discovers within oneself two, three figures. From each instant in our life, there are numerous other possibilities: randomness *always* contributes something to it![59]

"Every personality is first a *role*"[60] means that the individual does not have, as is the case in Hegel, for example, a substantial original reserve to bring to the light of day, an In-itself that calls for objective expression. The individual is not a substance, but exists and constitutes itself by entering various roles. But what is a role? Where do roles come from? How can they belong to the body? A role is not only an entirely external function that requires a certain predetermined behavior, but also an intimate agreement with what society requires of us in terms of the family, job, works. The collective impulses internalized by the individual are older and more powerful than individual impulses. The "roles" represent the masks of pre-individual impulses. As such they are ascribable neither to the "they" nor to the ego. A role, as well as the subject, to be sure, is neither anonymous nor unique; it is an "effect of the external world upon us, a world with respect to which we attune our 'person' in the same way as one tunes the strings of an instrument before playing it."[61] A role constitutes the matrix of the individual. It supplies a text that is not written by "me," but by others and whose script my body has learned. Hence the idea that the human being is an actor, and also that every actor has *several roles:*

> To What Extent Man is an Actor.
>
> Let us admit that the individual receives a role to play: little by little he grows comfortable with it. Finally he has the judgments, the tastes, the tendencies that correspond to his role

> and even the degree of intelligence that is usually connected with it—first as a child, adolescent, etc., then the role in connection with sexuality, then one in keeping with social standing, then profession, then works.
>
> But let life give him the opportunity to change, then he also plays another role. And often the roles in one and the same man are different depending on the days, for example an Englishman on Sundays and an Englishman on weekdays. Within the same day we are very different depending on whether we are awake or asleep. In a dream state we rest perhaps on account of the fatigue of the day role and we put ourselves in other roles.[62]

The roles that determine individual daily psychology are imposed from the outside. They are *de facto* conditions and produce the wealth of interiority (judgments, tastes, leanings, intelligence). Yet the major constellation that results from them is such that if the randomness of circumstances (the "opportunity") presents an individual with other roles, he will have a different psychology. With this point, Nietzsche suggests moving from fact to ideal, from the imposition of change to the willing of change: the idea is not to accept roles passively, but to *see* as roles all kinds of behavior and to *seek* new roles spontaneously. "Consider our way of living and acting as a *role* to play—including maxims and principles."[63] The *active* individual is one who does not turn himself into an *actor,* but takes upon himself *the actor that he is*. Through this, he claims as belonging to every life the connotation of illusion and lie traditionally associated with the acting of a comedian, the part of inauthenticity. But at the same time, he makes this part of inauthenticity light and free of the heavy responsibility of moral choice. The active individual is one who claims that, whatever his behavior, he is playing a role. In this sense he stands beyond all morals. "Everything that is imperative in morals is addressed to the *plurality of masks* that we carry within ourselves and requires that we show one and hide the others, hence that we *change appearances.*"[64] The process of "making amends," of "moral progress," the donning of "the garb of the new man," is indefinite, but illusory, because what occurs is nothing but a change in appearances. But because he knows that there is nothing besides appearances, the most affirmative man is one who refuses to be fixed in a privileged role (a determined rule for living) but who wants to experience a *series* of states or ideals, to live through a *series* of persons or characters. By living through them *successively,* isn't he externally similar to the one who only lives through few roles or is subjected to them? The one who would live, not in succession but *simultaneously*, many often contradictory characters would not be a man, but the Overman. Isn't the affirmation of the plurality of roles a transition toward the Overman?

In any case, certain fragments by Nietzsche stress that the aspiration to, or the acceptance of, a plurality of roles should facilitate the affirmation of the Eternal Return. "We must not *[dürfen nicht]*, we are bound *[müssen]* to *want to become periodical* beings = *similar* to existence (Fragment entitled "The Philosophy of the Return").[65] The plurality of roles—be they only our roles as awake or dreaming individuals—teaches us the cyclical character of existence. Further, the English word "role" as the German *Rolle* (the remark is not made by Nietzsche, but it would be part of the Nietzschean logic to think such consequences out) derives from the Latin word *rotulus,* itself from *rota* (wheel), thus meaning "small wheel." Isn't this small wheel, and the scrolling upon itself of the parchment that bears the text of the written "role," isn't each complete turning of the scroll like the axis of the great wheel of the Eternal Return, which is the return of multiple roles? The entire existence is role-playing, i.e., rotation of multiple roles. In another fragment that bears the title "The Ring of Rings,"[66] Nietzsche suggests, without saying it expressly, that to claim that the "person" is an illusion or a power of metamorphosis, teaches us how to let go of substantial individual identity and to affirm the cycle of always provisional identities—provisional because indefinitely or infinitely successive.

But the point of view of internal plurality is not only that of a *succession,* but also that of a "social" *coexistence* of *persons*. "The free man is ... a society of individuals."[67] "The individual is a society."[68] In fact, we maintain with ourselves and within ourselves social relations as complex and numerous as those we maintain with the individuals around us. The representation of internal life as monologue or as reflexive dialogue, mere self-duplication, appears as an arbitrary intellectualistic reduction of the interior and polymorphous social life described by Nietzsche as follows:

> Never do we treat ourselves as an individual, but as dual, as plural; all the social inclinations (friendship, vengeance, envy) we feel loyally toward ourselves. Our native and animal selfishness is gravely altered by our *social interaction*: we can no longer feel the unity of the ego, *we always find ourselves among a plurality of beings.* We have split into several beings and we always split anew. The *social instincts* (such as *hostility, envy, hatred)* that entail a multiplicity have transformed us: we have transported "society" inside us and shrunk it to our dimensions;

> to withdraw within oneself is no longer a way to escape society, but often *to prolong into a dream state*, or to *interpret,* what takes place inside us according to the schema of our past experiences.[69]

This intra-individual "social practice" is no longer connected to an external social life whose anticipation or memory it supposedly might be, as if those roles were the repetition of discourses we are about to make, or have made, to others. Instead, what is at issue is the interpretation of our "solitary" experience according to the schema of sociability. The fact that "we" address love, hatred, reward, or blame to ourselves is a datum and a fact observed by all, applicable to all, yet one that not everybody acknowledges. The "we" of the description is ambiguous here. Every individual is a society, but only the "free man" is capable of perceiving such a plurality as something positive, as worthy of acclaim, of transforming the fact into the ideal.

Yet the origin of the effectiveness of the schema of sociability seems to be located in the immemorial enslaving of the individual to the "herd." If the individual carries in him these social roles, it is as a trace, as a deep mark of a total and archaic dependency upon society. "Formerly the ego was hidden inside the herd, now the herd hides itself deep inside the ego."[70] Nietzsche formulates the hypothesis that in primitive eras, the individual first lived melted within the collectivity as a part of an organism. For long periods of time the collectivity used the individual as an organ. At the stage where there were no independent individuals, the only instincts, feelings and behaviors were those that concerned men as members of the society. That is why, even today, the hatred of, or the disgust with, what is nefarious to society is in us more "primitive," more immediately "ours" than any egotistical feeling. Later on, when society lost its overwhelming power over individuals, the originarily collective instincts began a struggle against the individualistic goals that had been assigned to them. Yet, it is not on the basis of a free self-invention but of a modification of the collective instincts that the individual who is emancipated from the organic society will find his own proper identity: he will succeed "in creating his *possibility of individual existence* thanks to a reorganization, an assimilation, an elimination of the instincts inside himself."[71] For Nietzsche, the "individual" has only a derived content: it is a transformation, a remodeling, a new interpretation of "social instincts," i.e., of socially determined practices and, ultimately, of judgment originally belonging to a social context (which from a historical perspective is now out of date). For it is necessary that a long time should elapse in order to allow social practices to become fixated as "instincts." It is therefore always against a society other than the current one that the individual revolts.

Let us note in passing that the Heideggerian conception of the "authentic" *Dasein* constitutes a variation on this Nietzschean theme: In order to conquer its ownmost being, the *Dasein* must claim as belonging to it those possibilities that were obtained from the "they." Just as the ego is first melted inside the herd, the *Dasein's* first and most fundamental identity is the "they-self" *(Manselbst)*. What radically separates Heidegger and Nietzsche is the fact that for Heidegger the possibilities are *"existentiell"* and transcendental views, not instinctive, i.e., bodily possibilities. The margin of freedom, of free self-invention, is weaker in Nietzsche inasmuch as the difficulty of reinterpreting the social instincts is greater than the difficulty of moving from the "they" to the ownmost individuation (i.e., from the "someone dies" I move to "I relate to my own death"); for the social instincts are ever more imperious and rigid: the patriot or the party man for example is capable of more passion and more "innocent" hatred, according to Nietzsche, than most individuals pursuing private goals.

It is this difficulty confronting the position of the individual ego which leads Nietzsche to a paradoxical critique of *egoism*. How can one speak of, and criticize, egoism since there is no true ego? Egoism is as inexistent, or as weak, as the ego itself. "Egoism is infinitely weak."[72] "Egoism is something belated and always still rare."[73] Before qualifying an action as egotistical, one must inquire whether there was an ego—and of what type—at its source. Because the ego is most often not emancipated from the collectivity, and because it is a link, conscious or unconscious, in the chain of living beings, a product, conscious or unconscious, of the historical past, most of the actions called "egotistical" are the effects either of "gregarious passions" or of the needs or tendencies belonging to the species or the specific group, and not to the individual! The concern for clothing, the desire to build a fortune, or political ambition are not more, or less, egotistical than the conservation instinct or the sex drive. True egoism is absent from these forms. The individual ego disappears when the individual entirely fulfills one *function,* whether it be simply biological (pleasure of food, sexual pleasure) or societal and diversified: the great "roles"—as for instance the prince, the prophet, the poet—entail the effacing, even the suppression, of the individual.[74] Nietzsche shows that the imperative in force here, especially when it is physiological, is quasi-impersonal, whereas, paradoxically, the moral imperative requiring one not to satisfy, but to restrain, one's desires, is undoubtedly inspired by the longing for a specific image of oneself. "In ordinary egoism, it is precisely the non-ego that dominates, profound banal being."[75] Whereas sensuousness is too banal to define true egoism, morals holds the ego in too high an esteem not to require an extraordinary egoism.

## Developing the Cosmic Dimension of the Ego.

It is not enough to observe that the ego never exists separately from the world. It must be concluded that the ego *is its* own world and gradually includes *the* world, or worlds: physical, biological and natural, social and historical, intellectual and spiritual. "We absorb within ourselves not only God, but all the beings whose existence we recognize without naming them; we are the cosmos to the extent that we have understood or dreamed it. Olive trees and storms have become parts of ourselves; the same applies to the stock exchange and the newspaper."[76] As is found in Heidegger, there is no subject facing the world, but Being-in-the-world. *The only "ownmost" possibilities available to man are those offered by the world.* There is no purely "external" world, which does not mean the absence of internalization and private sphere. Nietzsche scoffs at the ridiculous overestimation of man with respect to the world and the false symmetry inherent in the common formula "man and the world," as if there were the least equality between the two terms. The danger threatening Nietzschean individuality is not fallenness *(Verfallen)*, i.e., too extensive an identification with the surrounding world as in Heidegger, but on the contrary too loose a perception of the multiple links and intertwining with the world. The affirmative, noble being accepts and claims the widest cosmic standing.

The ego first experiences enlargement by being connected to the entire chain of evolution, by integrating itself to the tree of life, starting from the most elementary forms. There must necessarily be an absolute continuity through uninterrupted transitions from the first living form to this ego of mine. This continuity is bound to dismiss the absurd pretensions of the individual, who is not a detached fruit, but the summary and repetition of the ascending line not only of the species, but of the living in general. Each of our actions is seen as shorthand repetition of the entire history of life. Every act is a repetition, not of the "ego," but of the totality of life. In a great many fragments, Nietzsche tirelessly underscores that "man is not only an individual, but also the totality of the organic that continues to live inside him."[77] "The individual is life *in its entirety* such as it has developed so far, not its result."[78] "Each individual being is precisely the *whole* process in a direct line (not only "heir" to the process, but the process itself)."[79] "The *ego* is worth a hundred times more than a unit in the chain of members: *it is the chain itself in the absolute sense.*"[80] In every operation of the unconscious or in every perception—even more than in every conscious and pondered action—the entire organic past is reactivated and prolonged. "In every judgment of the senses, the whole organic prehistory comes into play."[81] As well as being the summary of the entire past of the biological line, the individual is also bearer of the whole *future* of that line. The individual plays and risks more than his own egotistical future even when he thinks he is acting in his own self-interest. "We are more than the individual: we are also the entire chain, with the tasks devolved upon all the futures of the chain."[82] "Man so far has been the embryo of the future man. All the plastic forces that tend toward this future are in him; and because they are prodigious, *suffering* is what results for the current individual inasmuch as he contributes to determining the future. Here is the most profound conception of *suffering:* conflicting plastic forces. The isolation of the individual should not project an illusion: in fact, there is a *common current* that goes through all individuals."[83] One of the most profound causes of suffering for the individual would then be the disproportion between his current reality and the forces (in him greater than himself) that work toward the preparation and birth of future humankind. By designating these forces as a "common current" thrown into the future, Nietzsche proposes an apparently substantialist and evolutionary version of the Will to Power (understood as the totality of the forces, a totality of forces which, on the one hand, forms a biological substratum common to all individuals and, on the other, is conjugated in the universal and progressive rush toward a type superior to current humankind). Such a "realistic" definition of the Will to Power would not permit it to be distinguished from forms of vitalism such as Schopenhauer's will-to-live or Bergson's *élan vital.* But this definition is in fact constantly doubled with, compensated and corrected by, a non-realistic, "perspectival" version of the Will to Power as an *interpretation* of phenomena from the "point of view" of such and such a force, or rather from such and such a relationship of forces. From the point of view of an individual who chooses his own values, i.e., his way of accomplishing the imperative "to be more" proper to life itself, there is a rupture with, a distance from, the "common current": the maximal index of this rupture—set in the future—is the Overman. But is it not *contradictory* to present the Will to Power *both* as the unity of the living realm and the play of forces dispersed into multiple perspectives, i.e., both as infinite identity and infinite difference? If there is a "contradiction," it is only for a logic that wants to avoid the contamination of the one by the many, that requires that pure identity should subsist somewhere. The Will to Power is both one and multiple, in itself, and in each of the individuals within which *it divides itself originally.* When Nietzsche states *"the hypothesis"* that one might "call *'Will to Power' every* acting energy,"[84] he takes care to warn against such a definition because it might bestow upon the world some "intelligible character," or (in Kantian terms) decide upon the "In-itself" of reality. But one should not turn the Will to Power into a substantial, underlying unity.

But then, why speak of a "common current"? Nietzsche allows himself to be tempted by the metaphor of a "current," whereas he means to affirm something very different from what was intended by a Schopenhauer or a Bergson. What does he claim? Not that an originally *unique energy* is sundered into multiple individuals when it becomes "world," as Schopenhauer would put it, or when it "creates" it as Bergson would say; but rather that every individual formation participates in a unique structure that takes the appearance of a unique source by dint of the fact that everywhere it obeys the *same rule.* After writing "It is the same force that is spent in artistic creation and in the sexual act," Nietzsche adds immediately, "there is one single *type* of force *[es gibt nur Eine Art Kraft].*"[85] Force is of the same kind *(Art)* everywhere; this is what appears.

It still remains that the affirmation of a unity that is non-substantial but structural and unifying, of the same *types,* suffuses with relativity the quest for multiplicity, especially intra-individual. Doesn't this quest rest on a deep quietness and assurance? However far one may go on the side of the division of the ego, isn't the danger—of a dispersion beyond repair, of fruitless chaos—conjured up in advance by the very existence of this unifying structure? Isn't Nietzsche able to manifest such an unreserved attraction for the multiple because he does not suspect that in a way the unifying *unification* constitutes "the ground of things"? The untiring search for plurality and the vision of the polymorphous character of the ego would then be the sort of counterpart to the very life of the One, the breathing, the pulsation, the "ebb and flow" of an identity that endlessly flees from itself and finds itself again. And when Nietzsche describes the "world" as:

> a sea of forces flowing and rushing together, eternally changing, eternally flooding back, with tremendous years of recurrence, with an ebb and a flow of its forces; out of the simplest forms striving toward the most complex, out of the stillest, most rigid, coldest forms toward the hottest, most turbulent, most self-contradictory, and *then again returning home to the simple out of this abundance, out of the play of contradictions back to the joy of concord,* still affirming itself in this uniformity of its course and its years,[86]

we must grant that the relation he establishes in this text between the multiple and the one functions according to a Platonic structure: Being (one and identical) is asserted of Becoming (multiple and dissimilar), Being bestows perfection, even "holiness," upon Becoming (as he states later in the same section). Yet there is no Platonism in the sense of the transcendence of the One, but rather in the sense of a participation—here immanent—of plurality within unity. From such formulations one must however avoid drawing general and definitive conclusions on the traditionally metaphysical character of the Will to Power and the Eternal Return, because subsequent formulas will be added, as we shall see, to correct or inflect the impact of those just quoted.

Now, concerning not so much the evolution of life but human history, it seems difficult to suggest that the individual could fuse within it and be integrated in organic fashion. How could the individual person summarize spontaneously the totality, or even a part, of the past of human beings? One's historical legacy is not received "automatically" as is one's "genetic capital." It is necessary that the collective past should penetrate into consciousness, should be evaluated, known. "We are the consciousness that history has of itself in an absolute sense."[87] By "we," Nietzsche means every individual. "Every man is a creative cause of history."[88] But how so? Wouldn't this amount to some sort of *inverted Hegelianism*, i.e., the gathering of the *totality* of the past not in the Absolute Spirit, but in the individual subjectivity opposed to the absolute? First, in Nietzsche the term "absolute" qualifying the relationship of the individual to history does not designate a totality, but *sovereignty*, in that the individual has to decide with *sovereignty*, i.e., in solitary *(ab-solute)* fashion and in an intimate and particular relation, upon the meaning of the historical past (because such a meaning is never established objectively once and for all, but is always a matter for reaffirmation, transformation, or denial and, in any case, for extending or prolonging). This means, secondly, that there is no room, either inside or outside the individual, for history to become universal, i.e., to reach its *conceptual* and retrospective synthesis. Outside of the fiction of historicalizing objectivity, the individual can relate "absolutely" to history only through identification or *affective* or *prospective* assimilation. The absence of totalization, the experimental and anticipatory point of view, are such that the fundamental Nietzschean notion of "historical sense" is unconnected with any sort of Hegelianism. From the second *Consideration Out-of-Season* to *The Gay Science* and beyond, Nietzsche constantly opposes the Hegelian import of "historical sense" to his own by describing such a "sense" as either the best or the worst of faculties or dispositions of the mind. It is the worst if it is conceived, as it is by

Hegel, with the meaning of determinism, of the weight of the past, of the irresistible and unavoidable movement of events that forces one to bow one's head and worship both "facts" and the "established order." It is equally dangerous if it amounts to the hypertrophy of a knowledge whose only goal is knowledge and which, by dint of the indigestible accumulation from the most various epochs, ends up in relativism and detachment, as well as in paralysis for action. Finally, the danger is that the "historical sense" might elicit a sort of frivolous game with the tawdry finery and spoils from the past that modern man dons with desperate compulsion. The nineteenth century constitutes "the first epoch that has truly studied 'costumes'—morals, pieces of belief, aesthetic tastes, religions."[89] The "historical sense" that allows us to locate all the moral, intellectual, artistic, and religious styles, to know all the fashions, to understand all the value judgments of the past, makes one incapable of being captive to any moment or figure of the tradition, any more than of the present. Modern man makes a nihilistic use of history: since he believes in nothing, he uses history as a sort of costume and accessory store. He takes the guise of the Classic, of the Romantic, of the Christian ... He floats and drifts everywhere considering the possible masks that haunt the backstage of universal history, this great theater with the front stage now filled by a tawdry carnival procession. The only release from the despair hidden within frivolity is to turn the game into satire and parody: instead of being comedians feeling the pangs of distress, the goal is to be deliberate actors, "parodists of universal history."[90]

If the project of a parody of universal history can still be interpreted as an anti-Hegelian reaction, there is still another meaning for the expression "historical sense," one that no longer has any connection with Hegel and consists of an individual's having the *force* to consider all human experiences as *his own experiences.* Such a disposition of mind has nothing to do with the intellectualistic and universalistic humanism whose adage is *nihil humani a me alienum puto* (I deem nothing human foreign to me). It claims nothing by way of an abstract knowledge of the human being in general, but is interested in the individual's affective participation in history as a collection of attempted experiences ("History is the great trial laboratory").[91] The first attempt would amount to apprehending history from the point of view not of the acquired results, but from the possibilities for the future that it reveals. *The Gay Science,* Section 337, describes what a future "historical sense" might be, unlike anything that was so far: a feeling of history that would no longer be dominated by the melancholy of the retrospective gaze, but rather by the delight in discovering new creative possibilities. First, the individual who might be "capable of experiencing the history of humanity as a whole as *his own history,"* who would know how "to condense into one single feeling" the defeat and the victories of humanity, would have to experience the phase of dejection, of bitterness, and of infinite exhaustion, i.e., the Hegelian phase, in facing the totality of the past. But if this hero of the twilight had the strength to affirm that this past only existed for the sake of a future, that this past in short was nothing more than a first attempt, a first trial, if he could be the hero that "on the second day of battle welcomes the dawn and his fortune," then this person would be filled with a feeling of superabundant and quasi-divine felicity. This person would incorporate the entire past history into *one single day* because of his sole belief in the "second day." Far from being passively absorbed in history, he would put the latter behind him through the simple affirmation of the "fortune" of a tomorrow.

Here the issue is no longer to seek, in the wake of what the second *Consideration Out-of-Season* calls "monumental" history, *examples* of great men or great actions to imitate. To assimilate history as "one's own history" means to be able to claim concerning history and oneself inseparably, "not only was I—and am I—this, but this 'matures' and continues through 'me.'" The apparently nonsensical formula often quoted: "at bottom all the names of history are me"[92]—a formula that indeed belongs to the scarce writings of Nietzsche's madness—has nevertheless "rational" equivalents:

> When I speak of Plato, Pascal, Spinoza and Goethe, I know that their blood runs through my veins.[93]
> In all that moved Zoroaster, Moses, Mahomet, Jesus, Plato, Brutus, Spinoza, Mirabeau, I am already present, and in many respects, it is only in me that the embryo, which needed several centuries, is maturing and coming to light. The historical sense is merely in the process of being born.[94]

The idea that the relationship to the past and historical continuity, at least on the level of the history of thought, constitute an organic link comparable to "blood links," to the transmission of hereditary characters ("their blood ... the embryo that needed several centuries"), such an idea implies a metaphoric assimilation between the formation of a thinking ego through various historical figures and the formation of a single organism through different phases. A more obscure but more narrow link, a "corporeal" link of kinship, of ascendancy, is substituted for the traditionally recognized intellectual relationships to a precursor, a model or a rival. This notion of kinship does not mean that the current ego of the philosopher is the result, the rational product of the logical development of the preceding great thoughts. It is indeed "in many respects" and not absolutely (i.e., in itself and for itself), that the current ego allows what was merely incubating in its illustrious predecessors to come to fruition. But what "ego" is involved there? What does *"I am already present"* mean? Is it certain that this is a *philosophizing ego*, a variety of the Cartesian *ego sum*? Let us note that Nietzsche does not say, "I am present in everything that Zoroaster, Moses, etc. ever thought," but in everything that ever "moved" (i.e., in everything that belonged to) the body of Zoroaster, Moses, and the Will to Power in them. In addition, only the first listing, Plato, Pascal, etc. provides a series of thinkers. In the second "list," dominated by the founders of religions and containing historical characters connected with violent events (Caesar's assassination, the French Revolution), there are only two philosophers. The issue therefore is not one of purely philosophical ascendancy, but of some wider point of resemblance dealing perhaps with the totality of the historical horizon. For these characters have nothing in common except the fact that they "left a mark in history," to borrow the ordinary expression. Nietzsche considers his revelation of Nihilism and Eternal Return as an event that "in all likelihood is going to break history in two segments."[95] "One day my name will be associated with the remembrance of something prodigious, with a crisis as never before on the earth."[96] The relationship—supposedly trans-historical—would then be the relationship to what *creates a destiny* in history. "I am a destiny."[97] Like the names on the "list," so the name "Nietzsche" is and always will be associated with a crisis, a turning, in history or in destiny, with a rupture and a new beginning, which each time presupposes some continuity. To what extent, and how, is this continuity—not only in the names of this "list" but also in "all the names of history," i.e., in all the figures that gained recognition in an era and that *are* merely names—*determined* by Nietzsche's ego? By inverting the thinking habit of identifying chronological succession with causality, and of deeming that the present ego can be nothing but the result of previous developments, Nietzsche does not formulate a paradox or a delirious idea of God's almightiness. His position rests on a double consideration concerning time. On the one hand, the past survives in the present (and the present has begun well before appearing as present); on the other hand, the future conditions the present—obviously—but also the most distant past (what comes next will modify the meaning of what was and what is). On the one hand, indeed, it is necessary to transpose on the level of historical individualities what pertains to the biological individual: he is not only himself, his narrow limit of actuality, he is "the entire chain" of the moments of history that led up to him. The thinkers with whom Nietzsche allies himself or against whom he struggles are not only present in himself, but he is present in them unbeknownst to them, as a sort of future development contained in a seed. This is the case for every fundamental historical relation. Napoleon could have said, "I am already present in the French revolution." On the other hand, such an anticipated presence means that the thought that Nietzsche made manifest—nihilism and the negation of the highest values in particular—must already be present in a latent, involuted, but clear form in the Platonic, Christian, and rationalist positions with respect to the highest values. The revelations of the future haunt, work through, the "past." Every thinker extends his influence not only upon his posterity, but far back upstream of himself. Nietzsche already haunts and defines Plato intimately.

But how can we accord this view of history, woven in legacies and secret lines of ascendancy—a history free of any strict chronology, and yet founded upon the idea of spiritual growth through multiple individuals—with the cardinal affirmation of Nietzsche's philosophy, the Eternal Return of the same? Doesn't the return of the identical preclude any genesis and development? Shouldn't one believe either in history or in the Eternal Return? Actually, there is a dilemma or a "contradiction" between historicality and the Eternal Return only if one conceives of the Eternal Return as a *fact*, as an actual mode of existence for the totality of beings. But the Eternal Return is no factual cosmic dimension, either "in itself" or as an "objective" universal law of nature (although Nietzsche did formulate hypotheses along these lines, but more in order to find confirmations by science for his "abyssal" thought than to *found* it on science). For the Eternal Return refers to the singular experience of an individual *in history,* or to the experience made by an individual at a particular time relative to his history and to history in general. The experience that "everything returns, has returned, will return," the experience of eternity is intrahistorical, but the one claiming its absolute validity escapes history conceived as an objective, homogenous, and universal development.

Nietzsche locates the announcement of the "Eternal Return" at the "center" of "world history." He also calls it rather frequently the "turning" of history. "As soon as this thought presents itself, everything takes another color and it is the beginning of *another history.*"[98] The doctrine of the Eternal Return must modify first the understanding of history, and then little by little the very style of its development: "The history of the future: increasingly this thought will be prevalent."[99] Nietzsche prophesies humankind's slow impregnation by this thought: it will take, he says, "millennia" to impose itself upon "all of future humankind."[100] Therefore it plays an intra-historical role. Yet it remains supra- or extra-historical: first of all because it is extra- or supra-temporal (the moment in which the return manifests itself contracts the future in the past, projects the past into the unlimited future); second because it depends upon so narrow and intimate a union of the individual with his *fatum* (as well as with every *fatum)* that this union cannot be manifested on the scene of history. Historical consciousness can only reject the idea of the affirmation of "I am such and such in the world once and for all times" because it sees it only as resignation, as the fatalism of weakness, as renouncing all progress. Finally, the idea of harmony, rather than a secretive and lack-free *fusion* involving the ego and the world (the one that is expressed in the formula "ego fatum"), seems to Nietzsche to be synonymous with being static and by principle eludes historical dialectics, based as it is on the *opposition* between the ego and the world and on their reciprocal transformation.

But this always singular fusion is announced only as a *possibility* (if you believed deeply that everything returns, what would result for yourself and for the world?), and not as an objective modality of the existence of things. Here it seems difficult to follow Heidegger's interpretation of the Eternal Return as akin to the metaphysical category of *existentia,* with respect to which the Will to Power would be *essentia*. "The mode in which beings-in-their-totality, whose *essentia* is the Will to Power, exists, i.e., their *existentia,* is the 'Eternal Return of the same.'"[101] The accord of this function with the Eternal Return is made possible because, according to Heidegger, the Eternal Return concerns the principle of the totality of beings. But along the way, Heidegger fails to mention the numerous reserves Nietzsche associates with his formulation of the concept of totality (particularly the idea that the totality of the circle of the return is bound to be shattered, lacunary, imperfect: *circulus vitiosus).* In addition, Heidegger fails to mention the impossibility underscored by Nietzsche of assigning to such a totality the character of both subjectivity and objectivity. The Eternal Return cannot be erected as a universal and objective law of nature because it depends upon an affirmation made by the individual. But it cannot be maintained either that "everything returns" is purely subjective, because this would amount to asserting that everything is the fictional double of an objective "In itself" situated outside a perspective. For the individual who affirms the return, extreme subjectivity meets extreme objectivity. But this degree of affirmation is so high that there is as yet no humanity capable of reaching it (man is the nihilistic being who prefers to believe in his disappearance forever rather than in his return). The only individual who would affirm the return might be the Overman. This is why it is necessary to maintain the necessarily conditional and hypothetical character of this degree of affirmation. In order to make the Eternal Return into a classical metaphysical proposition, Heidegger set aside the conditionality of Nietzsche's statements and claimed that "the Eternal Return of the same enunciates *how* beings in their totality *are*."[102] In fact the Eternal Return enunciates *how* the totality *should be* for the one who would affirm it without restriction, without the least reserve with respect to an eternal *da capo*. If Nietzsche can distinguish those who will not believe in it, and will be conscious only of some fleeting existence, from those who, believing in it, will have their life marked with the seal of the eternity, it is precisely because, contrary to Heidegger's interpretation, the Eternal Return does not constitute *the* mode of existence of the totality of beings. That is why, rigorously speaking, the Eternal Return escapes metaphysics, because no metaphysics can be founded on a *hypothetical* proposition, but on the contrary always searches for an *unconditional, anhypotheton*. Every metaphysics is a discourse on *phusis,* a physics, a realism. The thought of the return as a thought of a *possible* experience of the world is non-real and non-realistic.

By the same token, the Eternal Return contains an implicit critique of the realistic tendency toward an enlargement of individual subjectivity, toward its rootedness in the organic and historical world. Developing the "cosmic dimension" of the ego represents a new conquest of fleshly density, of the "earth," of those links that ensure that the subject is never insular. In this sense, the formula is not to be rejected. But this conquest remains flimsy in contrast with the true transmutation of subjectivity that might obtain after the suppression of the age-old opposition between the ego and the world. To speak of a "cosmic dimension" of the ego is to take the ego again as basis and point of departure. In formulas such as *ego fatum* or *amor fati,* who is the subject? Is it not, just as much, *fatum?* For "love" in *amor fati* is not, contrary to what Heidegger thinks, the supreme effort of the will in willing the "highest object," the totality of beings in their continual return.[103] This "desire of destiny" does not have merely the sense of an "objective" genitive, but also of a subjective one, inasmuch as it is the totality itself, the *"fatum,"* that takes this desire or this will upon itself. And since there is willing involved, it is a will to receive, a will to accept, an attitude that is not objective. Aren't the will and the subject metamorphosed, "neutralized," inasmuch as they are willed by the *fatum?* The unreserved affirmation of the *fatum* means that the *fatum* affirms itself through "me." Such a reversal *transfigures* the will (Heidegger interprets *amor fati* as "a transfiguring will to belong to destiny,"[104] but is it not rather a will transfigured by its belonging to destiny?) by suppressing the primacy of subjectivity.

But what is *fatum?* In no way is it the "objective" connection, one posited outside myself, of all those events in the world susceptible of concerning me and conceived of as inevitable and determined in advance. *Fatum,* from *fari* (to say), is the "spoken" that does not come from me; the "spoken" (words heard from whence? from a superhuman power, god or demon?)[105] whispers to me the overwhelming and exalting revelation, "you are this, you were this, and you will be this" and "everything is coming back, has come back, will come back." In the formula *ego fatum* it is impossible to separate what belongs to the "subject ego" and what belongs to the *fatum,* which is no "object," but more intimately the "subject" than the subject. Here the *ego* does not posit itself with every assurance and every transparency, as in the traditional metaphysics of subjectivity. It owes its emergence to speech, to the spoken word, and cannot be understood without the totality of the *fatum* that contains it, while containing itself within it.

Facing the richness of the critical analyses and attempts made by Nietzsche to treat the question of subjectivity, it is not possible for us to accept at the end of this examination the Heideggerian idea that Nietzschean philosophy merely perpetuates in modern times the classical model of the metaphysics of the subject and brings it to "completion." To be sure, Heidegger is right in showing that the essence of subjectivity does not reside in the privacy bestowed upon the *ego*, but in the position of a *sub-jectum,*[106] i.e., to an underlying substratum that takes the role of ultimate and absolute foundation. Nietzsche seems to concede this unconditional, underlying, and foundational function to the Will to Power as *body*. But such an interpretation is reductionist in many respects. First, it neglects the fact that the Will to Power is never identified with a substance, and most of all does not constitute a basis upon which phenomena unfold, but only their interpretative structure.[107] Furthermore, this interpretation does not take into account Nietzsche's radical questioning of the subject-object opposition. The traditional metaphysics of the subject implies the notion of an object-facing and objectifying representation. Now, Heidegger himself recognizes that the "aesthetic state" as it is described by Nietzsche is a state that manifests "the most transparent expression of the Will to Power" and escapes the subject-object duality. "Beauty is not the given object of a pure representation. ... The aesthetic state is neither something subjective nor something objective."[108] Just like beauty, the *fatum*—whatever meaning one gives to it—is neither objective nor subjective. At the very least one must acknowledge that the notion of representation of an object on the level of subjectivity ends up being strongly shattered. Finally, the Heideggerian interpretation fails to recognize that the *ego fatum*—be it as the *hypothetical* expression of the Eternal Return, as the *possible* suppression of the antinomies of the *ego* and *non-ego*, of freedom and necessity, of activity and passivity—brings about the ruin of the *sub-jectum*. It can be concluded that the subject capsizes into an abyss, into the vertigo of the return, or into madness, but in no way that the metaphysical subject remains unaltered as the venerable and unshakable foundation. It remains to elucidate what reasons pushed Heidegger to build up this hardly defensible construction. His own aspiration to find "authentic" identity, a certain totality, and complete finitude for the *Dasein,* and his distrust for the dissipation of the subject in multiplicity (namely, the multiplicity of occupations) are certainly not foreign to these reasons. However, this inquiry must be taken up another time.[109]

Can it be said that Nietzsche changed the essence of subjectivity? The "plural *ego,*" the "cosmic *ego,*" are merely attempts to sidestep the obstacle, the mountain of the *ego*. And yet, against a long tradition (to which the early Heidegger still belongs in part) that identifies the individual and the completion of conscious self-possession and against the quasi-sacred search for the *ownmost* (for the private sphere), Nietzsche sketches out the possibility—perhaps more oriental than occidental—of an *open individual*, or one at least whose limits are defined neither by self-consciousness, nor by self-positedness, nor by the assurance of an indivisible identity. Returning beyond Plato to Heraclitus, he reminds us of a sentence of the Ephesian, "You could never reach the limits of the soul, no matter how far your path takes you, so deep the *logos* is that it shelters."[110] Heraclitus' *psyche* is not the limited openness of the *Dasein* but the limitless and bottomless disclosedness of *Phusis*.

# Chapter 6

## LIFE AND NATURAL TOTALITY

*Chaos sive natura*[1]

Isn't Nietzsche a modern Stoic? Couldn't it be claimed that the model ruling over the Nietzschean philosophy of nature, and perhaps even over the thought of the Eternal Return, is a Stoic model—albeit one in reverse? Doesn't his philosophy posit a totality which is not reasonable but devoid of reason; a fatalism not merely ataraxic and resigned, but Dionysian and exuberant? Numerous indications reveal in Nietzsche an affinity, surely with some ambivalence, toward Stoicism. This affinity is characterized by an approval and a rejection, which are both so vigorous that they allow us to propose the expression *Stoicism in reverse.* Supporting this claim, we have texts such as: "Let us remain *hard,* we the last Stoics."[2] "The doctrine of the Eternal Return, that is, of the unconditional and infinitely repeated circular course of all things, this doctrine of Zarathustra *might* in the end have been taught already by Heraclitus. At least the Stoa has traces of it, and the Stoics inherited almost all of their principal notions from Heraclitus."[3] Stoicism again is mentioned as an example of "what is essential and of inestimable value in each morality, namely that it is a long-lasting restraint."[4] In spite of their illusory belief in the moral order of the world, the Stoics understood the necessity of self-tyranny inherent in the Will to Power; they understood that it is "in tyranny—and not in *laisser aller*—that 'nature' and 'the natural' reside."[5]

On the other hand, in the same manner in which Nietzsche occasionally alludes to the overcoming of Christianity by "hyperchristianity," he also affirms the need to become somehow a "hyperstoic," i.e., to possess *at the same time* hardness and softness. "For it is nothing to be as *hard* as a Stoic; by dint of insensibility, one has detached oneself from everything. One must have the opposite in oneself—a tender sensibility *and* the opposite capacity not to lose one's cool, but to be able with plasticity to 'make the best' of any misfortune."[6] Everything depends, for Nietzsche, on the magnitude of the force that carries the approval. In Stoicism, there was a great force, such that a Seneca who dared to say "Deus nudus est"[7] might well have thereby shaken off his own moral straightjacket.

For it is obviously with regard to the moral rigidity of the Stoics that the Nietzschean rejection is absolutely radical. The Stoic sage is a caricature, a "barbaric exaggeration."[8] His mistrust and hatred of pleasure allow us to have serious doubts about his professed love for a life and a world with which he wants to fuse. By dint of this repudiation and dismissal of the passions and pleasures, he gains access to a *total insensibility* and to *self-petrifaction.* And the god he embraces, says Nietzsche, is itself a mere statue! "What does it mean to kiss a statue in the winter, since one has then become insensitive to the cold?"[9] The Stoic does not love the world; in his claim of a *fatum*, he asserts nothing but a series of abstractions: order, goodness, beauty, reason, providence. He does nothing but indulge his love of himself, and of his own coldness and reasonings.

The ideal of *amor fati,* of universal approval, of individual existence fusing with the totality, can be meaningful, according to Nietzsche, only if this totality has been stripped of its "moral," i.e., anthropomorphic, attributes. This does not mean that the world should be conflated with life, and granted the character of a living being. On the contrary, one must forcefully reject the Stoic idea that the world is a great living being, *the* Great Living One. Supporting this claim, two reasons are given. First, the "presupposition that everything is organic contradicts the essence of the organic."[10] An organism needs an element exterior to itself in order to sustain itself and upon which to feed, for it would be absurd if it grew by feeding upon itself. In what direction would it grow, if it is everything there is? Second, an organic totality would necessarily be guided, as the Stoics do require, by a universal *logos,* a divine reason or soul. Thus, a biological representation of nature would supply "perhaps the ultimate form of the representation of God."[11] Seneca said: *"Quid alius est natura quam deus" (What else is nature if not God?)*[12]. But then, what is the world if it is not God? "The world is absolutely not an organism, it is Chaos."[13]

This rejection of the organicity of the world and this affirmation of "chaos" as defining the very life of the Totality raise several questions, which are all metaphysical because they concern the issue of the ultimate being of this totality. How can one think a totality without a unity? How can the totality be a living, yet not organic, being? What does the concept of "necessity" mean, when, for Nietzsche, it is the only one that can be applied without anthropomorphism to chaos, to nature, or to the world (these last two terms not being really distinguished in his lexicon)? Let me quote an essential passage: "The total character of the world, however, is in all eternity chaos—not because of a lack of necessity, but because of a lack of order, arrangement, form, beauty, wisdom, and whatever other names there are for our aesthetic anthropomorphisms."[14] Is the concept of chaos merely a preventive concept, one forbidding us from essentializing, eternalizing, and deifying nature? *"Chaos sive natura,"* says Nietzsche. Yet is it not precisely the eternalization of the world that the experience of the Eternal Return is bound to produce: *Haec est vita sempiterna tua?* The divinity of the whole in no way seems excluded by the concept of chaos, since it reappears both in the invocation to Dionysos and in the enigmatic formula, *circulus vitiosus deus.* What credence, then, should we lend to the injunctions that Nietzsche proposes: "One must rehabilitate nature, not deify it," or else "My task: to dehumanize nature and then naturalize man after he has acquired the pure concept of 'nature'."[15] What can "pure nature" mean for a philosopher who demonstrates that all our feelings of nature—to say nothing of our concepts—are entirely acquired, entirely "inherited," i.e., never immediate or spontaneous? What would an idea of nature be that would no longer be human? Isn't this idea humanized at the outset by the fact that it is a human thought? Isn't the negation of anthropomorphism still a human operation *[une humanisation]*? We shall see that Nietzsche attempts to capture the concept of "pure nature," by operating a relativization of the living in the face of the inorganic, and by proposing an insistent definition of life as immorality.

Doesn't the Nietzschean philosophy of nature lead, however, on this very road, to restoring the theology it sought to avoid—which takes place under the double characteristics of a *negative theology,* with the concept of *chaos*, and of a *theodicy*, with the concept of a *necessity* pertaining to imperfection itself? Beyond this inexorable outcome (the destiny inherent in the internal logic of metaphysics), isn't there in Nietzsche an ontology of nature that might already be a theology?

## Life Is not the Totality, nor the Good, nor the Evil, but a Logic of the Impulses, which Is the Origin of every Conscious Logic

There is no unconditional exaltation of life in Nietzsche. Life is not a totality, and is not the object of the highest affirmation. True, the Will to Power is thought, along the model of life, as the faculty to conserve and expand oneself, to exercise the perspectivalism of one's forces. But "life is only one instance of the Will to Power." The domain of the Will to Power extends far beyond the realm of living beings. It is Nature as a whole that is Will to Power. Hence, there is a rehabilitation of inorganic nature in the face of life. Every body, every atom extends its force and its action as far as it can. "Every moving force is a will to dominate."[16] Nature as a whole is neutral not only toward Good and Evil, but also toward life and death. In any case, it is not *by a necessity of essence* that it sides with life. "There is in nature no partiality toward what is alive, or against what is dead. If something does not manage to maintain itself in life, *no goal is missed as a result!* The character of 'finality' is accidental, human ..."[17] Thus, life is not the ultimate end of nature. "The living is merely a type of what is dead, and a very rare type."[18] Nature is indeed dehumanized, but at an exorbitant cost, since the superior unity, of which the living is a mere genus, must be one devoid of life! This view seems therefore to entail the preponderance, even the *superiority,* of the inorganic world. This superiority is paradoxical, because it comes about from the fact that elementary nature too strives, acts, perceives, and even "thinks," i.e., produces shapes. "'To think,' at the primitive (pre-organic) stage, is to *realize shapes,* as in crystals."[19] Apparently, Nietzsche grants even greater clarity to the action and thought he assigns to inanimate nature than to those of life, which is essentially subjected to illusion and "error." "Admit it: there are *perceptions* in the inorganic world, and perceptions of absolute exactness, wherein 'truth' reigns! With the organic world, *imprecision* and *appearance* begin."[20] When one moves from the inorganic to the organic realm, one moves from what is clear and certain to what is obscure and indefinite. As compared with a chemical substance, a protoplasm, says Nietzsche, "has only an *uncertain* and *vague* perception"[21]of the forms exterior to it, precisely because they are legion.

It is the uncertainty of life—its need to grope and err—that finally accounts for its power. Life is forced to invent cunning, as it finds itself faced with multiplicity—its own and that of external forces. It must, first and foremost create simplifications behind which to hide. "In the inorganic world, dissimulation seems to be absent—one brutal power against another; in the organic world only does cunning emerge."[22] Cunning is spontaneous illusion, and does not result from a prior calculation. A living being can only present itself as different than it is. It is bound to deceive, inasmuch as it deceives itself, i.e., essentially confines itself to its own limited perspective. To live entails for the living the act of extracting from the world what is necessary for its conservation and growth, and of abandoning the rest. To live entails accepting or rejecting, and hence abstracting.

Nietzsche conceives interpretation—the faculty to choose unilaterally according to one's point of view—as the essence of life: "The organic process presupposes a continuous interpretative activity."[23] In conformity with the logic of Platonism, he calls the vital principle itself *illusion, error,* because it is unable to seek a truth other than perspectivalist. Hence the formula: "Error, mother of the living."[24]

Life plays cunningly with the inorganic, as it plays cunningly also with its environment, and with itself. It can neither entirely dominate nor dissolve the absolute force of the non-living. It can only *feign* giving way to it. Consequently, an always unstable equilibrium of forces comes to pass. The link between the organic realm and nature is a link of reciprocal domination, amounting precisely to the reciprocal domination and infinite intricateness of truth and error!

If one accepts the definition of life in terms of *error*, it seems at first quite surprising that Nietzsche should associate the notion of *immorality* with all the definitions he gives of the *organic*. "Life rests on immoral presuppositions."[25] Why such presuppositions? What meaning do they have? With them, Nietzsche aims at a reversal not only of the optimistic naturalism of the Enlightenment, or of the Rousseauean myth of the original goodness of nature, but also of the Stoic idea of the essence—both divine and moral—of nature. He also wants to dismiss finalistic views, Providence, and any kind of theodicy. But doesn't anthropomorphism—even inverted—remain just that? Saying that life is the contrary of the Good conceived as virtue, and the perfect antithesis to Stoicism, inevitably leads to the same conclusion: it is *necessary,* it is *good,* that things be that way! Among the negative attributes that predominate in qualifying life are *injustice, lie, exploitation.* The inversion concerning the term *"injustice"* reestablishes the most transparent affirmation. "Absolute justice *[unbedingte Gerechtigkeit]* is what leads to the idea that life is essentially unjust."[26] "Injustice"—which affects the very essence of life—cannot be unjust. It is only unjust in the eyes of those who ignore its fundamental perspectivalism.

But let us quickly examine, one after the other, the three negative attributes. They appear in a fragment of *The Will to Power:* "In great men, the specific qualities of life—injustice, falsehood, exploitation—are at their greatest."[27]

According to what has just been said, the sense of injustice is apparently more metaphysical than moral. It is possible also to detect in it the inversion of Plato's *dikaiosunè*. Still, the injustice and violence inherent in the Nietzschean definitions can hardly be mitigated by—or reduced to—a pure ontology devoid of ethical consequences, as Heidegger seemed inclined to think. Let us quote four texts, which Heidegger never quoted:

> Life itself is essential assimilation, injury, violation of the foreign and the weaker, suppression, hardness, the forcing of one's own forms upon something else, ingestion and—at least in its mildest form—exploitation.[28]
>
> Doesn't living mean evaluating, preferring, being unjust, being limited, wanting to be different?[29]
>
> Life operates *essentially,* i.e., in its basic functions, through injury, assault, exploitation, destruction and simply cannot be thought of at all without this character . . . . From the highest biological standpoint, legal conditions can never be other than *exceptional conditions.*[30]

One would ruin the source of life if one wanted to abolish whatever was in some respect harmful or destructive.[31]

The ambiguity of these texts, as well as of all the so-called "immoralistic" propositions made by Nietzsche, is twofold On the one hand, they address life simultaneously as an organic process (Nietzsche talks about living cells, metabolism, nutrition, secretions, and excretions), and as the social existence of man entailing the concept of *right [droit].* On the other hand, they have a meaning that is ontological, descriptive, and practically phenomenological, and also a normative and prescriptive meaning. Thus, Nietzsche says that "the strong and free man acts in the same way as an organism":[32] the latter assimilates and rejects by using cunning, praise and blame, "enslavement to somebody else," i.e., submission. The organic realm becomes a model. This shows that immorality is inverted moralism. Nietzsche does not make a claim for injustice in the absolute sense, but insists that what traditional morality calls injustice is just. Justice, as the "supreme representative of life itself," is nothing but the essence of every estimation, of every position of value. Since "justice" has thus become, as Heidegger stressed, the name for truth, conceived as the adequation of life and the values it affirms, rigorously speaking, nothing can be characterized as unjust. Characterizing life as unjust would amount to an operation of rhetoric and sophistry. Nietzsche, said Fink, is a philosopher, as much as a sophist.

The same inversion applies to the negative attributes of lie and exploitation. Life is a lie inasmuch as it is appearance, dissimulation, endless mask-donning. In order to live, one must necessarily believe in fictions, in surface phenomena. By the expression of a "living lie," Nietzsche understands the fiction produced by the artistic Will to Power, which is itself a power of nature.

"This ability itself, thanks to which [the philosopher] violates reality by means of lies, this artistic ability *par excellence,* he has in common with everything that is. He himself is after all a piece of reality, truth, nature: how should he not also be a piece of *genius in lying*?"[33] In other words, in order to be part of the truth, one must take part in lying. In sound logic, this means that the lie is an essential attribute of the truth. Hence, when Nietzsche says that "life is a lie," he means to say that life is, in this way, the truest of truths.

On closer inspection, the term *exploitation* expressly refers to the Will to Power: every stronger sphere dominates, assimilates, or shapes a weaker sphere. This applies to nutrition as well as to social relations. "'Exploitation' is not a part of a vicious and imperfect or primitive society: it belongs to the *nature* of living things, it is a basic organic function, a consequence of the will to power ... "[34] Here too, the immoralism postulated and displayed dwindles and vanishes, while making room for a sort of levelling of, and indifference to, the essence of the phenomena. Isn't it nihilism to equate the relations between rulers and ruled to the process of digestion? The inversion of metaphysics that leads to asserting that everything is natural, raises the unpleasant—nay, despairing—question of the absence of any hierarchy in pure nature. Nietzsche never found the true hierarchy, which lies neither in the herd, nor in the Overman, who by essence is isolated, uncommunicative, and as incommensurable as a "splendid solar system."

If the negative definition of life constantly finds itself in an unstable position as the result of the anti-Platonic struggle entailed by it, doesn't the true originality of Nietzsche reside in the positive definition of life as creative power, as the capacity of the instincts and impulses to bring about a shape? Here too, unfortunately, the consequences of the inversion, not only of Plato but also of Hegel, constantly weigh upon the phenomenology of the living being. Nietzsche's greatest intuition consists in grasping life as a faculty of *incorporation, Einverleibung*. In this sense, the fundamental faculty of the living being is nutrition, bringing Nietzsche to write: "What we call 'life' is a plurality of forces, linked together by the phenomenon of *nutrition* that is common to them."[35] In order to accomplish nutrition, the organic being must be capable of sensibility, appetite, but also of evaluation, choice, assimilation, and elimination; hence, says Nietzsche, it must be capable of thought. "Every organism thinks," i.e., orders, condenses, establishes a hierarchy in beings. "Every organic being acts as an artist."[36] The phenomenon of incorporation, whose form is most obvious in nutrition, not only presupposes the presence of interpretation and selection, but also of memory. The organism never forgets anything. It incorporates not only the foreign element, the inorganic, but the non-foreign, the ownmost, in the sense that it integrates and coordinates its own experiences. It incorporates, finally, the *totality* of organic life that continues to press within it. "I presuppose memory and connection of spirit *[Geist]* in every organic being." "We must revise our idea of memory. It consists in the mass of all the experiences from the entire organic life, living experiences that order themselves, that shape themselves by reciprocal action (the ones struggling against the others), that simplify, summarize, and transform the facts into numerous units. Necessarily, this entails an internal process analogous to what happens when, from numerous isolated cases, one draws a concept; ... the feelings of inclination, repulsion, etc. are symptoms of an already formed inclination; our 'impulses,' as they are called, are such formations. Thoughts are what is most superficial."[37]

It is in texts of this kind that the inversion takes place. Here, the living body with its absolute memory has taken the place of the absolute spirit. For conscious thought is not merely a symptom of life. Life is the spirit itself. "The logical element is the impulse itself *[Trieb]*,"[38] or elsewhere: "What is commonly attributed to the *spirit*, so it seems to me, composes the essence of organic life."[39] "The logic of our conscious thought is nothing but a *crude and simplified form of that thought, which our organism, and even more each of its organs, needs.*"[40] Distinctions, nuances, the sense of haste, of concurrence, and of progression—intuited by our bodies—are much more refined than, much superior to, a mere category such as causality, which is available to our intellects. The extraordinary refinement of organic thought is capable of apprehending endless fluctuations in a flux of becoming, without fixating the process under rigid forms and arbitrary identities. Here we may think of examples, such as the descriptions that Nietzsche makes of the manifold relationships obtaining between consciousness and body. Consciousness is a simple organ, a very partial—in both senses of the word—instrument that is kept separate from the overall processes occuring within the body. Consciousness has the illusion of ruling, of deciding, but govern it does not. It is the instrument that executes choices and decisions that have already been made in our depths. Everything that emerges to consciousness is the reflection of a temporary equilibrium in the interplay of the impulses. What makes the decision concerning this equilibrium? The "great reason" is the body, namely, is organic thought that never stops computing the subtle and spontaneous estimates of relations between *quanta* of force. Life is incarnate logic, which combines the totality of its forces for the best, that is, according to the greatest advantage for its conservation and enhancement. This view is very Leibnizian. *Dum vita calculat, fit mundus* (While life calculates, the world comes into being), Nietzsche could have said. Such a point justifies the idea that he was the precursor of technology as universal instrumentalization—where each impulse becomes an organ—and integral computability.

Yet isn't there a flaw in this Nietzschean system of life? For Nietzsche grants to himself—in the same way that Schopenhauer and the Romantics did—the *intellectual intuition* of this organic thought, to which we can, however, gain no direct access, and about which, rigorously speaking, we should know nothing, because everything comes as the result of the deforming and superficial handling of consciousness and language, and is nothing but a falsified, or infinitely diluted, image. "Great reason," rigorously speaking, is ineffable. Since the elementary and subtle phenomena of life are inaccessible to our crude thinking, isn't the superior thinking attributed to it, if not a perfect fiction, at least a mere hypothesis?

From this derives the importance of the concept of chaos. Isn't the chaos some sort of indispensable correction to the hyper-rationalism of the Will to Power facing it? Isn't it the somewhat regulative idea that preserves the enigma of the world, in the face of the extreme requirements of an inverted—but nonetheless unrestrained—rationalism?

## As Soon As The Chaos of the Totality Is Affirmed Absolutely, It Becomes Divine Necessity. The Eternal Return May Be Viewed As A New Theodicy

But what is chaos? Is it not a name to designate the superabundance of the forces of becoming, that are too rich or too diverse to be limited to life? "Universal chaos" means that the totality is not subjected to the logic of the living, to "great reason." That such a chaotic totality forms nevertheless one single world, *"the world of the Will to Power and none other,"* is undeniably a radically metaphysical presupposition, one absolutely undemonstrable. Likewise, the notion of a finitude of forces, "whose totality is an invariable quantum," strictly and eternally confined within limits, is another presupposition that admits of no possible proof, but only of the affirmation—actually, the self-affirmation—of the world itself. This view is articulated in an admirable text in which Nietzsche describes this world as the divine, since its name is Dionysos. Let me quote the text, which, at the outset, provides the answer to the question, "Whence comes the unity of the totality of chaos?" It comes from the *affirmation* of the Eternal Return by itself, in which chaos is gathered, contained without being suppressed or surmounted.

> And do you know what "the world" is to me? Shall I show it to you in my mirror? This world: a monster of energy, without

> beginning, without end; a firm, iron magnitude of force, that does not grow bigger or smaller, that does not expand itself, but only transforms itself; as a whole, of unalterable size, a household without expenses or losses, but likewise without increase or income; enclosed by 'nothingness' as by a boundary; not something blurry or wasted, not something endlessly extended, but set in a definite space as a definite force, and not a space that might be "empty" here or there, but rather as force throughout, as a play of forces, at the same time one and many, increasing here and at the same time decreasing there; a sea of forces flowing and rushing together, eternally changing, eternally flooding back, with tremendous years of recurrence, with an ebb and a flow of its forms; out of the simplest forms striving toward the most complex, out of the silliest, most rigid, coldest forms toward the hottest, most turbulent, most self-contradictory, and then again returning home to the simple out of this abundance, out of the play of contradictions back to the joy of concord, still affirming itself in this uniformity of its courses and its years, blessing itself as that which must return eternally, as a becoming that knows no satiety, no disgust, no weariness.[41]

This world, insists Nietzsche, is "without goal, unless the joy of the circle is itself a goal, without will, unless a ring feels good will toward itself."[42] Only the circle of the Eternal Return "saves" chaos from non-sense, and conversely chaos saves the world from the trap of rational and moral finality. "The chaos of the whole, as excluding any teleological activity, *does not* contradict the thought of a circular ring; the latter is indeed an *irrational necessity,* flying in the face of any formal or aesthetic consideration."[43] There are, therefore, both a negative concept of chaos and a positive one. Negatively, the term has the preventive role of holding at bay two possibilities: the ancient representation of a great cosmic living being, and the various optimistic themes of the order, beauty, and finality of the world. Positively, chaos aims at designating all the raw forces of nature, animate or inanimate, taken in themselves, as they lend themselves to the schematizing action of the Will to Power. When Nietzsche says: "The Will to Power is the schematization of chaos," he implies that chaos "survives" this imposition of an order or of forms. Chaos is the zero degree of Being that eternally changes forms, not because of entropy (Nietzsche rejects it), but so as to be able to engage in a new cycle, by moving through nihilism (chaos would then be the "natural" name for nihilism). Since this imposition of forms upon forces is not a process that occurs from outside, but, instead, the imposing of a self-hierarchy, chaos is in effect the bottom, the base, or the primary material of the Will to Power. Since the Will to Power is always hylemorphic, chaos must be its hyletic component. Heidegger devotes many pages to the interpretation of this concept, and quite appropriately stresses that, for Nietzsche, chaos means metaphysically a specific relationship between multiplicity and unity: never will the multiple reach unity, never will becoming reach a stable state, Being. "Chaos is a multiplicity originarily exclusive of any unity and any form."[44] But Nietzsche in Heidegger's view equates *[reconduit]* chaos, arbitrarily it seems, to the *impulsive essence of life* in the process of organization, taking chaos to be the apparently ungovernable vital flux,which always "aspires to constancy".[45]

It is remarkable to observe the extent of Heidegger's efforts to reduce by all means possible the chaotic within the concept of chaos and to rationalize it. This reduction is evident, first of all, at the level of the very essence of the impulse. The latter, says Heidegger, would be diluted and would destroy itself if it did not find within itself the force to stabilize itself. There is in the essence of the impulse the necessity to resist itself, to *hold firm* against the impulsive rush, in order not to tumble and disappear under its own irresistible thrust. The impulse rests upon itself, and, in this fashion, surmounts its chaotic impetus.

The three interpretations of chaos that Heidegger gives are all highly positive. First, he associates chaos with a particular conception of *phusis* and *aletheia*. Chaos is pure nature, in the sense that nature is pure openness. Etymologically, chaos means the fissure, the crack, and the abyss that widens. The concept of chaos, inasmuch as it refers to an original upsurge and to the spontaneous development of the totality, seems essentially directed against the concept of creation by a personal god, be he Greek or biblical. The great Living One of the *Timaeus* presupposes the demiurge. This termination of the deification *[dé-divinisation]* of nature must not be crudely reduced to materialism, or hylezoism, and to atheism. Heidegger writes: "Metaphysical thought anticipates a path toward the extreme denial of deity, a path without phony escape ... a path that would be the only one—if that were ever possible in the history of humankind—where the gods encounter humans."[46] What is at issue is not exactly a projection upon Nietzsche of the Heideggerian expectation. Think of the famous sentence: "How many new gods are still possible!" Such a possibility is undoubtedly connected to the new relation between multiplicity and unity.

From there, the second interpretation follows. It is located in the extension of this quest for the deity. The thought of chaos conceives that nothing can be said concerning the supreme being, the world, or the totality. This *arrheton,* this unspeakable, constitutes a sort of "negative theology," essentially because it denies any human attributes to the totality.

The third interpretation presents such a distortion or so crude a denial of the incontrovertible Nietzschean doctrine—which states that "the world is in no way an organism, but chaos"[47]—that at first the reader is perplexed. For Heidegger identifies world, chaos, and living organism: "Chaos is the name of all-incorporating life, of life as a great living body ... Chaos is the name of a particular antecedent project, relative to the world in its totality. This project represents the world as a living body, extended so to speak to gigantic dimensions. In it the fundamental experience of the world as chaos is rooted." "The world as chaos means beings in their totality projected with respect to the image of the body and of the incorporating operation."[48] Such a blunder can be nothing but intentional. It reveals the unease that this concept produced in Heidegger, and the fact that it is difficult for him to renounce the metaphysical notion of order immanent in the totality. Heidegger repeats that one must not conceive of chaos as confusion, disorder in itself, upon which order would be applied from the outside, but as this "element of impulse, flux, and movement, whose order is *hidden,* whose law is not immediately known to us."[49] What is this *hidden* order, this law, if not precisely the order and the law of the Will to Power? Heidegger suggests erroneously that the Will to Power reveals, or contains, *the* intrinsic, definitive, and absolute order and law of the world, when in fact it is not a unique essence (Nietzsche says that there are always *several* partial Wills to Power), and when in fact it only brings out—here and there, and provisionally—*one given* order, *one given* law, which stand like islands of meaning destined to disappear later on. The belief that nature follows rules, as would ideal citizens, or civil servants, is anthropomorphic. In no way can it be compared to *the* secret order of the world! Instead, there are temporary and local orderings, i.e., a hierarchical ranking of forces, but, overall, chaos returns and dominates. If chaos is a necessary attribute of the natural totality, this is precisely to save it from "universal order in itself."

But if nature is this mass of forces without unity, form, and identity (for circular movement is none of these), what could the insistent Nietzschean theme of chaotic nature—in need of being retrieved, "reestablished," and "rehabilitated"—possibly mean? Chaotic nature seems unable to offer a model to imitate. However, first of all, there are the requirements of the imitation of the cycle: they urge us to become cyclical beings, to identify with existence, to be capable of experiencing several contrary points of view, several opposite philosophies, to view health from the perspective of sickness, and *vice versa*. Next, the absence of a moral order of nature must lead us to rehabilitate "physiology." At issue is the possibility of progressing in the acceptance of instincts that are devoid of rationalization, or of sentimental idealization, of accepting what he calls "naked nature." "A period when the old masquerade and moral decking-up of the affects arouses antipathy: naked nature."[50] Nietzsche is far from taking a radical stance against the naturalism of the nineteenth century. He wants to liberate it from the naive scientific positivism and its oppressive uncouthness. "There are signs that the European of the nineteenth century is less ashamed of his instincts; he has taken a goodly step toward admitting to himself his unconditional naturalness, *without becoming embittered*."[51] *Naked nature*, the expression means nature considered without judgment, without goodness or evil. Immorality, here, means in fact morality. Why do we feel at ease in the middle of nature, a forest or a mountain? The reason is not that it presents us with the image of goodness itself, as Rousseau believed, nor that the air is healthier to breathe; the reason is that "free nature has no opinion about us."[52] "To return man to nature" amounts to exhibiting a "primitive text," devoid of grotesque interpretations. But what does this "primitive text" say? What do we learn from "naked nature," which, for us, is no longer a model of virtue, which is not innocent or good, or beautiful, but only a little more *primitive* ("but instead of despising it on that account, we have felt more closely related to it ever since, more at home in it)?"[53] "Physiology," once more, is what "naked nature" is. It entails, for example, that friendship, love, artistic creation depend on physical dispositions. For centuries, the human body was poorly understood, or despised and mistreated. In contrast, our task is now to admire and imitate its wisdom, to let it teach us how to live, i.e., to be instructed in what is appropriate to health. Thus we must deem that taking an interest in climate, in location, in regimen, and in a choice of recreation, may not be unworthy of the philosopher.

Let him listen to music; let him walk; let him not read too much. "To read a *book* early in the morning at sunrise when one is still fresh, while one's strength is barely arising, this is what I call *vice*."[54] To know oneself is to be able to implement one's own regimen, to take the right steps in one's own life rhythms: "All of us die too young, from habits fraught with innumerable errors and ignorance."[55]

Understood in this sense, the return to nature, or rather the "progress in naturalness," is nothing metaphysical. Following nature's path becomes for us a prudent prophylaxis that takes into account the insertion of humans in their living environment. We are made up of the same elements as nature and, as Nietzsche points out, of more inorganic than organic ones. The link with the cosmos is asserted here. "We are the shoots of one single tree."[56] "Man is absolutely dependent upon cosmic forces, their distribution, and their motions."[57] With such a view, Nietzsche endorses the ancient idea—present in Stoicism and during the Renaissance—of an *organic* relation between the microcosm and the macrocosm. But isn't this idea contradictory to the affirmation of universal chaos? In order to observe a dietary regimen, or seek the benefits of one climate as opposed to another, mustn't one believe in a universal link?

Here again, we face the problem of totality. If nothing in the universe can be taken away, and if—as Nietzsche claims, in terms quite reminiscent of Leibniz—"the smallest detail implies the whole," how could we escape the fact that, in spite of the preventive concept of chaos, the Nietzschean philosophy of nature—notwithstanding its attempt at removing all deification *[dé-divinisation]*—is led to the rational justification of the totality? In Nietzsche, we find much more than fragments of a theodicy. First, there is the necessity of the whole; then, its supra-moral "goodness"; finally, its divine character. The texts that support this claim are numerous and well known. I shall quote only a few that in addition express the thought of an active and joyful fatalism. In *Twilight of the Idols,* concerning the strong man according to Goethe, he writes: "A spirit *thus emancipated* stands in the midst of the universe with a joyful and trusting fatalism, in the faith that only what is separate and individual may be rejected, that *in the totality everything is redeemed [erlöst] and affirmed—he no longer denies.*"[58]

The thought of *fatum* is the absolute antithesis of any idealism, which Nietzsche views as "cowardly in the face of necessity" and as exhilarating for the one who knows he is part of it.

"One cannot disentangle the fatality of one's nature from the fatality of all that has been and will be." Hence there is no equivalence between necessity, fatality, totality, and innocence: "One is necessary, one is a piece of fate *[man ist ein Stück Fatum]*, one belongs to the whole, one *is* in the whole—there exists nothing which could judge, measure, compare, condemn our being, for that would be to judge, measure, compare, condemn the whole ... *But nothing exists apart from the whole.*"[59] Quite obviously, this conception contains a sophism. In the absence of a measure appropriate for the evaluation of the whole, and with the impossibility of assessing the value of the totality of the world (in opposition to Schopenhauer), the universal link still is no obstacle to internal distinctions, such as the assertion that certain things, or certain human beings, are not as beautiful, not as good, as others. Furthermore, isn't such a proposition contrary to Nietzsche's philosophy, which requires a hierarchy between beings and the possibility of saying of some individuals that they shouldn't exist, because they are nothing but ressentiment against the world? But the totality is to be affirmed as it is, without adding or subtracting one *iota:* "Seeking 'what should be, but is not,' or 'what should have been,' is to condemn the total course of things. For in it, nothing is isolated: the smallest detail involves the whole ... . The smallest criticism raised against a detail is raised against the whole."[60] How could we not conclude that the world is perfect, down to its minutest detail, or, at the very least, reasonably satisfactory—as in Leibniz—in spite of various dark shadows? Nietzsche does not hesitate to voice this opinion, thereby obviating his own interdiction concerning any judgment of value on the totality: "It is certain that, assessed *[gemessen]* from an economic point of view, all in all the forces of nature are good *[allesamt gut]*, that is to say, useful, in spite of being the source of the most terrible and irrevocable fatality *(Verhängnis,* fatal power)."[61] The fatal and destructive power leads Nietzsche to observe that, once more, he sees the good in the totality, and evil in the details. He immediately reacts against his own reasoning, and concludes—temporarily—with the injunction to rid ourselves of the totality! "It is in my view important to get rid of the whole, of who knows what absolute: it would be taken for God—inevitably. ... The Whole would always bring back the same problems: 'How is evil possible?' etc ... *Hence, there is no whole.*"[62]

We are now facing the antinomy of which the Eternal Return must be the solution. *Either, there is a whole;* and in this case, one cannot fail to justify it rationally, to attribute to it also "totalizing power," "a universal sensorium," and therefore to reintroduce God as "the consciousness of the totality in becoming"—an operation that would be, according to Nietzsche, "the greatest objection to Being."[63] *Or else, there is no totality,* and thus no joyful fatalism, no supra-individual link, and becoming loses itself in indefiniteness. Every being sinks into dispersion. "Everything is a fragment, an enigma, a horrible randomness."

But isn't the Eternal Return an idealistic solution? For I am the *one* who says that there is a whole. *Ego Fatum.* The unity of the world is not organic, but depends upon a "yes." This "yes" may or may not be uttered. In any case, one thing must be said. "To state that *everything recurs* is the most extreme case of approximation *[die extremste Annäherung]* by the world of becoming (the only world) of the world of being (a fictitious world)."[64] Claiming that Becoming is Being,

Identity, Oneness (in Plato's sense), that it is abundant and perfect, such is the summit of contemplation, i.e., of the highest interpretation—yet it is nothing but an interpretation. To reach this "Dionysian affirmation of the universe as it is, without possibility of subtraction, exception, and choice,"[65] such an affirmation needs to rest on *necessity*. The interpretation needs to be reversed into pure necessity, the affirmation originating in the *ego* corresponding exclusively to the absolute self-affirmation of the world. In other words, it is the totality, "the eternal cycle, the same things, the same logic, or the same absence of logic of events," *that wants its own return,* and that affirms it through the individual affirming it—in order that his own affirmation be the affirmation of a self-affirmation. We have reached here the ultimate degree of the inversion—the inversion of the highest interpretation into the affirmation of affirmation—as we find it in "The Drunken Song" of the *Thus Spoke Zarathustra* or in the *Dithyrambs to Dionysos:*

> May you be eternal!
> May you be *necessary!*
> My love, eternally,
> Is kindled by necessity alone.
> Symbol of necessity,
> Sublime constellation of Being,
> Unreached as you are by no wish,
> Unsoiled as you are by no denial,
> The eternal "Yes" of Being,
> For ever I shall be that "Yes."[66]

I can utter the unlimited "yes" because Being has already granted itself the "yes," has already granted itself an eternal *blessing.* It has already said to itself that it is good. It loves itself, and that is why I love it. *Amor fati* is nothing but the echo of the love—both jubilant and rational—that Being has for itself. Being is again, incontrovertibly, *the* Model.

It is clear that Nietzsche did remain inextricably entangled within the metaphysical terms and themes he overturned, which, because he failed to think more originally, he confirmed and inevitably reestablished. Why is his ambivalence toward the models he borrows particularly intense with respect to the ones dealing with Greece? His love-hate relationship with Plato is no longer to be found in the relationship with Descartes or with German Idealism. Some Platonic themes—hierarchy and justice—remain unaffected in spite of, and through, the inversion to which they are subjected.

Likewise, *amor fati*—the affirmation of the totality inspired from Stoicism, once stripped of its moralizing rationalism—keeps its power. To be sure, the reason is that, from Plato himself to the Stoic decadence, there obscurely survives the same ideal of unity and totality which had been that of the Pre-Socratics. This is the "Dionysian ideal of the Greeks, the religious affirmation of life, life whole, to which nothing is denied, from which nothing is severed."[67] Pre-Socratic Greece, says Nietzsche repeatedly, is a "model of life." This concept of life does not have a biological meaning. It is the idea of "total life," without sundering, without *chôrismos*, between the intelligible and the sensible, good and evil, Being and Becoming, divine and human. The notion of "total life" is meant to retrieve a sense of being that precedes those divisions. Stoicism, which does not reject the unity of the world and stresses that "the world is the common house of humans and gods," keeps alive the memory of the unity that obtained prior to the Socratic catastrophe.

For Nietzsche, Greek culture "in the tragic age" had been able to achieve a vital equilibrium, based upon the harmonious continuity within even the most frightful "natural instincts," social practices, works, institutions, acts of worship—all of which took instinctual life upon themselves and managed a cultural outlet for it. The Greeks before Socrates had the strength and courage not to denounce the impulses—even wild and "immoral" ones—before the court of the Virtues. Natural forces *are integrated within* culture without being either repressed, extirpated, or tamed from the outside. Thus, envy becomes the fine *Eris,* who is emblematic of competitiveness set within limits. Let me quote a text, one of the most provocative among several dating from the same period (1874–1876):

> The pleasure of *inebriation*, of *cunning,* of *vengence,* of *envy,* of *insulting*, of *obsecenity*—all of these the Greeks acknowledged as human, and therefore integrated in the edifice of society and morals. The wisdom of their institutions rests upon the absence of a distinction between good and evil, black and white. Nature, such as it shows itself, is not disavowed, but *integrated*, assigned to worship on special days. ... A release appropriate to the forces of nature was sought, not their destruction and denial."[68]

Nature, *as it shows itself* in its disquieting eruption as *phusis,* is greeted and affirmed *in toto,* without being condemned in advance in some of its aspects. Greek life embodies the ideal of a life that is no "mere embellishment," but *life itself:* "A new and improved *Phusis*, without distinction of inside and outside, without dissimulation and convention, culture as the consonnance of life, thought, appearing, and willing."[69] But the secret of this harmony has been lost forever. Although the faith in the Eternal Return predominates, to us moderns nature is impenetrable in its own ground, and its *logos* is inaccessible: the totality, which is torn apart, chaotic, labyrinth-like, unfathomable, finds a cohesion, a sacred character, and a necessity only in *moments* of joy, in *moments* of full affirmation. Do these moments form a continuous link, because of some substantial connection or because of the repeated act of affirming? In most formulas of the Eternal Return, the supreme harmony is more akin to the unity of lightning (upon which, each time, the night closes) than to that of a constellation forever inscribed in the night skies.

## Chapter 7

# METAMORPHOSIS OF THE DIVINE

> The supremely original matter *[die ursprünglichste Sache]* ... the *originary* cause *[Ursache]* as *causa sui,* this is the right name for the god of philosophy. Man can neither pray nor sacrifice to this god. Before the *causa sui*, man can neither fall to his knees in awe nor can he play music and dance before this God.[1]
>
> Martin Heidegger

To ask about "Nietzsche and the divine" means to assume from the start (an assumption that remains to be verified) that the famous phrase "God is dead," however one interprets it, does not put an end to questions about God, gods, or the divine, but rather raises anew the question of the very essence of divinity. It assumes that Nietzsche's declared "atheism" is relative to a particular definition of God. His "atheism" is not concerned with the simple possibility of God, but rather asserts a distinction between a heavily conceptualized and domesticated God and a divinity free from the conceptual weight of metaphysical theology. Nietzsche initiates a questioning, which makes him, as Heidegger wrote, "the last German philosopher who was passionately in search of God."[2] As always with Heidegger, the expression "in search of God" is not an idle phrase but one rigorously coined in a specific context. The statement is not a psychological conjecture about Nietzsche, the man; nor is it an allusion to Dionysos (for in those contexts the god is not searched for but found—or about to be found); nor a reference to some of his famous sayings, such as "How many new Gods are still possible!"[3] or "Two thousand years and not one new God!"[4] Rather, the context is that of *The Gay Science* (Section 125), where for the first time, before *Thus Spoke Zarathustra,* the phrase "God is dead" is uttered by a strange character, the

Madman *(der tolle Mensch*—a reference perhaps to Anselm's *"insipiens"*?). For what does the Madman say, as he lights a lantern at high noon—or rather what does he shout, while running across the market place? He shouts, "I am looking for God, I am looking for God." As for Zarathustra, his proclamation occurs at the beginning of a long inquiry during which the possibility of a God is not excluded at all. On the contrary, there are several allusions to the possibility of another god: "I like the one who chastises his God because he loves his God" *(Thus Spoke Zarathustra,* Preface, Section 4), "I would believe only in a God who could dance" *(ibid.*, "To read and write"), and "Could you create a god?" ("On the Blessed Isles"). One of the so-called "Higher Men," the Old Pope, makes an allusion to this other God that Zarathustra is searching for, when he says to him, "O Zarathustra, you are more pious than you imagine with such unbelief! There is some God present in you that is inspiring you in your impiety. Is it not your piety that prevents you from still believing in God? ... You have eyes, hands, and lips made from all eternity for blessing." ("Available," "Out of service").

Whatever Nietzsche's position with regard to God and the divine, it is nothing like the dogmatic and easy atheism of the kind encountered in Diderot or in Sartre. To be sure, the atmosphere surrounding the announcement of the death of God in *The Gay Science* is one of anxiety and terror in the face of a catastrophe of cosmic proportions. It is most certainly not a happy event. For while—at least in Section 125 of that text—God does not simply die, the text does not insist on the fact that this is a crime, a murder. The emphasis is not on human responsibility, even though it is asserted: "God is dead; *we* killed him," but rather on the terrifying and apocalyptic nature of the catastrophe. The ancient God was as sun to the earth. Man split them, tore one from the other and henceforth the earth, detached from the sun, is falling into an infinite night. The earth has no more center, neither intellectual nor sensible light. "What were we doing when we unchained this earth from its sun? ... Is it not night always, night closing in on us?" asks the Madman. This catastrophic event is represented as an unbearable crisis, whose continuance will result in our own death, the death of the human race. Nietzsche insists on the fact that this is a rupture, an event unique in history, but also that it is a transitory, incomplete phenomenon. This event will inevitably complete itself, introducing—after the crisis, after the schism, after the "caesura" (as he calls it) in universal history—a new form of time: "this tremendous event is still on its way,"[5] and again: "the greatest recent event, that God is dead, that belief in the Christian God has become discredited, is already beginning to cast its first shadows over Europe."[6]

But what kind of discredit is this? Can discredit kill? How did God actually die? As we shall see, two simultaneous versions of his death are given in *Thus Spoke Zarathustra:* one that he simply died of sickness; the other that he was killed, that there was an assassination. Both scenarios are spectacular, dramatic, but not in the least tragic. It is the same God who died: the moral God, the God of consciences. The other version of the ancient God, namely the God of metaphysics, of the other world, creator and governor of the universe, did not die in a spectacular fashion. Rather, he wore out and vanished along with metaphysics. Undoubtedly, Nietzsche attached greater importance to the end of morality than to the end of metaphysics. The death of the God of morality necessarily brought with it the death of the God of metaphysics. The God of morality is the one Kant defined as the "ruler of the kingdom of ends," distinguished from the "Author of the world." He is the supreme Judge who rewards and punishes not only at the Last Judgement, but who now and forever "fathoms the loins and hearts," sees into the souls and their intentions, and through His Providence guides the course of the world. It is these moral determinations that in the end have turned against the idea of God. The centuries-old religious practice of the examination of conscience gave birth to a spirit of scientific scruple, which itself engendered a methodological atheism, forbidding appeals to "hidden causes" to explain phenomena, requiring adherence to facts. Nietzsche, who did not particularly believe facts to be sacrosanct (in his day any more than we do in ours), thought that such a moral-scientific atheism, far from destroying the essence of the divine, would liberate it for a rebirth in a new—and as yet indeterminate—direction. In two later and posthumous fragments, which both differ and harmonize, he affirms, without additional precision, the reappearance of God or of a god, and the disappearance of the God of morality:

"The refutation of God: finally only the moral God has been refuted."[7]

"You call this the self-decay of God: but he is only shedding his skin; he is only casting off his moral epidermis! You will soon see him again, beyond good and evil."[8]

This affirmation obliges us to ask what this God stripped of moral determinations would be like. If a rebirth of God remains possible, is it not because some immemorial, trans-historical, or pre-religious divine dimension subsists? Can this divinity have personal expression, or is Dionysos simply a symbol of the sacred? If this divinity exists outside of any establishment or institution, outside of even any tradition, as a pure possibility, why did Nietzsche call it by the ancient name of Dionysos? What link is there between the Greek Dionysos of *The Birth of Tragedy* and the new Dionysos, the internal

Dionysos, who—in Section 295 of *Beyond Good and Evil*—is called "the genius of the heart"? What suggests this continuity in the name of God? Is there a relation between this second Dionysos and Christ as conceived of by Nietzsche, a post-Christian Christ as innocent as Dostoevsky's, or a pre-Christian, quasi-Buddhist, Christ, identified with neither the moral nor the metaphysical God? Is Dionysos a god who has already come, or is he a symbol of the god or the divine still to come? Why is he not simply referred to as the "Nameless One" *(der Namenlose),* as in *Thus Spoke Zarathustra,* the One whom future hymns will name?

## The Death of God as the Self-Suppression of Bad Conscience

Each of the two versions of the death of God in *Thus Spoke Zarathustra* is linked to a symbolic character (of the category of the so-called "Higher Men," who are looking not for a completely new God but for an ideal to replace the old God): the Old Pope who says that he watched God as he died, and the Ugliest man, who says he is the murderer of God.

The preceding chapter shows us, through the intermediary of another very nihilistic character, the Enchanter, just where the drama of God's death takes place. The Enchanter is a poet-comedian who parodies and caricatures religious interiority. This character probably contains allusions to Wagner, as the founder of a pseudo-religion. In the manner of a cheap melodrama, the Enchanter acts out a masochistic relationship between God and the guilty conscience, a conscience that suffers for its sins, but wants to suffer even more than it wants to be seen suffering. God, its supernatural partner, is reduced to a purely sadistic divine stare that tortures it for no apparent reason (since the term "sin" is not even mentioned) while watching it suffer. This conscience both adores and detests its torturer:

> Why are you still staring at me, you who are
> eternally hungry for human suffering, why do
> you strike me down with your divine and cruel eyes?[9]

This strange God, a Voyeuristic God (recalling the Sartrian "stare"), "Tormentor God" and "hunter" of souls, is not explicitly identified with the Christian God, since he is called "the Unknown God," "Thought, Unnameable". The comedian acts out the soul's despair when God is absent or has disappeared. Suddenly, he is gone and the soul is left with nothing but nostalgia for the continual staring and torment, and regret for the token of love in the pain. The soul would now prefer the company of this "divine tormentor" to its loneliness.

> Disappeared!
> Flown away, even him,
> my last, my only companion ...
> my divine tormentor!
> No ! Come back, with all your tortures ...
> Oh, come back!
> My tears stream
> towards you!
> The last flame of my heart
> flickers towards you!
> Oh, come back
> you, my unknown God, my pain, my last happiness![10]

What is the meaning of this text? Why the *acting out* of this perverse relationship with God? Nietzsche wants to show a moment of extreme crisis in the development of the bad conscience. It has discovered a cause of its suffering outside of itself, a cause whose absence it can then no longer bear. The Enchanter says to Zarathustra: "I played the role of the *Penitent of the Spirit* ... the man who freezes on contact with his bad conscience." This text represents the passive version of what the chapter, "The Ugliest of Men," presents in its active form: the difficulty for man to accept the absence of a transcendent spectator of his suffering, a spectator whose constant presence is the very target of the assassin of God. Both versions represent the same morbid hypertrophy of an interiority that refuses to accept its dereliction. The text also suggests that no one believes this play-acting any more, it cannot even be performed: "The distaste [for your performance] alone is true *[echt]*" says Zarathustra to the Enchanter. The impossibility of presenting God as a hypostasis of bad conscience, the disproportion of such an image, its unbelievable quality, foreshadow the imminent disappearance of such a God.

It is at this point that Zarathustra meets the Old Pope, who tells him that he was the last Pope and served the ancient God to the end. He also tells the story (which Zarathustra will immediately suspect of being a fable, a fiction) of the decline of the Judeo-Christian God: "Hard and vindictive in his youth ... he ended up growing old and soft and limp and compassionate, more like a grandfather than a father. ... One day he ended up dying, choked by his excessive pity."

Much earlier ("On Pitying"), this interpretation had been attributed to the Devil, who says: "God died of his pity for men." Why is pity so dangerous, why can it be fatal? For Nietzsche, pity is a shameful glance at the suffering of the other. This glance is bad in itself, because it weighs down the shame of the one who suffers, and then it weighs itself down and falls even lower under the weight of its own shame. "I was ashamed of his very shame when I saw the suffering one suffer" ("On Pitying"). Pity is shame at witnessing a suffering, which is already humiliating. As shame about shame, pity is a paralyzing backwash of subjectivity against itself, a backwash that causes a congestion, a choking. Pity can neither let be the suffering of the other nor assist it by means of what Heidegger calls "*Fürsorge,*" so that he might overcome it. "If your friend is sick, give shelter to his suffering, but be a hard bed for him" *(ibid.).* Tenderheartedness belongs to a sentimentality enamored of itself and caught up in itself, so that pity loves itself and its own pitying more than it does the other. When taken to an infinite degree, this tenderheartedness, this suffocation, this narcissism become fatal. Through pity, God's love for men becomes infinite love of self.

This idea of suicide by pity, a self-decomposing of God from a surfeit of good feelings, is not presented by Nietzsche as something to take seriously as an interpretation of the nature of God. Rather, it is a psychologizing, human, all too human, interpretation borne in the mind of the Pope. He does not believe that God could support his own infinite pity. His version gives rise immediately to Zarathustra's ironic, doubting comment: "Did you see that with your own eyes? Surely, it might have happened this way, or another, for when Gods die, they always die several kinds of death." Zarathustra suggests that perhaps the Pope saw nothing, that he invented the whole story. A Pope who had lost the faith discovers that God is not viable, is sick unto death; but the idea that God is but a monster of pity and must die of it only demonstrates weariness and distaste for pity.

The succeeding chapter puts the theme of pity in the foreground once again. This time, pity is the direct cause of the murder. The "Ugliest of Men" wanted to suppress the witness to his shame. He killed him out of hatred, out of resentment for God's pity at his shame. Why is the murderer of God hideous, horribly ugly, without form ("he looked like a man, but had almost no human shape, an unnameable being")? One might think that his ugliness came simply from his shame before God, or his resentment of him. But for Nietzsche, just as all beauty is affirmation, so all ugliness originates in non-acceptance of self. The ugliness of the "Ugliest of Men" comes primarily from ressentiment for himself. He does not love himself; he does not love man; he does not love the world. He becomes a murderer because he cannot bear that an omniscient and always vigilant conscience should know and see constantly the mass of suffering and hatred within him. Thus, the murder is by a sick man, the act of someone unbalanced. There is something mad, something paranoid in the discourse of the murderer of God, a folly with an element of truth—namely, the fact that man, whose being is rooted in ressentiment, must finally deny himself: what man denies in God is in fact his own unbearable essence:

> But he, he had to die *[er müsste sterben]*: he saw with eyes that saw *everything,* he saw man's depths and ultimate grounds, all his concealed disgrace and ugliness.
> His pity knew no shame; he crawled into the dirtiest recesses, this most curious, over-obtrusive, overpitying one, he had to die.
> He saw me at all times. I wanted to have revenge upon such a witness, or to cease to live.
> The God that saw everything, even man, had to die *[er müsste sterben].*
> Man cannot bear to let such a witness live.[11]

At this point, metaphysics seems to have turned into a bad detective story. The idea that God's lack of discretion, the morbid pleasure he would have in scouring the deepest—necessarily dirty—recesses of the human heart, comes from psychopathology. It is the dysfunctional projection of a persecution complex and a delirium of self-accusation. God is only the hypostasis of a delirious bad conscience, magnified by the metaphysical dimension into a constant presence. What is unbearable about the "divine" look of pity is its metaphysical, tireless, and infallible constancy; that God is endowed with inexhaustible, unflagging attention: "He saw me at all times."

In *The Genealogy of Morals,* Nietzsche defines bad conscience as the profoundly morbid state that occurs when the aggressivity of the subject, which a certain development of the social order prevents him from exteriorizing and turns against the Ego. God's murder, the hyperbole of aggression, is the desperate attempt by man, suffering from himself, to get rid of the cause of his suffering. The murder of God reveals the impasse represented by a certain fixation on the very essence of man. Without bad conscience, no humanization, no internalization would exist. But this internalization is now secured, and man must move on to a new stage in which bad conscience is no longer necessary. The hypostasis of bad conscience as God, and the suppression of that hypostasis, are man's clumsy efforts to free himself from his reactive essence. But that reactive essence is already bypassed, already dead. The theme of the death of God and the fiction of his murder are part of a mourning ceremony, mourning which has as its true object the traditional essence of man. Man must overcome the loss of himself, overcome grief for himself, lest he remain enclosed in his former essence. "If we do not make of the death of God a great self-denial and a perpetual victory over ourselves, we will have to pay for this loss."[12] Grief over God's death can only be overcome by a new affirmation, by an evaluative principle other than that of a moral conscience thought of as self-accusation. Nietzsche calls this new principle for evaluating the world as a whole "the innocence of becoming." It implies not only the death of the moral God, but also, as we shall see now, the death of the metaphysical God, that is, God conceived as the leading conscience of the universe, as the operator of universal finalism. The innocence of becoming means the exclusion of universal ends in nature, in the world, as well as in history. "Becoming must appear as justified at every moment, so that it is impossible to devalue it,"[13] justified without recourse to any global completeness or intention, or any "final state." The metaphysical God originated from reactive nihilism, from the post-Platonic denial of becoming (understood as the world of sense, whose "truth" is a "world of affects"), for the benefit of a supposedly immutable true world. Totalization, finalism, absolute goodness and immutable truth, identical with God or rooted in God—all these depreciate becoming and relegate it to a passive role in the achievement of the Absolute.

Such a God cannot die a violent death. Does it contain some element of the divine essence that is changing, that is metamorphosing itself? The moral God was personal, yet neutral, "objective" with the pure gaze of total overview. The metaphysical God was simply an impersonal, universal organizing principle. Contrasting with these abstractions, it seems, Nietzsche calls his Dionysos "the genius of the heart" and gives him a secret, furtive, intimate, and totally individual, not to say incommunicable, character. Does this amount to abandoning any idea of a universal divine power, a power gathering all together, implying the participation of all beings, and of which the metaphysical God was an all too rational example? We will see that something of the universal element, something Pan-like, something of the Greek Dionysos, is retained.

## The Refusal of a God Conceived as "Universal Consciousness of Becoming," or as "Total Sensorium," or as "Total Process."

The criticism of the idea of God as "total consciousness of becoming" is addressed more to the principle of totalization than to the principle of the absolute supremacy of the consciousness hypostasized as God. The common error among philosophers is to make consciousness a supreme measure, a regulating principle of the living, whereas consciousness is an instrument, a simple organ (of superficial unification) in the service of life, a translation of the necessities of life into simple codes or abbreviations, a "numerical language." "All philosophers instinctively tend to imagine a total consciousness, a conscious life and a conscious will of everything in existence, a 'spirit,' 'God.' But it must be said that such a hypothesis truly makes existence a *monster;* that a 'God,' a universal sensorium would be sufficient to *condemn* existence ... To have eliminated this global consciousness which sets ends and means is our great *relief*—it is that which permits us to be *obligatory* pessimists ... Our strongest objection to existence was the existence of God."[14] To admit the existence of God as an omniscient consciousness that governs the totality of the world from above and beyond, from the *geometric focal point*, i.e., from a fictional geometric point that serves as the focal point of all perspectives, that imposes an order on the totality, a necessity, a transparent finality—all this amounts to demoting the world because it is tantamount to measuring it against an external quantum. A point of view which from the outside could cast a gaze upon the totality does not exist. Given that there is a totality, it must contain all things including all interpretations that are given of it. Given that there is a necessity, it could not possibly be imposed from outside, like the necessity of the laws of nature, those laws which Descartes's God established as a monarch would in his kingdom. If there is a necessity, it could not certainly be an immanent rational necessity, as is the case in Spinoza. The only "admissible" necessity for Nietzsche would be one that embraces everything, that encompasses all contraries, suffering and joy, creation and destruction, chance and reasonable freedom, chaos and law. The necessity that appears in the idea of the Eternal Return, the "ring" uniting all things, the Divine Ring, a Circle "perfect" in its very defectiveness, *circulus vitiosus deus,* a defectiveness that is nothing else but the impossibility of totalization—this Nietzschean "necessity" is a category without contrary and, in addition, linked to an undecidable. Indeed, it is impossible to say whether this "necessity" is the self-affirmation of becoming, or whether my affirmation is what engenders this necessity; in other words, whether my affirmation inscribes itself in necessity, or whether it makes an originary appeal to it. Such is the ambiguity of the *ego fatum* of *amor fati* (or rather, the ambiguity resulting from the identity of these two contrary formulae).

> Symbol of necessity,
> Supreme constellation of Being,
> Eternal 'Yes' to Being,
> Forever I am your 'Yes.'[15]

In any case, Nietzsche rejects a God who communicates a necessity of becoming while being himself outside of becoming.

> "Necessity" [is not to be represented] in the shape of an overreaching, dominating total force, or that of a prime mover; even less as a necessary condition for something valuable. To this end it is necessary to deny a total consciousness of becoming, a "God," to avoid bringing all events under the aegis of a being who feels and knows but does not *will:* "God" is useless if he does not want anything, and moreover this means positing a summation of displeasure and unlogic which would debase the total value of "becoming." Fortunately, such a summarizing power is missing (—a suffering and all-seeing God, a "total sensorium" and "cosmic spirit" would be the greatest objection to being).[16]

Here Nietzsche intends to refute theodicy by means of two arguments. In the first place, if God were not only omniscient, but also an omnisentient Absolute (absolute sensorium), he would suffer all the pains of the world. But the projection of suffering into an all-powerful sensibility would either annul it (which would suppress the problem of divine compassion) or would give to the suffering a hallucinatory and truly fantastic intensity. Nietzsche reverses the reasoning of theodicy. The existence of God as absolute will and consciousness of the good, as absolute feeling of evil and suffering, cannot diminish the "total" suffering (from a perspective where the suffering would be reconciled by being included within a universal compatibility), but can only intensify it and make it more absurd. There is only one way to exonerate God from evil, and that is to say that he knows nothing of it, that he can do nothing about it, even though he is "power," albeit power devoid of finality. Hence the surprising aphorism, "Let us separate supreme goodness from the concept of God ... Let us separate supreme wisdom in the same way; it is the pride of philosophers that has imagined this absurdity ... No, God is *Supreme Power.* That is enough. From that, everything results, from that results the 'world!'"[17] But—and here comes the second argument against theodicy—a theodicy is in any case impossible a priori, not because, in Schopenhauer's words, the sum total of suffering is greater than the sum total of happiness, but because such a totalization does not make sense. There is no "process of the whole," there is no making compatible with the "whole," because there is no "whole."[18] The world is neither a system nor an organism. The depth of Chaos that it includes cannot be reduced or reabsorbed, no matter what the point of view.

The refusal to hypostatize finality into God, the criticism of a universal, transcendental teleology, is each time simply a corollary to the rejection of totalization. The finalistic, providential interpretation of the phenomena of nature, of history, or of individual existence appears to the scientific spirit—trained and brought up in the ascetic ideal of probity inherited from Christianity—as a mystification, as an edifying fiction whose goal is to explain everything, as being part of a total plan of God.

> Considering nature as if it were a proof of the goodness and the protection of God; interpreting history for the glory of divine reason as a permanent witness of the moral finality of universal order; interpreting one's own experiences according to the meaning given to them long ago by the pious, as if *everything* were merely aptitude and illustration of love and as if *everything* were conceived in order to lead to the salvation of the soul: this is what has come to an end, from now on, this is what consciousness has against itself.[19]

The paradox that Nietzsche underscores in *The Genealogy of Morals* is that this 'atheism' of interpretations is the self-destructive consequence pure and simple of applying the Christian ideal of rigorous and unconditioned truth.

Nihilism as "psychological state" is thus for Nietzsche the manifestation of an enormous lie, of disillusion, and, ultimately, of despair in the face of the crumbling of universal meaning, which results from the absolutization of becoming taken as a whole by means of logic and the moral order. "Psychological nihilism manifests itself when one has presupposed a *totality*, a *system,* even an *organization* within facts and between *all* facts."[20]

The excessive meaning turns into an excess of meaninglessness. "The soul longing for admiration and veneration," which draws its strength and its self-confidence from its relationship with the whole, which thinks of itself as "a mode of the divine," loses "the faith in its own value"; it feels no longer connected to anything, no longer guided by anything, no longer held to anything. "We have arrived at the feeling of the nonvalue of existence, when we have understood that it can no longer be interpreted as a whole either with the aid of the concept of 'end,' or with the aid of the concept of 'unity,' or with the aid of the concept of 'truth'"[21] (in the sense of a world both true and moral in itself). The moment of the complete dedivinization of the world, the complete dissociation of becoming and the logico-moral divine, constitutes the gravest crisis in the history of humanity. With the disappearance of the true world, the apparent world initially loses all consistency.

The reaffirmation of the divine beyond such a crisis is everything but evident. Man has several possible "outcomes"—actually, however, all dead ends. He can wallow in pessimism and in a new "Buddhism," in forms of indifference and frivolity; he can take refuge in a mediocre search for happiness, as does the "Last Man," or, again, in the adoration of the mere surfaces of things, in the admiration of anything whatsoever lacking significant depth (which is simply a version of reactive nihilism, the nihilism of ressentiment against excess of meaning). "We will no longer take anything to heart, we will chose the mask as supreme divinity and as redeemer."[22] Nietzsche prophesies a long reign for the substitutes of the dead God, which since the nineteenth century have been Science, Progress, and Happiness for All. According to Nietzsche's prophecies, the nihilistic crisis (with such terrifying symptoms as, for example, the decomposing of intra-individual unity and the economic and political struggles for planetary domination) will last two centuries, the twentieth and the twenty-first!

One might ask to what extent the doctrine of the Eternal Return is itself prisoner to nihilism, caught up in the reactive cycle subsequent to the destruction of the ancient gods. At first glance, the doctrine *seems to reverse* the nihilistic conclusion of the death of God ("Nothing has meaning anymore," because there is no end to becoming, no universal and transcendental goal), by making the contrary affirmation: "All is perfect, divine, eternal."[23] The phrase, according to Nietzsche, is pantheistic, but is not that of the Eternal Return. There is indeed in the Eternal Return a dimension that comes close to pantheism, insofar as the Return is the self-justification at every moment of the world, as good, infinitely precious, infinitely worthy of being affirmed, and completely assured of returning. But Nietzsche expressly rejects the idea of the divinity of the world, or rather of the world as divinity. The world is not a new god. The process is "divine," but it is not guided by divine intentions, nor by the opposite intention to be without goals whatsoever. For we wish at all cost the movement of the world to be "controlled," even if it means that no end could ever be produced. We keep "this nostalgic need to believe that the world is at least at some point similar to that ancient and well-beloved god, that infinite God of unlimited created power."[24] This is precisely Spinoza's nostalgia for *Deus sive Natura,* which wants to believe that "the god of old still lives." For Nietzsche, the world must not be thought of as an infinite substratum, unlimited in extension, eternally new, but eternally repeated, resounding within itself. We must be able to affirm of everything that it is divine without affirming the divinity of the All, without even affirming that there is an All. For there is certainly no All, which would be a subject conscious of all and settling everything. Dionysos, so enigmatic and diversely present in the later texts, most often represents not a god but rather explicitly a *faith* and attitude which Nietzsche calls "a joyous fatalism." "The faith ... that generally speaking everything is resolved and affirmed ... this is the faith, the highest possible of all faiths, that I have baptized in the name of Dionysos."[25]

## From the Revelation of the Divine to the Naming of a God

In the period of nihilism, all new naming or determination of a god appears provisional, hypothetical, and multifaceted in its formulation. For between the long perishing of the metaphysical moral god and the upsurge of a new meaning of the divine or of the god, the most that can be hoped for is that a space of expectancy remain open, a period of latency and maturation in which, when it is capable of emerging, the new meaning will appear indeterminate and surrounded by many blanks and question marks. The divine undergoes a metamorphosis without reference to any destination and any decision. There is no question of a "controlled" transmutation by any sort of will whatsoever. In the interregnum, when nothing is fixed, when the divine is—as it were—indecisive, free-floating, scattered, the philosopher must above all know how to wait. "We must wait and prepare ourselves to spot the welling up of new springs, prepare ourselves in solitude for strange visions and unexpected voices,"[26] writes Nietzsche in those fragments which also refer to Dionysos. After the death of God, the divine is to be reinvented.[27] It is to be rediscovered according to its own, "wild" apparition that we must not rush to categorize under an already established name and identity. It is obvious that for Nietzsche, Dionysos is only a name for expectancy, and not at all the definitive and final name of God. Despite this name, the god remains "the unnamed god" evoked in *Thus Spoke Zarathustra*, or again the "unknown god," the "ungraspable god" *(Du Unfassbarer)* previously invoked in an early poem (1844). "Oh, you, the ungraspable ... I want to know you and love you."[28]

The name Dionysos seems the most powerful Nietzsche could find to designate a divinity still to come and a sacred form, both surprising and beyond classification, ever abounding and beyond limit. One must emphasize that the path of polytheism, which he sometimes urges, never leads to any sort of naming. Apollo disappears, forgotten in the Apollonian principle. The ancient Dionysos is dead. No other god is named. The *epoche* of the unique Name seems demanded out of respect for the very force of the experience of the divine. Lack of knowlege of the Name is tantamount to a negative condition for a new blossoming or a free redeployment of the "religious instinct." "The religious instinct experiences a vigorous surge, but rejects with deep suspicion the pacification of theism."[29]

In his later years, after the positivist critique of religion as an aberrant form of causality (in *Human, All Too Human*),[30] Nietzsche forced himself to describe the primordial, elementary, or transcendental conditions of the religious instinct, when it manifests itself outside a determined tradition or revelation. For him, faith and piety rest above all on the feeling of a "necessary link" between all things, of an immanent unity, of an original cohesion of the world that can possibly include transcendent beings. "Piety towards God is piety towards the necessary link between all things and the belief that there exist beings superior to man."[31] Only on the basis of an ancient sacredness predating all revealed faith could a god arise. Contrary to Heidegger, this sacredness resides less in Being itself than in a *fundamental feeling*, the feeling of the necessity of the universal link, the *amor fati*. This is a paradoxical pantheism where it is not the all that is divine, but rather the feeling of the link, or the link itself, and where each thing is sanctified and transfigured insofar as it participates in this link. "In solitude, where I experience all things as necessarily linked, every being is divine for me."[32] The divine character of the cosmic cohesion might well be one of the primitive contents of religious "revelation" taken in its originary indeterminateness as pre-religious, predating every constituted dogmas. The indissoluble feeling of a marvelous belonging-together of all beings would be the source of the "religious instinct." "I, in whom the religious instinct—namely the one giving rise to the shape of a god *[gottbildende]*—is sometimes set in motion inappropriately, in how many different ways have I not received the revelation of the divine!"[33] In how many different ways? Nietzsche remains rather discreet concerning these experiences, which he calls "encounters." But through all the different aspects he describes (joy, surprise, the uncanny, the *stopping of time*, and *instantaneousness:* "I have experienced the sight of so many things in these moments out of time"),[34] the Revelation is that of a link at once supremely necessary and supremely harmonious. "Five, six seconds, no more—suddenly you experience the presence of eternal harmony."[35] This is an almost unbearable, overwhelming feeling of joy, approbation, a feeling "superior to love."

In his mortal shell man could not withstand this: he must either

> transform himself physically or die. Clear and indisputable feeling. You have the feeling of contact with nature in its entirety and you tell yourself, "Yes, this is true!" When God created the world, at the end of each day he said, "Yes, this is true, this is good!" *This is no emotion, my friends, this is joy.* You forgive nothing because there is nothing to forgive. You love no longer—oh, this feeling is superior to love. Most terrible is the awesome certainty through which this is expressed, the joy that overwhelms you. If this lasted longer, the soul would not withstand it, it would depart.

And the end of this text is surprising. For Nietzsche talks about "the understanding of the symbol of resurrection." A feeling that "the goal has been reached." The divine appears as a break in ordinary time, an *ecstatic* sight when the veil of interpretations is removed and when the universal link reveals itself to understanding, that is to say, affirms itself with irresistible and unlimited evidence and force. The "saying-yes-and-amen" without measure, without limit *(das ungeheure, unbegrenzte Ja- und Amen-Sagen* from *Thus Spoke Zarathustra,* III, "Before the Dawn") imposes itself before one can even express it. This "yes" is indistinctly the "yes" of man and the "yes" of Being, as in the *Dithyrambs of Dionysos* already cited: "Eternal 'yes' of Being, forever I am your 'yes.'" This is not the revelation of a particular divinity—nor of an unchangeable, divine essence of things that would eclipse what is human—but rather of an irresistible inclusion in Being. For Nietzsche, only moments can contain this "revelation," and that is why it is destined to remain indefinitely wild and untamed, since it is part of no continuity and always appears in the flash and lightening of the moment. On the side of man, let us recall, the Dionysian attitude is defined as "*instantaneous* identification with the principle of life."[36] On the side of the Will to Power, the divine or god is an apogee (one can find several positive definitions), a climactic state of the forces: "'God' as culmination."[37] "The only possibility of retaining any meaning in the concept of God would be to represent God not as the moving force but as the *maximum gradient* of forces."[38] "God" would be a state of perfection of the Will to Power in which the superabundance of forces arrives to an equilibrium with respect to which earlier stages of perfection could later be understood and linked in a *history*: "God" is explicitly named as an "epoch."

But the divine in Nietzsche is not synonymous with a perfection that would preserve itself free of all possible degradation, fallenness or destruction. Supreme perfection includes imperfection, as the highest joy includes suffering. "Perfection is nothing else but the prodigious *expansiveness* of the feeling of power ... (that would extend so far as wanting obstacles)."[39] Perfection is not in fact an objective state of affairs, but a *Stimmung,* specifically the very *Grundstimmung* of joy. Divine is the moment, *movimentum*, the movement of transcendence in immanence, the *apogee* when joy severs the links, reunites what was sundered, reaches the limits of existence, and without reducing them gathers the negative, evil, suffering, and all forms of imperfection. At this juncture, "The Drunken Song" of the fourth part of *Thus Spoke Zarathustra* must be recalled: "Said ye ever Yea to one joy? O my friends, then said ye Yea also unto *all* woe. All things are linked, enlaced and enamored." And also "All joy wants the eternity of all things, it wants honey, it wants the dregs, it wants drunken-midnight, it wants graves, it wants the consolation of mourners' tears, it wants the gilded splendor of sunset."

The affirmation of the "circulus vitiosus deus" in *Beyond Good and Evil* (Section 56) is only meaningful against the backdrop of the repetition of the transfiguring affirmation of joy, hence against the backdrop not of a temporary leap for joy, but of an "insatiable" call for a *da capo!* issued to existence *such as it was and such as it is.* The joy that renders possible the Eternal Return is thus transformed, to be sure, into a permanent, and in that sense metaphysical, will for repetition. But in itself Dionysian feeling is more the joyful feeling of the *necessity of a universal link* than the will that follows from it. The Dionysian feeling, which is also called "tragic wisdom," is that of the *necessity* of coexistence and mutual relativity of contraries such as perfection/imperfection, joy/suffering, creation/destruction: "the fact of experiencing the necessity of imperfection itself from the superabundance of the form-imposing, Dionysian force."[40] The Dionysian is defined elsewhere as "the great pantheistic participation in every joy and suffering, which blesses and holds as sacred even the most awe-inspiring and enigmatic properties of existence ... the feeling of the necessary union of creation and destruction."[41]

Is this not Heraclitus transposed on the plane of feeling? For Nietzsche does not say: "God is night and day, winter and summer, famine and abundance" (Fragment 67, Diels), but rather: *the feeling* of this necessary unity of contraries is *divine.*

Does not such a displacement of the divine toward feeling, toward the interiority of man or of the Overman render all the more difficult the encounter with an identifiable and personal god? Isn't the feeling of the divinity of the world tantamount to a blinding and narcissistic projection of subjectivity which sees nothing else but itself in the mirror of the world (evoked by Novalis' disciple to Sais)? The "unnamed god" of *Thus Spoke Zarathustra* is a "hidden god": the god is "veiled to us because of his own beauty," we read in the hymn called "Before Sunrise." In such a climate, which is so close to pantheism, the god seems to be located everywhere and nowhere. However, in a tone part serious and part humorous, Nietzsche, in his later texts, tells of some strange encounters with his Dionysos. He bears little resemblance to the Dionysos of *The Birth of Tragedy,* clearly he is now a god half Greek, half Asiatic (of the Mysteries), a God of sacred drunkenness at the same time beneficial and cruel, a god of nature. He seems to have experienced a Christian metamorphosis. In the version given in *Beyond Good and Evil* he has become in part a god of interiority. "The genius of the heart" is indeed a god of consciousness, "flute-player, enrapturing the consciousness," whose single message consists in being seductive for the sake of existence. But how does he become seductive? Not because of the attraction for the vital element, the surface appearances or the masks, but by dint of revealing to each one "the hidden and forgotten treasure" he carries in himself. Dionysos is the "tempting god," the "seducing god" inasmuch as he teaches man to discover and to follow what is divine *within himself.* Dionysos is the revealing agent of an internal dimension that makes possible "a new path toward the Yea."

We must stop here for a moment to mark the strange proximity and—at the same time—the distance between this interiority of Dionysos and that of Christ, at least such as Nietzsche describes it in *Antichrist.* For the message of Christ in Nietzsche's reading (a message that was subsequently falsified by Paul and diverted in the direction of ressentiment and the ascetic morals) was only that the "Kingdom of God" resides in the pure interiority of the heart, in the intimate feeling of joy and love. "My kingdom is not of this world" signifies no ressentiment whatsoever toward the world, no negation of the "world" in the ecclesiastical sense. "Negation is something of which it is quite incapable."[42] Christ is deemed to have taught withdrawal from the world of established reality and great institutions. The "Good News" is the affirmation of the internal kingdom of God. "What does the 'Good News' mean? True life, eternal life has been found—it is no longer promised, it is here, it is *within yourselves:* life in love, without exception and without preference, without any feeling of distance."[43] Thence Christ is an antirealist, a "symbolist" par excellence, who does not negate the "world," but who detaches himself from the entire institutional order. "Jesus attaches no importance to anything established: the letter *kills,* everything fixed kills." For him, true "life" is immediate, *internal life,* beyond every formula and every representation. "He only speaks of what is most internal: "life," "truth," "light" are the names that he gives to this internal world."[44] He holds all the rest as inconsistent. He considers every exteriority merely as sign or symbol. "He locates himself outside of any religion, of any idea of worship, of any history, of any science of nature ... of any politics, of any psychology, of all books, of all art."[45] What he calls "the reign of God" is the feeling of transfiguration of all things that produces the total acceptance of *oneself.* Every reality is eclipsed in the face of this feeling of happiness. The Gospel would then be the original sketch for a Buddhist peace—which would be a novelty in the West—and the announcement of happiness on earth, yet outside time and space. "If I understand something in this great symbolist, it is the fact that he took as realities, as 'truths' nothing but the *internal* realities and that he conceived the rest, everything natural, temporal, spatial, historical, as signs, as occasions for parables."[46]

There is a resemblance between Christ thus presented and "the genius of the heart," inasmuch as this genius is an intimate voice, a call (a sort of joyful, non anxiety-ridden *Gewissen)* leading the individual to turn away from the clatter and noisy hubbub of the world, teaching him or her to turn aside and to *divine* himself or herself. For in this rediscovered interiority there is an abyss of strangeness and dispossession, a profound inadequacy that translates—in the description of the Dionysian effect—into uncertainty, frailty, scattering and yet indeterminate hope. "The genius of the heart"—an expression that is used four times in *Beyond Good and Evil*—brings no marginal benefit nor any elaborate doctrine on "spirituality." Most especially, this "genius" does not provide us with a god-sent "grace." Everyone is not so much "thrown into a state of grace, ... *fulfilled and oppressed with goods from elsewhere,* as enriched from his own being, renewed in his own eyes, fulfilled, bathing and wafting in a spring breeze, perhaps more uncertain, more tender, more frail, more strewn, but filled with still nameless hopes."[47] Such a divinity resembles the purely internal Christ inasmuch as the identity proper to the god is dimmed, so to speak, behind his message. In the end, Dionysos is nobody but that voice. This demonic dimension of a "genius" that inspires now fades. He is the "Great Hidden One"[48] without a contour and without worship. The principal element that distinguishes the new Dionysos from Christ is that in the other late texts of Nietzsche, Dionysos is not only associated with an internal affirmation, but appears as the symbol of an unlimited affirmation, the symbol of the sacred character of the *yes* that can only repeat itself infinitely and eternally. Dionysos then means the "saying *yes* to the world as it is, without subtraction, exception, or selection."[49] Such a saying yes includes the acceptance of all deaths. This Dionysos—akin to the Great Pan and a double of creation/disappearance ("under the name Dionysos it is becoming that is experienced in active fashion")[50]—has nothing Christian about him. But is he a god? Do we know what a god is? Is he anything other than the *symbol* for a philolosopheme? Is he anything other than a *lived experience?* Anything other than the one *and* the other, the one *in* the other? "Becoming felt and interpreted *from within,* this would be the continuous creation ... of a god."[51]

In a preliminary remark to the reduction of the transcendence of God, Husserl notes in Section 51 of *Ideas:* "A world-god *[Ein mundaner Got]* is evidently impossible," and he adds: "The immanence of God in absolute consciousness cannot be grasped as immanence in the sense of being as experience *[Erlebnis]*—which would be no less absurd."[52] Husserl excludes as absurd that the absoluteness of the phenomenological lived experience and the absoluteness of God could coincide in immanence. But mostly (in the first part of the remark) the immanence of God in the world seems to him as something to be excluded.

For Nietzsche, neither the immanence of a god in the world nor the coincidence of the lived experience and of the divine are absurd. In this he is heir both to the Greek tradition (the Greeks have thought their gods as immanent and as susceptible of appearing under familiar guise in the world) and to a certain mystical tradition, or one of negative theology, that conceives the coincidence of the soul and of the divine principle in a happy *ecstasy,* i.e., in a nontragic fashion and without the annihilation of man. Paradoxically, what Nietzsche calls "tragic" is this ecstasy or this ecstatic coincidence felt in the midst of joy. The paradoxical theme of "tragic joy" exalts a sacred link to the world, a *re-ligio* in the strong sense, yet without worship and dogma—a faith, yet one without a creed.

## Chapter 8

# TRAGIC JOY[1]

The Dionysian, with its primitive joy felt even in the midst of pain is the common matrix to music and the tragic myth.[2]

I am the first one to have discovered the tragic.[3]

Tragedy is a tonic.[4]

Nietzsche is far from the first to expand the concept of tragic well beyond tragedy as a theatrical genre, which is the staging of a myth of destiny, in the attempt to encompass a fundamental determination of human existence.[5] For Plato, "tragic" is an epithet that characterizes "life" *(bios)* in its entirety, or this immediate world, or all the things here below. He has Socrates give this truth in *Cratylus*[6] when he asserts (as he rarely does), "Logos expresses the whole" *[ho logos to pan semainei]*, "the true *[alethes]* is free and divine *[leion kai theion]* and dwells with the gods on high; but the false resides below with the crowd and is rough and tragic *[trachu kai tragikon]*; for it is down here that myths and lies about tragic life *[peri ton tragikon bion]* abound the most."

Immediately thereafter, Socrates insists upon the double nature of beings within the double nature of *logos:* "two-natured son of Hermes, smooth *[leios]* on one side on high, rough and tragic on the other here below." In this way Plato plays upon a subtle difference between two adjectives, *tragikon* and *tragoeides* (both derived from *tragos,* the scapegoat, the sacrificial animal of legend, predating the institution of the religion of the gods of Olympus). The first adjective *tragikon* designates that which is literally, empirically or in itself, tragic; the other *tragoeides* designates that which through *logos* belongs to one face, to one "idea" of the tragic *(tragoeides* derives from *tragos-eidos).*

In Nietzsche's reversal of Platonism, not only does the tragic become *alethes,* but also divine. It characterizes the whole, or rather that which can be affirmed of a nontotalizable whole. Our lot is simply and exclusively to give our blessing to "tragic life," whether deceptive or non-deceptive, not to escape it, but to love it as such. But then in what sense is it "tragic"? Tragic for Plato is the incarnation, the separation of the above from the below, the blinding shadows so difficult to redeem, the quasi-dereliction of this ambiguous and mortal world. For Nietzsche the tragic would be the inseparability of the above and the below, of truth and falsehood, of good and evil, for he *accepts* this dichotomy so as better to *reject* an antinomy of Being. Tragic would be the infinite mixture flawlessly woven once and for all. Why does the non-sundering, the unity of Being (called originary Oneness in his early writings), remain tragic? What meaning could there be in the words "tragic knowledge or wisdom," words that seem to imply a final *clarification,* a non-illusion regarding the falsity of all antitheses? Does not such a *pantragism* necessarily include a new *panlogicism,* as Jean Hyppolite commented apropos of Hegel?

Nietzsche's philosophizing began in 1869 with (and was interrupted, rather than completed, in 1888 by) a reflection on the significance of the phenomenon of the tragic. "I have every right to consider myself the first *tragic philosopher,"* he wrote in *Ecce Homo.* The reversal of Platonism entailed first the unlimited fragmentation of Being into inimitable appearances, and later, the sundered unity inherent in all the major "final" concepts (active/reactive Will to Power, Overhuman/last man; infinite linear lost time/infinitely finite cycle of the Return): these are the first and last words of an ongoing and unique philosophy of the tragic. For, well before and after Nietzsche's double "turning" came in 1875-79 (well before and after his passage through positivism in *Human, All Too Human* and his rupture with Wagner's music), the same intuition of the tragic constitutes the most consistent orientation of his thinking, his intimate fidelity to himself. This intuition was present from the very beginning of his itinerary in *The Birth of Tragedy* and guarantees that the tragic—even considered in "the sublime and terrifying"[7] spectacle of tragedy—is not synonymous with resignation, with pessimism, and with the overwhelming and crushing of man by fate. Rather, the intuition of the tragic amounts to a symptom of power, even an "excess of power" as he said in 1880, a phenomenon of pure affirmation of existence or *redoubled* affirmation. This paradoxical approval rests on one fundamental disposition, or affect: joy, but a joy very *different* from ordinary joy, a *religious* joy.

However, we shall see that this religious phenomenon (of which the tragedy is an official *liturgy* since the staging of performances was financed by rich elected citizens) does not originate for Nietzsche in a public, dogmatic, and codified religion, a *temple religion*, but in a secret, mystical religion, without articles of faith, in what one might call a "religion of the moment." This religion is discontinuous and magical, a source of surprise for its involuntary faithful, seized by the divine transformation of pain into joy; it is a *religion of the high-intensity theatrical moment* evidenced in the death of the hero. How shall we conceptually account for such a phenomenon whose ultimate meaning is "musical"?

From the "objective" point of view, the exterior of the drama, the death of the hero, or his fall, or his ruin, is, one might say, his triumph (although for Nietzsche the *essence* of the *tragic* is neither in myth nor in drama). "The most universal form of tragic destiny is victory snatched from defeat."[8] Prometheus, Oedipus, or Antigone (whom Nietzsche does not mention) bring their "causes" to triumph through annihilation. Oedipus's cause is the will-to-know everything for himself, an excess of *libido sciendi,* his "one-eye-too-many" as Hölderlin would put it, and his symbolic "death" is the self-piercing of his eyes and his demand for ostracism. From the subjective point of view of the spectator, which is more important to philosophers, there is a celebration *[jubilation]* allowing the vision of the collapse and destruction of the hero—agonizing in itself—to pass into the superior dimension of *aesthetics. Tragedy is aesthetically sublime. Sublime* in the very precise sense Kant gives to the term, or rather according to one of Kant's definitions: "a feeling of the expansiveness of life ... a pleasure produced by the feeling of the cessation for an instant of the vital forces, followed immediately by an all the more powerful *enlargement* of the same."[9] Tragic joy is linked to the sublime as taken in this *sense alone,* and not at all according to the other definitions, such as "the presentation of the supra-sensible" or some "inadequate symbolization of freedom," or else a "negative pleasure." Tragic joy is not simply and crudely sweet-and-sour, merely an *oxymoron.* It accompanies, and perhaps makes possible, the grasping and the approval of a power that exceeds every finite form. There is in the Nietzschean feeling of the sublime a playfulness with the infinite, a game which for all its seriousness and reality, is not weighed down, or reappropriated, or twisted away, by the heavy-handedness of morality. His sublime is not edifying.[10]

While it might well be true that "joy within the tragic"[11] *(die*

*Lust am Tragischen)* reveals the emergence of the sublime, one should nevertheless not confuse the sublime that gives birth to the tragic with the moral sublime, which is what the entire tradition has done since Aristotle. Every finite loss (such and such beauty, such and such greatness destroyed) is compensated for on another plane, without being repaired, by an infinite gain or regain of ... *life.* For the Greeks, tragedy is the power of healing *(Heilskraft),* or a means of preventing disease. And yet, nothing destroyed is restored, reestablished or dialectically preserved; rather, it *returns,* only perhaps for the joy of the One and not for the transcendental self-satisfaction of the subject in its enactment of pure practical reason, or for the logical self-satisfaction of the world-historical Spirit. How are we to understand this conjunction of the vital and the sublime, the strange knot, this vital sublimity, the sublime vitality, called the *"tragic?"*

## Joy and Serenity of the Hero and Joy of the "Spectator-Artist"

But before taking up this question, once more let us ask, Why is joy involved? How is Nietzsche justified in breaking with the whole tradition and the traditionally established connection between the experience of the spectator and the tragic affects, the feelings of *phobos* (extreme fear, anxiety) and *eleos* (pity)? Nietzsche calls these traditional affects "reactive" or "depressing": the first one entails an intense *fear* for the life of the hero or (by projection or identification) for oneself, and the second an intense *sadness*, a poignant *grief* (the German *Trauerspiel,* literally the "play of grief," is yet another word for *Tragödie)* in the face of the lucid and terrified precipitation, of the unavoidable slipping into the abyss of a great, admirable and superb individual. How can one not *suffer* in seeing the end—disastrous, cruel, and moreover never entirely deserved—of the hero or heroine, who was beautiful, happy, glorious, powerful, respected, sometimes good, always *noble*? Isn't it true that none of these tragic heroes is endowed with a mean soul and seeks (at least in Aeschylus and Sophocles[12]) merely his or her own interest, vengeance, or satisfaction of a selfish or vile passion? How is it not possible to see here with Hegel the wrenching *sundering* of the universal?

From a Hegelian point of view, joy could originate in the conviction—one internal and ownmost (from *Meinung,* meaning "opinion" and literally "mineness")—of "being right," of "possessing" the universal. Fatal illusion! "I wanted it, I foresaw it," says Prometheus repeatedly. "Voluntarily I committed this fault." "The future I already know in advance and entirely. No misfortune that I have not foreseen will ever befall me" (*Prometheus,* lines 101–103; 265–266). But Nietzsche's rupture with the Schopenhauerian doctrine on art as negation of the will to live (and on tragedy in particular as the school of "resignation, renouncement and even abdication to the will-to-live"[13]) no longer suffices to explain the rejection of melancholy as such. Melancholy is indeed pushed outside, set at a distance by beauty, and experienced as "foreign"; it is an "effect of strangeness" *(Verfremdungseffekt),* as Brecht was to say. Yet this melancholy is transformed in Nietzsche into an exaltation, a paroxysm of pleasure, and most of all the unlimited approval of existence and of the "totality" that "permits" such an evil. "The tragic hero is serene *[heiter],*"[14] exuding that "sereneness" *(Heiterkeit),* which Nietzsche finds in Homer and considers as the most fundamental *Stimmung* in the ancient Greeks. Their gaze "sank into the horrible depths of nature" but, whereas our eyes are wounded from having looked at the sun directly and see dark spots dancing behind our eyelids, theirs were able to draw from the unbearable vision of the night those luminous images: the heroes of myths. These are "luminous spots, capable of curing eyes hurt by the ghastly night."[15]

The joyful serenity of the tragic hero is not as paradoxical as it might seem. Section 9 of *The Birth of Tragedy* evokes the exemplary serenity of Oedipus, who has taken refuge at Colonus, exiled, blinded, symbolically dead already, a sage whom the Christian tradition has been tempted to understand as a saint, and the serenity of Prometheus: they belong to the Apollonian principle of the separation between individuals and abstract universality. Here the tragic dimension is, as it turns out, oddly truncated. Oedipus has reached a "mysterious serenity" by means of a supraterrestrial transfiguration; and Prometheus, moved by the rational desire for universal justice, has introduced or discovered, after the sacrilegious theft of fire, what today one calls "the rights of man." Both have lost the original link with the phusic sphere of the Dionysian. Devoid of anything chtonian or vitalistic, they remain nonetheless "masks" of Dionysos, fabulously complete projections or mirrors of the One that originally is split between pleasure and pain, one and multiple, good and evil.

Oedipus at Colonus—groping and giving the eerie spectacle of death warmed over, a prophetic old man who broke down as the result of the monstrosity of his crimes and of his archetypical destiny—"attains his highest activity, extending far beyond his life," and gains a "superterrestrial serenity,"[16] thus leaving behind Dionysian vitality. Prometheus, the robber of divine fire and consequently the founder of every human hearth, hence the originary author of every polis and culture, symbolizes "active sin," by contrast to the "glory of passivity" of the first Oedipus; he manifests the affirmative impetus for transgressing the limits of what is human, which he believes have been arbitrarily set by the jealousy of the gods. His *hubris,* his overweening pride, consists in putting himself not only above the present gods but above the divine generations: he knows that Zeus castrated his father Kronos, he anticipates that Zeus will be brought down, made powerless by his child, the son of a mortal. "Knowing in advance" ("Pro-metheus" comes from *pro-manthano)* the twilight and the death of the Olympian gods, he puts his Titanic and archaic force (as the son of the Earth) and his *pro-mathesis* at the service of future universal justice. From the Dionysian he draws the revolutionary energy to promote a purely Apollonian, egalitarian universality. He has no goodness, no sentimentality, but marvels at, and brags of, being right against everyone and everything, against all his enemies, against all the gods. He finds *his solitude* exalting. For wanting "to become the *one* world-essence,"[17] for equating himself with the One, which entails offending the truth of the internal originary dissension of the One, he must "perish," as much as this is conceivable for a god or a Titan; in other words, he must remain enchained until Zeus later, according to other myths, becomes reassured and releases him, or until Heracles releases him. His absurd *[folle]* serenity is the result of the absolute but irrepressible will-to-*know.* He does not risk losing his life because he is immortal: Zeus can only torture, not exterminate, him. Prometheus's generosity is devoid of discrimination, his justice is without measure, in the image of an already infinite cosmos. His indignation in dealing with sufferings inflicted by Zeus upon mortals is a rhetorical, already slightly sophistical, game. His absurd joy resides in the senseless affirmation that all gods will die. The later Nietzsche would say that his enjoyment is moved by the spirit of vengeance, by the ill-intentioned prescience of Zeus' removal from power and of his fall into forgetfulness: "I am one who knows how Zeus will perish" *(Prometheus,* line 915). He does not *announce* the advent of another god, the son of the Earth; he does not affirm it, although he *knows* about it. Himself a son of Earth (who is prophetess par excellence), he uses his gift for divination and knowledge poorly, i.e., merely to imagine himself above the gods and first and foremost above time, and thus loses his Dionysian grounding.

However, the serene joy of the hero (even if it is more Dionysian than Antigone's, where it is connected to obscure blood links) is not "true tragic joy." As a result of his partial belonging to the metaphysics of subjectivity, Nietzsche remains *de facto* blindly dependent upon "aesthetics" in the Kantian sense of the word, i.e., upon the definition of aesthetic pleasure as a pleasure of "reflection," as enjoyment in the creator or the spectator. Creator and spectator share the same ecstatic affects, because the goal of art is for the creator to communicate the highest tonality of inebriation that will bring him to creation. It matters little what the content, what the message is: it is the *aesthetic creative state* that must be transmitted, somehow, as the "inspiration" received by the poet in Plato's *Ion.* This subjectivity, however, is neither that of an individual nor an abstract transcendental subject: neitherthe one rejoicing in the tragic spectacle nor the one singing in the lyric poem emerges at all as a poor, destitute individual subject; each is "the only truly existing and eternal I," the ungraspable "subject," whose grounding is the abyssal depth of things, "the genius of the world itself."[18]

If tragic joy belongs to a higher dimension, it is because it is the metaphysical joy of the One that celebrates itself, ecstatically wrapped within its overabundant plenitude and its perfection in spite of suffering. "It is absolutely not possible, to be honest, to deduce the tragic from the essence of art such as it is conceived traditionally under the single category of appearance and beauty: that joy could be reborn out of the annihilation of the individual, is only comprehensible from the spirit of music."[19]

In order to understand the phenomenon of tragic joy, the Kantian category of the beautiful is insufficient. One must resort to two dimensions: First, the *sublime,* thought anew, outside of the influence of practical reason and the moral infinite; and second, the difficult notion of *Geist der Musik,* where *Geist* contains nothing Hegelian or spiritualistic, but means the *Grundstimmung,* the *preobjective rhythm* that "inspires" every production of forms, a difficult notion to elucidate because it points toward the very root of the "musical." Let us postpone this double elucidation until the next two sections of this chapter.

In the second half of *The Birth of Tragedy,* Nietzsche underscores with extreme intensity the theme of "metaphysical joy." Let us read two of the most vibrant yet obscure passages, because the "phenomenological" explanation of the irruption of joy in the spectator is to come only in Section 22. At the end of Section 16 we read:

> The metaphysical joy that arises from the tragic is the translation of the instinctive and unconscious Dionysian wisdom into the language of images: the hero, the highest manifestation of the will, is negated for our pleasure, because he is only phenomenon, and because the eternal life of the will is not affected by this annihilation.

At the beginning of Section 17 we read:

> We are really for a brief moment the primordial being itself,

> feeling its raging desire for existence and joy in existence; the struggle, the pain, the destruction of phenomena, *all of a sudden* appear necessary to us, in view of the *excess [Übermass]* of countless forms of existence which force and push one another into life, in view of the exuberant fertility of the universal will. We are pierced by the maddening sting of these pains just *when we have become, as it were, one with the infinite joy in existence, and when we anticipate, in Dionysian ecstasy, the indestructibility and eternity of this joy*. In spite of fear and pity, *we experience the happiness of being alive, not as individuals, but as the one living being, with whose orgiastic pleasure [Zeugungslust] we are united.* (stress added)

Let us note that the words "joy" and "pleasure" refer back to the unique German word *Lust.* The idea that "every true tragedy" is permeated with "the thought that life, in the depth of things and in spite of the changing character of phenomena, is entirely joy in its indestructible power" is introduced earlier without development in Section 7.[20] Before explaining how this irrepressible disposition is possible and leads man to unity with himself and the cosmos beyond the social and below the individual, we must investigate the difficult complementarity of the Apollonian and Dionysian. Nietzsche never ceased going back to the problem, except during the years of the so-called "intellectualistic" critique (from 1874 to 1879), in the attempt to show with ever greater clarity that *there is no true unity.* Both "principles" are inseparably "physiological" (dream and intoxication), protoartistic (two varieties of *rhythmos,* one being a stabilized form, the other mobile and unstable) and "theological" (Olympian divinity and a more archaic divinity). They are as fundamental as sexual differentiation (see the first sentence of Section 1 of *The Birth of Tragedy):* they can only communicate one to the other, one inside the other, each corresponding to the other and indefinitely exchanging its attributes. The symbolic richness of the couple Apollo/Dionysos is inextinguishable. Their eternal struggle can give rise only to temporary reconciliations, which are no syntheses, but just momentary: at the moment of the myth when Apollo heals Dionysos of his laceration (I shall return to this point), at the moment of tragedy when the exchange becomes the "fraternal alliance of two divinities: Dionysos speaking the language of Apollo." There can be no other language since Dionysos' "language" is music, but "Apollo, *finally,* speaks the language of Dionysos,"[21] which means that Apollo has been metamorphosed by the all powerful spell of the Dionysian sublime.

On an external level—in no way superficial, yet calling for innumerable nuances—Apollo and Dionysos, as the masculine and the feminine in the unity of the proper body and in sexuality, are opposed and transform into one another, forming a series of non-antinomic antitheses or a vast non-dualistic system of complementarities. One can produce a succinct and simplified table of these contraries (one necessarily incomplete, because unfinished), as in the following list without "logical" or deductive order:

Apollo/Dionysos
day/night
sight/hearing
static/dynamic
limit/unlimited, Pan-like
concentration principle/principle of expansion
forms/forces
arrest/upsurge
beautiful/sublime
surface/depth
"dream" (as *vision* of forms)/ inebriation (as production of the forms through rhythm)
regular rhythm/staccato rhythm
conscious/unconscious (collective)
individuation/fusion
reality principle/"self-dispossession," orgiasm
Occident/Orient
culture/"wildness,"[22] barbarity, natural chaos
work/festival
language/music
melody/harmony
law and order/nondelimitation of borders
State/nomadism
wisdom/madness
measure/nonmeasure
healing/disease
appearance/indeterminate ground
identity and *eidos*/disindividuation—mask—internal chaos
memory/forgetfulness

(chiasmus?)
*space* as distancing and separation/*time* as principle of simultaneousness, artistic ecstatic *moment* in which forms collapse (later in the Eternal Return)
*time* as chronology or succession/*space* as principle unifying and scattering, as originary spatiality prior to time

visible divinity/hidden, masked divinity

Is this "system" "metaphysical"? Yes and no. It is metaphysical inasmuch as it brings a *semblance* of "total" explanation to the world. It is not metaphysical insofar as it is not a closed totality, as it does not congeal into a system in the Hegelian sense, as duality is endlessly articulated and disarticulated, and as opposed terms constantly change roles and intertwine in an endless play of compensations of successful or failed attempts at equilibrium.

The originality and the difficulty of the thought of *The Birth of Tragedy* is in keeping with the fact that at the outset Nietzsche thinks the One as Dionysos or Dionysos as the One, and yet exposes both principles and their *history*. For Apollo becomes the one he is only by facing the intrusion of the barbaric god who originates in Asia and now storms against him. He is ignorant of the fact that he is Dionysos' own brother and with him forms a parental couple; he does not recognize his own sublime parents in the eerie stranger, who is at once his guest and enemy *(hostis)*. First, Apollo is merely beautiful. Dionysos, as we shall see, makes him sublime later. But above all *there cannot be a system* because the Dionysian One is itself internally divided and already contains the sun-like *[solaire]* principle of appearing (of *Scheinen),* it is hermaphroditic, split and divided within an irreducible double nature *[duplicité]:* in no way is the Dionysian principle pure withdrawal or pure night simply because it is the first principle of ecstasis, of being-outside-of-oneself *(Ausser-sich-sein).*[23] The Apollonian is not originary, it is only the visual projection of the Dionysian abyssal ground through an "originary desire for appearance"[24] in the One. The Apollonian is set on stage or in imaging, it is the *elucidation* of the Dionysian. "What we name 'tragic' is precisely this Apollonian elucidation of the Dionysian."[25] As early as the 1870–71 fragments, the focus is entirely on the sufferings of Dionysos: according to certain myths he is lacerated by the Maenads, by Prometheus himself, or by the Titans who rebelled; according to others, it is Promethean man, the enlightened civilizing agent, who lacerates and shatters Dionysos. The focus is also the transfiguration of these sufferings. Then the Dionysian is the one and only "subject": "To a Dionysian *chorus*, under the enchantment of some Apollonian action, is revealed *its own state* in a *vision*."[26] Vision is now considered as action, personified into living images that struggle by means of dialogue. Everything that is externalized is destined to veil the terrifying ground that on occasion juts forth to broad daylight as a "grotesque and brutal power."[27] Against this power, which is quite noxious, one must radically protect oneself and find remedies: Apollo is healer; the Apollonian is *pharmakon,* but it is a remedy that "poisons" because it dissociates the surface from the roots.

Because it hides the ground, the Apollonian dissimulates above all the ambivalence that is constitutive of such a ground, its double nature which it is bound to detest, to negate, or to attempt to reduce. For the Dionysian harbors an essential or unsurpassable ambivalence, "gentleness (voluptuous fusion with nature) *and* cruelty"[28] (mythical dismemberment of the god and abyssal loss of identity for the human consciousness), or in other words *joy AND suffering*, a contradictory unity for the Apollonian logic of the affects of pleasure and suffering; it is in other words the unity of a crucifying unleashing, which Hegel calls "Bacchanal revelry," identical with "translucent and simple rest." Nietzsche reappropriates the double nature (vital and deadly) of Dionysos attested by Heraclitus in fragment 15, which he quotes in part in the posthumous fragments that are contemporary with *The Birth of Tragedy* "The same *[houtos]:* Hades and Dionysos, which strikes [men] with delirium *[mainontai]* and enthusiasm from the divine wine press." Quoting the chorus of Euripides' *Supplicants,* he recalls that Dionysos bears the eponym *"Zagreus,"* a contraction of *Zeus* and *agreus,* the primitive hunter who kills animals and eats them alive or eats their meat raw. And Dionysos is called either *"agronios,"* the hunter (an allusion to some archaic, pre-Greek hunting rites where the kill was eaten in a ceremony of communal and propitiatory brotherhood)[29] or *"omestes"* (the one who eats raw meat) AND *"meilichios"* (sweet as honey). This sweetness, which symbolizes reunification with nature, is evoked in a posthumous text[30] that is suffused with extremely sensual pantheistic magic, with "eroticism," with the "musical inebriation of musical transfiguration." Nietzsche's description is all the more surprising as it *remains totally silent* on the violent scene, which in *Supplicants* immediately follows this paradisiacal scene. For then the Maenads devastate the rich plain of Thebes, slaughter the herds peacefully grazing, cut the bulls to pieces, "tear the young heifers to shreds," cover pine trees with blood, with "flames coming out of their hair, yet not burning them," they wound and scatter the poor herders who cover them with arrows which they scarcely notice, because the god heals the wounds immediately (See *Supplicants,* lines 669–780). Let us read now the summary made by Nietzsche of the preceding, idyllic, and magical scene:

> A messenger tells that in the heat of noon he was grazing his herd on the mountain tops: it is the right moment and place to see what no one else has seen. For then Pan sleeps, the sky is the motionless backdrop of a glory, the day is in bloom. In a meadow the messenger notices three choruses of women resting

> on the ground in the most decent positions: several lean against the trunks of pine trees; all of them slumber. All of a sudden, Penthea's mother begins the jubilation, sleep is banished, all get up in a leap—a model of noble restraint. The girls and the women let their curls drop on their shoulders, their roe hides are readjusted if, during their sleep, the ties and ribbons have loosened. They surround their necks with snakes that lick their cheeks with familiarity, several women take wolf or roe cubs in their arms and breast-feed them. All adorn themselves with ivy crowns and garlands. At one strike of the thyrsus on the rock, water springs out. At one strike of the wand on the ground, wine springs forth. Soft honey drips from tree branches: if one touches the ground merely from the tips of her fingers, milk white as snow flows from it—This is a world bewitched, nature celebrates its reconciliation with the human being.

For the young Nietzsche, benevolent and cruel Dionysos is not far from designating the essence of the world, "the mutual penetration of suffering and pleasure in the essence of the world,"[31] but against a backdrop of joy, that is to say, in the ecstatic movement of becoming One, not in a stable essence already settled. Ambivalence itself only exists in the act, in the exaltation of the festival, in the commotions of music, in the magic of the dithyrambs, in the artistic "jubilation" of the archaic celebration, which preceding the establishment of a ceremony is not ritualized: unbearable voluptuousness, pleasure born of suffering itself, coupled states, inverted but similar *pharmaka* ("the remedies [of Dionysos] recall deadly poisons," see Section 2) through which the duplicity of the god is incarnated in the dance of the raving, i.e., the "possessed of Dionysos": "The surprising mixture in the affects and the duplicity of the possessed of Dionysos, this phenomenon in which pleasure emerges out of suffering itself and jubilation tears from their chests intonations of torture—at the peak of joy resounds the cry of terror or some complaint arises, filled with desire, over an irrevocable loss."[32]

This archaic prefiguration of the strange joy of a spectator of tragedy allows us to anticipate its essence: on the one hand, the eclipse of the Apollonian surface, the collapse of the visible; on the other hand, the identification with this double nature of the Dionysian and the victory of the "spirit of music."

Let us underscore in passing the profound continuity between Nietzsche's views in 1872 and in 1888 concerning this double polarity of the Dionysian and Apollonian, in spite of the preponderance of Dionysos. First, with respect to the Romantic idea of an art directly dictated by nature (which proves that his 1886 self-critique is not to be taken literally): *"Apollonism—Dionysism.* There are two states in which art itself bursts out in man as a force of nature and takes complete hold of him—willing, nilling: on the one hand, compulsion of vision *[Zwang zur Vision],* on the other, compulsion to orgiasm *[Zwang zum Orgiasmus].* The two states are prefigured—more weakly however—in normal life, in dream and inebriation."[33]

Elsewhere both states are described as two degrees of "inebriation," that is to say, of extreme receptivity and lucidity but merely with a difference of rhythm *(Tempo Verschiedenkeit).*[34] I will return to this point. Next, the idea that Apollonism as "will to measure, to simplicity, to submission to rule and concept"[35] imposed itself upon the Greeks after a long struggle: it had to be conquered and secured by them "in the struggle against their own Asiaticism," against the "taste for the measureless, for the complex, for the uncertain, for the horrible."[36] Nietzsche views the Apollonian as constructed from "a Dionysian underground," which is the spontaneous nature of the Greeks. Hence the later Nietzsche is in agreement with Hölderlin for whom the Ownmost of the Greeks is first the Pan-like ecstasy, the Asiatic unity with nature, whereas "Occidental and Junoesque sobriety" comes to them only as the result of a sort of expatriation.[37] A change of views occurred (since for the young Nietzsche it is Apollo, unconscious of his essence, who precedes the arrival of Dionysos, and Dionysos is the one who brings about his metamorphosis) but did not change the relationship of dependency and derivation between both principles. The later Nietzsche maintains that the legislating, regulating, unifying and simplifying power that the Greeks call "Apollo" is a mere figure of the Will to Power, Dionysian in its essence because it is able to confront the broadest horizon of forces in contention—Chaos: "Dionysian, an Overflowing *[Überströmung]* and the unity of multiple, partly terrifying, excitations."[38]

The joy of the spectator-artist is obviously trans-individual, *metaphysical.* On the most elementary level, it links back to the artistic self-affirmation of life: "Joy *[Lust]* is more originary than suffering; the latter is no more than the consequence of the will-for-joy (to create, to shape, to assign to destruction, to destroy) and under the highest shape, a *sort [Art]* of joy."[39] In the situation of the spectator, joy results from a stage event that ruptures the delicate equilibrium between the musical Dionysm of the chorus and the singular heroic figures. I speak of a delicate equilibrium between Dionysos and Apollo, because it is in no way a "reconciliation" in Hegelian fashion as some interpreters[40] have believed hastily, but a pause in the hostilities, a cease-fire at a point of suspension in the endless struggle. In that struggle Dionysos always has the upper hand. *"To end it* Apollo speaks the language of Dionysos."[41] What is the "language" of Dionysos? It is originary "music," the infinite rhythm of the oscillations of the will—from joy to suffering and from suffering to joy. The language is indeed audible, but remains unintelligible to logical and chronological thought. The words of the Apollonian hero are always clear and serene, devoid of babbling and ambiguity, and nonetheless they bespeak the *abyss or the relativity of every figure,* which the ground is on the verge of capturing back within itself. And at the culminating moment of action, when the hero is on the verge of sinking, the manifestation of the gaping hole and the gaping openness of forces produce in the spectator an extraordinary effusion of joy inexplicable in Apollonian terms. The entire visual realm, the "images," the beautiful sculptural figures of the myth, the staged scene, collapse under the unfurling of "sacred" energy, a "numinous" energy (in the sense of Rudolf Otto[42]); this collapse brings about a mystical ambivalent revelation not of joy pure and simple, but of terror (the spectator "shakes with terror"[43]) and voluptuous ecstasy, mixed together. "He anticipates an infinitely higher and more powerful enjoyment," a joy that is all the higher as it encompasses and overcomes suffering. The *mysterium tremendum et fascinosum* is to be seen in the *evidence* of a *blinding* joy: in this vision, which fills him or her with the shadows of catastrophe, the spectator "wishes only to be blinded" *(ibid.).* Such is the truly religious moment of tragedy, when the "clear night" of Dionysos eclipses the illusory brightness of representation. Put differently, in terms of *phusis* or *physiology,* "the impulses of visualization and transfiguration" pushed to their highest degree suddenly perceive their essential "object" (the hero who so far stood irrecusable and firm) as quasi-derisory, precarious, infinitely weak. Under the upsurge of an impulse that is colossal and "enormous" *(ungeheure),* the veil of the phenomenon is cast aside and the "truly artistic spectator" participates in an *active,* affirmative destruction. He no longer identifies with the suffering of the hero, with the process of the action reaching its unavoidable term, but rather with the process of creation/destruction in and beyond the tragic artist himself. The spectator is reunited with originary Oneness toward which this "moment" causes him to return. This "moment," the only *metaphysically* tragic, *magic* moment of the "Dionysian" *(dionysischen Zauber),* where nothing remains except Oneness, Nietzsche calls the "break of the Apollonian in its very peak." Let me quote merely a part of this description, which should be quoted in its entirety.

> Here [the spectator] beholds the transfigured world of the stage and nevertheless *denies it.* He sees the tragic hero before him in epic clearness and beauty and nevertheless rejoices *in his annihilation.* He comprehends the action deep down, and yet likes to flee into the *incomprehensible.* He feels the actions of the hero to be justified, and is nevertheless still more elated when these actions annihilate their agent. He shudders at the sufferings which will befall the hero, and yet anticipates in them *a higher, much more overpowering joy.* He sees more extensively and profoundly than ever, and yet wishes he were *blind.* How must we derive this curious internal *bifurcation,* this blunting of the Apollonian point, if not from the Dionysian magic that, though apparently exciting the Apollonian emotions to their highest pitch, still retains the power to force into its service his excess of Apollonian force? The *tragic myth* is to be understood only as a symbolization of Dionysian wisdom through Apollonian artifices. The myth leads the world of phenomena to its limits where it *denies itself* and seeks to flee back again into the womb of the true and only reality.[44]
>
> His vast *[ungeheure]* Dionysian impulse then devours his entire world of phenomena, in order to let us sense beyond it, and through its destruction, the highest artistic primal joy, in the midst of the primordially One.[45]

At the paroxysm of the Apollonian force, a sea of compelling joy submerges—and drowns under successive waves of joy—the entire lengthy sequence of those images that preceded the moment. Nietzsche then quotes the text of the death of Isolde in Wagner's opera:

> in the world's breath
> wafting whole—
> to drown, to sink—
> unconscious–highest joy.[46]

The Wagnerian heroine would no longer incarnate the serenity and joy of the ancient hero, but the joy of the spectator-artist, himself foundering in confusion of subject and object. The overcoming of the visual by the musical could be nothing more than a self-overcoming that *sketches in advance the ontological structure of the Will to Power:* the epic ordering of the dramatic development, the self-sufficiency of figures of sculpture, their plastic development sufficient to give rise to pity by means of human, all-too-human compassion, all these

Apollonian passions are eclipsed and make room for a euphoria that is higher than the joy/suffering now left at a distance. This higher euphoria—a strange and unjustifiable happiness—is ultimately in its essence foreign to the thematic unfolding of the action, indifferent to the fate of the protagonists and to the cruelty of devastating destiny. This euphoria effaces in one recoil the horror of the inevitable crisis, loosens up and unties the "spectacle" in a way *different* from the logically deadly outcome of tragic intrigue. And the spectator realizes as in a flash that the true theme of tragedy does not lie in myth, and that the strange happiness he or she feels is connected to, or grows from, a prior ground *[arrière-fond].* Such a prior ground has always been dominated by a musical resolution, perhaps an accord of dissonance, without words, outside of any meaning reducible to the principle of reason. "Music has nothing to do with beauty."[47] "Sound emerges from the night."[48]

## The Joyfully Fraternal Struggle between Two Sublimities

*"It is in the annihilation [Vernichtung] of even the most beautiful appearance [Schein] that Dionysian happiness [dionysisches Glück] reaches its apex."*[49] Several times before, in the same fragment, Nietzsche proposes a difference between two forms of "happiness," or supreme perfection or joy: on the one hand, the joy of existence *(Glück am Dasein),* connected as he claims to the "joy of appearance;" and on the other the "joy of becoming" *(Glück am Werden)*, the latter emerging from the "destruction" *(Zerstörung)* of every "beautiful appearance" *(schönen Anschein)* or of every goal that collapses as illusory. Tragic joy is the happiness of becoming experienced in the collapse of "Being," understood in the sense of illusorily eternal eidetic "form." Here, however, a new and higher precision is indicated. What is destroyed is "appearance, *even the most beautiful one*": the superlative indicates the overcoming of the beautiful. It is a beauty already sublime that collapses in front of the eyes of the spectator under the irresistible unfurling of the *Dionysian sublime.* The tragic effect results from the intertwined exchange of two sublimities, when the stronger encompasses, takes away, and elevates the weaker, although the encounter is deadly for the weaker. For Nietzsche, *the beautiful is sublime* inasmuch as it tames and masters a formless or multiform manifold–just as previously this was the case for Schopenhauer ("in his main determination the feeling of the beautiful is the same as the determination of the sublime")[50] and for Schelling ("the sublime in its absoluteness contains *[begreift]* the beautiful, as much as the beauti-

ful in its absoluteness contains the sublime")[51] and as it would later be the case for Rilke ("the beautiful is nothing but the first degree of the terrible").[52] But how can Apollo—the divinized "principle of individuation," the god of the limit, measure, and firm beauty—be exalted to the level of the sublime, which in one way or another entails a movement toward the infinite, the unlimited, the excessive? How does the Apollonian sublime distinguish itself from the edifying sublimity of Kantian morality that Nietzsche detests?[53] Upon which textual evidence does the idea of a double antagonistic sublimity, which would form a momentary coupling to produce the tragic work of art, rest?[54]

From the outset, the Dionysian excess, with its ecstatic dissolution of the subject and the social world, the dissolution of every ground or grounding, the wrenching opening in abyss, is itself set within the abyss. It is, says Fink, "an opening to the somber, nocturnal face of life," and belongs phenomenologically in a way that is quite "classical" (Kantian and Schellingian) to the category of sublime: "The *chaos* [of nature] is the fundamental *intuition* of the sublime," writes Schelling.[55] But what about the Apollonian excess? Is it not absurd to claim that Apollo becomes unlimited? How could he elevate himself beyond or above himself? Is this not contrary to his very essence? Would the Apollonian image be sublime simply because it participates in the sublime game or in "the aesthetic game where the will plays with itself,"[56] or in the "sublime recreation"[57] of the tragedy? Is it sublime only inasmuch as it is the *transposition* of the abyssal sublime, the "manifestation *[Manifestation]* and the translation into images *[Verbildlichung]* of Dionysian states (the visible symbolizing of music, the dream world that arouses Dionysian inebriation)"?[58]

In fact, Nietzsche distinguishes two properly Apollonian sublimities. The first is pretragic, and can be classified as "idyllic" or "epic"; the second, he says, is derivative from a "phantasmagoric delirium" *(Wahnvorstellung)* and is nothing else but the *compensatory illusion* destined to cause us to lose the memory of horror and *monstrosity,* of the abyss, into which inebriation was able to reach. This therapeutic illusion also results from a "mechanism of illusion" aimed at erasing the bitterness of a popular pessimistic wisdom, more ancient than that of the Olympian gods, the wisdom of Silenus, who was Dionysos' lugubrious and sinister companion and shadow (reminding us of Zarathustra's dwarf). For that wisdom, "the supreme good is not to have been born, *not to be*, to be *nothing;* the next good is to die soon." The "gods of joy," the gods of the radiant sky, were called and invoked by the Greeks in order to negate such a Silenian and horrible wisdom, this Schopenhauerian resignation, this will to die. According to Nietzsche, the Greeks "overturned" this atrocious and suicidal wisdom that arises out of the genius of negating life, and they learned from their gods how to affirm, justify, and transfigure existence by agreeing with Homer that the greatest evil is that one must die one day, that one must forsake light, the tenderness of sunrise and the glare of noon. The Greeks could deem the most humble swineherd happier than the king of Hades *(a-eides,* the nonvisible, what is withdrawn from visibility). But at the same time that the Apollonian gods are the negation of horror and suffering, of nihilism before it unfolded, they are also the negation of vital excess, of the *ecstatic pleasure,* and they foreshadow therefore the advent or the blueprint of a first form of *asceticism,* which subsequently culminates in Plato.

The double sublimity of Apollo is inscribed within the original Greek epithets for his majesty, which correspond to the three meanings of the word *Scheinende.* The word applies to the Appearing[59] (or the Making Manifest); the Radiant;[60] the Seeming.[61] But each of these three attributes contains an intrinsic ambiguity. For Apollo is:

1. one who makes manifest, who reveals, *and* one who hides, who speaks cryptically through the oracle of the Pythia[62] (Heraclitus wants to *reconcile* both aspects: "the god whose oracle is in Delphi neither speaks nor hides, but intimates"); in other words, both one who shows the way *and* one who leads you astray in a labyrinth of appearances;
2. both one who throws his spears far away, spreading death with cold indifference (killing the snake Python that kept vigil on Themis, Delphi's former chtonian oracle, thus sever ing one link with earth), who sends a plague that decimates the Greeks in front of Troy, who protects the Trojan Paris to allow him to kill Achilles all the more easily, *and* also one who heals, purifies, who is the inventor of all philters, the father of Asclepius (the famous, skillful surgeon who is able to sew back and to heal Dionysos himself after his tearing and cutting-apart by the Titans): he is Life which from its own highest point and through exceptional lucidity and vision invents those *instruments* for its own regeneration;
3. one who teaches prophetic knowledge to the divines (e.g., Calchas), informing the future and one who produces beneficent *illusions*, propitious or misleading hallucinations after a certain divine madness; in other words, he is both one whose magical lyre or flute inspires poets and sober and well-rhythmed musicians (the peaceful and sylvan god, the candid *shepherd,* the musician playing with the Muses on Mount Parnassus) *and* the implacable warrior, slaughtering Niobe's children without vicious cruelty but in cold blood.[63]

The Apollonian *idyllic* sublimity, which Nietzsche called "naive" by borrowing from Schiller's concept of the spontaneous, dreamed harmony between man and nature, is epic, pre-Dionysian, Olympian, Homeric. For us, such a naivete has become impossible. We are *sentimental beings,* indefinitely aspiring to an unattainable harmony, and *Romantics*. And it is so asto end with Romanticism that Nietzsche strikes the blow of the double affirmation, the fatalistic voluntarism of the Eternal Return, whose precise formula "Impress upon life the seal of eternity"[64] is already inscribed in Section 23 of *The Birth of Tragedy,* fifteen years before being fully articulated. Homer's naivete is sublime: "What inexpressible sublimity does Homer touch upon, Homer who, as an individual, is to Apollonian civilization what the dream artist is to people's or nature's ability to dream in general."[65] *Integral Apollonism* appeared in the course of Greek post-Socratic decadence *after Homer* (its characteristics are the "theoretical man," the delirium of knowledge, the delirious illusion that science can comprehend the enigma of the universe when in fact it is an "endless vise") and could only come out negatively: as abstract, anti-naive *and* anti-Dionysian, as inimical toward nature, and as forgetful of music. Homeric "naivete" is itself a "mirage," says Nietzsche, an illusion destined to mask the ground of monstrosity and frightful uncertainties, of suffering and joy, that moves forward and always works in the background. The idyl, the dream of the absolute transfiguration of nature, is itself already a phantasm.

The Apollonian sublime is not "true," each time it is a hallucination *(Wahnvorstellung)* or a delirious idea, a "fixed idea," especially once Dionysos has been recognized. Apollo is no longer purely Apollonian, but Apollonian-Dionysian. It is not the Apollonian element that produces by itself alone the effect of *catharsis* (the pathological discharge that heals and purges the sad affects, as Aristotle proposes) or brings about the "triumph of the moral order"[66] (as Hegel suggests). All these superficial interpretations are perhaps true to a certain immediate and relative degree, but they forget that Dionysian power is what rules over all phenomena. Under such a power and in the equilibrium of the tragic work of art, the Olympian gods cease to be naive and beautiful, and become sublime. For an immense tide of despair threatened the Greeks when the darkest figures of the abyss (the Furies, Medusa, Gorgon) appeared. "The gods of Olympus were in great danger. The tragic work of art ... [let us leave aside comedy, which for Nietzsche has the same healing effect] saved them by immersing them in the sea of the sublime. They ceased being 'beautiful,' absorbing so to speak within themselves the ancient divine order and its sublimity."[67] Thanks to the play of the tragic *and* comic stage, Dionysos became double once more: he became sublime and ridiculous; yet his sublime was idealized, no longer the true and original, chaotic and barbarian sublime. The absurdity of and the disgust with life, the wisdom of Silenus, the negative side of the Dionysian, all these find a counterweight stronger than the mere veil of appearances. Horror can be conjured up and can dissolve only in the artistic play and with natural inebriation, "not through a total immersion into inebriation."[68] Tragedy is the middle term between divine beauty from above (henceforth without strength) and the unbearable "truth" of the abyss below. The tragic work of art is midway between ecstasy and disgust. It provokes a transmutation of the world of beauty pure and simple under the effect of musical inebriation: by shattering this world to its core, the tragic work of art energizes and spurs it on again. Apollonian will—which is weakened and softened into too loose a harmony, when it is not conquered from chaos—finds itself reaffirmed in the disquieting jolt between these states of climactic ecstasy, comparable to vertiginous ascending scales: "In Dionysian inebriation, in the mad, raving race through all the soul's scales, provoked as they are by narcotic stimulants and the unleashing of spring-like impulses, nature expresses itself with its highest strength; it *unites* again isolated beings and makes itself felt as *unity;* so much so that the *principium individuationis* appears as a prolonged state of weakness for the will."[69]

At this point a new human type comes into the world, *a third term,* between the all-too-natural satyr and the unmovable, all-too-reasonable, all-too-"cultural" sage: this type is the "actor," the instinctive "poet-singer-dancer, the Dionysian man in the act of *playing.*"[70] By *playing* artistically with inebriation the man of this type cures himself of such an inebriation, he transfigures appearance and overcomes horror. What is under consideration here is not a single individual, but a small group, a Dionysian mass welded into one, a dithyrambic chorus of "raving individuals;" in their singing and dancing dramatic action emerges as a phenomenon of spellbinding, of *being possessed,* and of successive discharges of the Apollonian impersonations of Dionysos.[71]

In any event, for the humanity that has fathomed "the infinite of the Dionysian abyss," Olympian serenity no longer has the character of beauty. The height of pacification and conciliation that is henceforth required by the terrifying passions of creation and destruction now becomes sublime. The transfiguration in Aeschylus of the bloody vengeance and murderous rage of the Furies into the Athenian tribunal of the Eumenides is one of the clearest examples of this new sublimity. "In Aeschylus, disgust disappears in the *sublime* shudder felt in front of the wisdom of the order of the world, which man has trouble recognizing because of his weakness. In Sophocles, the shudder is still greater because this wisdom is unfathomable."[72] "Whereas Aeschylus finds the sublime in the sublimity of Olympian justice, Sophocles—strangely enough—sees it in the sublimity of the impenetrable character of Olympian justice."[73] This is the *enigma* of the gods as repetition *[duplication]* of the enigma of the existence, which henceforth appears as *sublime.* A Dionysian "magical" power pushes Greek humanity to affirm the *enigma as enigma,* to find "just" even the terrifying destiny of undeserved suffering, to affirm *everything.* The wise Apollo—the god of the ancient sages, the pre-Dionysian god, whom Socrates wants to restore to power, the one who requires that man find his limits in the "Know Thyself"—has metamorphosed into a healing, salutary power of *illusion.* Healing evil takes place through his affirmation. "Reconciliation with reality because it is enigmatic! Refusal to solve the enigma *because* we are not gods!" Sublime wisdom dissolves the woe of existence into a *possessed* transfiguration. The self-blinding of art allows myths to emerge as so many delirious illusions. *"The illusion, hallucination [Wahn] is at its apogee"*[74] and *Apollo himself has become possessed by Dionysos.* He does not believe in beautiful appearances. Appearance is no longer experienced as an *image,* but as the *living symbol* of "truth." Carried, transported beyond itself by the wave of musical intoxication, the entire world of the stage and everything visible enter a dance as in a *miracle.* All sing; sight is dismissed, reduced to the role of support.

"The clearest sign of this contempt for appearances is the *mask."*[75] With three black openings on a Dionysian night the mask is sublime: although in Latin it is named *"persona,"* the mask actually offers nobody and nothing to see, no face, no psychological identity, but rather a monstrous and quasi-anonymous impersonation of the abyss. Apparently, the mask was not used to amplify the voice, and thus was not a *tool.* Hence it amounted to the sublime overcoming of the principle of individuation by Apollo himself, possessed with Dionysos: this overcoming is both transcendence and sublime immanence. Behind the mask, there are two elements: first, obviously, a character with a name and a destiny *and,* second, the nihilating and ungraspable force (no-thing, nò-where) that carries everything. The union of the two, behind and in the mask, obviously is no "synthesis": it is absolute victory of the nocturnal and musical over the realm of the solar and its measures.[76]

If we follow the unfolding of *The Birth of Tragedy*, as well as its conceptual construction, the *Dionysian* sublimity is strongly articulated: the primitive dithyrambic chorus, made up of Dionysos' servants who feel themselves metamorphosed into mythical satyrs, is called "sublime." "The satyr was something *sublime* and divine."[77] Such he was, as the companion of the god in ecstasy and also of suffering; to him the god directly communicated his *wisdom*, a wisdom that was not contradictory with the myth of sexual superpotency, with the symbol of the inextinguishable energy of the cosmos. "The bearded satyr possessed with his god"[78] was the patron saint of the Dionysian man, his model. And in the theatrical ceremony, the unity of fusion (what we call "identification") of the spectator and the actor was made possible through the intermediary of this satyric model: Beyond the opposition between those who were formerly possessed by the god (and have since disappeared) and the simple citizens who come merely to a spectacle, a *regression* toward a previous culture has taken place. Contrary to what Schiller holds on the chorus as "ideal spectator," the chorus for Nietzsche remains the fundamental point of rest, the *imaginary locus* of *sublime* reunifications with the Dionysian, the "spiritual" space where there are *no longer spectators nor actors*. Even for the educated Attic spectator (one far removed from all the barbarian dances and all the Asiatic rhythms, between the walls of the theater, experiencing a paradoxical mixture of derealization and reincorporation within the City, of civic concreteness and forgetfulness of civilization outside) the original dithyrambic state could be found again and again, and "everything was nothing but a sublime and vast chorus of satyrs singing and dancing"![79] There was no question of a *faith* in such or such a divinity or in its hypostases, but of participating in the *festival of a new beginning*. This festival of a new beginning refers back to an *in illo tempore,* to the archaic institution of a first mythical time when earth and world had, in fact, "in a time gone by," sealed their union (as Mircea Eliade has shown for a number of cultures). Tragic joy is, in fact, "outside of time," and as such, according to the word of Nietzsche, always *joy of the origins (Urfreude)*.

Nevertheless, the encounter of the two sublimities (each one redoubled) confers upon this joy specific features that distinguish it from every other form of joy. Tragic joy is unique ("joy of the One") and subjected to dispersion, but this contrast is not its specific feature. Tragic joy contains mourning, the sorrow over the loss of even the most beautiful appearances. Even sorrow rejoices tragic joy. Yet every joy, however closed and wrapped up in itself until forgetfulness it may be, bemoans and secretely harbors the heaviest sorrow concerning every limit—unless it be the extreme joy of affirmation of the Eternal Return *of joy*. Isn't every joy, except the last one, too humanly tragic, in the sense that it can only rarely be strong enough to be eternal joy of the *totality?* Doesn't the Eternal Return stand beyond the tragic as the immeasurable, which in advance has approved—not surmounted, but accepted and gathered—all sorrow? Tragic joy trembles in front of its own phenomenon (in front of the withdrawal of the phenomenonal realm as such and of its standing base), it is *Erschütterung* (a quake of the Earth), it is the tonality that *brings closer* to the Original, to the Sacred. This joy does not "unveil" the origin (which can be neither revealed nor disclosed) but allows the anticipation—in sublime shuddering—that all given, accessible, serviceable, manipulable, assessable reality is *nothing* in front of the abyssal ground from which each emerged. To quote Heidegger: "What is joy? The character of springy upsurge[80] of joy is to familiarize *[heimischwerden]* with the proximity of the origin *[Ursprung]*."[81] We have already settled within the proximity of the origin, but we endlessly forget such a settlement. Joy awakens us from this forgetfulness. Joy is one of the upsurges that make us find again what we have always known, that give us back what we thought we had lost, and yet what we cannot lose.

Both sublimities unfold from the same source. Apollo and Dionysos, as sons of Zeus, are brothers, and both are persecuted in their tender age before their reign begins. Their fraternal struggle is the flash of the Difference, not between Being and beings, but between *phusis* (which bears obscurity) and Being as the serene, imperturbable, and high dimension of the *Clearing*.

Nietzsche conceives the original pulse of this *phusis* as "the spirit of music," a music that comes *before* any *externally* audible music, before any played music, the very *essence* of the Dionysian (hence the word "spirit"), "power that puts the spectator *in the condition of believing in a miracle,* of seeing everything as enchanted,"[82] which deprives of its force and seduction the very force of appearance, thus "compelling it to its service,"[83] exalting it before eclipsing it.

## The Musical Essence of Joy

Contrary to what he sometimes seems to say, or what he would have the reader believe,[84] especially in the insistent[85] homage to Schopenhauer's doctrine on music in the very first versions of *The Birth of Tragedy,* Nietzsche is radically opposed to this doctrine, essential though it was as a spring-board for his own innovative approach. It is well-known that Schopenhauer assigns music to a new place "quite outside of the other arts,"[86] because instead of producing copies, as the other arts do, of *the phenomenal world*, music absolutely does not depend upon that world. "It could so to speak continue to exist while the rest of the universe would no longer exist," because, like the world, music is an immediate reproduction or copy of *the will in itself.* In Schopenhauer's remarkable words: "Music *speaks of Being*": it imitates none of the beings, but only the intimate essence of the phenomena, i.e., their effective essence, which it unfolds outside with mathematical precision. It is "the copy of a model that can never be directly represented itself." There exists an immediate analogy between the degrees of life in nature and the pitch of sounds. The bass, or what Schopenhauer calls "fundamental bass," corresponds to *inorganic matter, to planetary mass,* whereas the higher sounds on the scale express the entire ascending scale of beings "from crystal to the highest animal." In similar fashion the harmony that represents first the heaviest bodies, second vegetation, and third the animal realm, rises in a graduated series up to the melody sung in clear voice by the human being, which symbolizes this human being's development of reason and the crowning of his desire. Whereas harmony directly represents the obscure natural ground common to all individualities—underlying and sustaining them in existence—melody symbolizes the free upsurge of a separate individuality that, little by little, gains momentum *(andante* or *allegro),* "tells its suffering" in the *adagio,* and after such a crisis often finds a resolution in a new *allegro con moto* or *vivace.* Schopenhauer says that music does not express a *given joy, a given affliction.* It directly reveals the *very essence* of these feelings, inasmuch as this essence is eternally contained in the will. It does so with simplicity through the magic of tonalities, according to major and minor modes, and "without motivation." This utmost restraint is what excites the imagination to conceive figures on a given stage with musical background.

In his initial destruction of Schopenhauer's system, Nietzsche breaks with the idea that music *imitates* the will and is an immediate and penetrating intuition thereof. There is no possible distinction or segregation between a pure eternal will and its musical phenomenalization, just as there is not Oneness on one side and multiple projections or appearances on the other. The will *is* music, as the One is Division into images. There is no pure willing beyond music. Music does not *speak* of Being, nor does it tell of its trials and tribulations in the process of nature. It is Being itself, not its first *re*production. Hence, it follows that because of its originary status, music as conceived by Nietzsche precedes every kind of musical composition. The music of the world is pre-harmonic and pre-melodious. It is silent. In other words, it is a *Grundton,*[87] and the *"tonal backdrop,* echo of sensation of pleasure and displeasure," a fundamental harmonic bass, one that cannot possibly be transcribed and is perhaps even undescribable (hence the paradoxical expression "harmonic chaos" that he uses frequently)—"an originary melody of pleasure and displeasure,"[88] or "musical fluctuations of the will" that the composer hears in silence preceding every work of musical composition. These are tonalities—still unheard by the world—that the composer gathers and "condenses" *(dichtet)*. Nietzsche maintains that such latent musicality is not a symbol, but the thing itself, i.e., the unstable states of *the* "will" (itself formed from a plurality of impulses that are continually on the way to concordance and discordance or, if it is preferred, are formed of differences between forces in a situation of equilibrium and disequilibrium, namely pleasure and displeasure constantly changing into each other). Symbolization for music does not mean being referred back to a dynamic ground whose key one might be presumed to hold (and toward which, anyhow, one cannot retrace one's steps); rather, symbolization amounts to suggesting, to acting upon senses, muscles, imaginations and thoughts. The music of Being is originary symbolization. This primordial musical symbolization is nothing but the working of productive imagination, the shaping of plastic force immersed in "pure" rhythm, that is to say, rhythm without image and form. As early as 1870–72, Nietzsche denies himself any sort of Romantic, post-Kantian "intellectual intuition" of the pre-ontical musical essence. This essence is accessible only indirectly, through its manifestations. We have no possible introspective intuition of the musical essence that founds all symbolics: gesture, language, all imagined representations. Intuitively we know "the forms of intermittence"[89] of the will, which give rise to rhythms, but "the essential being of sound hides itself—irreducible to comparisons—in harmony."[90] Rhythm and harmony constitute, so to speak, pure schemas and a "pure logic," which reveal the essence "not merely of feeling, but of the world."[91] Facing this pure logic, the concept is radically powerless, as we shall see. In any event, no path will be able to give us access to the very origin of music, to its "spirit." There is "no bridge" that could take us back toward the core of the world, and make it intuitable.

We know only the symbolized. The symbolizing power, "essence" itself, is to elude us forever, and we shall be able merely to conjecture its existence by means of an afterthought or retroactively. "All of impulsive life, the play of feelings, sensations, affects, acts of the will—all this is known to us—*I must add this here against Schopenhauer*— ... only as representation and not according to its essence."[92] Even the body, which is prey to the hallucination of music, cannot use its self-intuition to reach a knowledge or an immediate apprehension of the essence. Nietzsche remains perfectly Kantian. The essence Schopenhauer thought he grasped, i.e., the In-itself of willing, is merely the phenomenon "of something else that furthermore remains entirely undecipherable."[93] Music is Being. Being is music—Dionysos is the ground—but Being eludes itself, the symbolizing power veils itself under its symbols.

That is why nowhere in the 1872 book or in the Fragments or even later does Nietzsche give any definition of the "Spirit of music," *Geist der Musik.* This silence is necessary. The Nietzschean *Geist,* the flame that encompasses all, the leap, the primal mover, all this collapses as a ghost when one seeks to capture it, to embrace it, to conceive it. We only have its body in a trance, or its bodies, as moving signs. *"Es ist der Geist, der sich einen Körper baut,"* ("It is the spirit that builds a body for itself") said Goethe. The architect is nowhere but in his moving constructions, in his building/destroying, in elementary "rhythm."

The immanent music of the world, whether it be harmonious or discordant with respect to the play of the world, is more like chtonian music, a music of the elements, of the winds, waters, trees, stones, of the insects and animals—replete with undertows, howlings, buzzings, whistlings, bellings, ripplings, sighings, wailings, cooings, gurglings, rattlings, growlings, crackings, cracklings. This music is both grave and light; it is cosmic music in circular expansion, not the concentric Platonic music of the spheres, the music of the sky. The music of the world can be heard before it resonates through beings. It would be illusory to reduce such a natural harmony (which comes prior to any music on a score, to any music played on instruments, although such music is what is always understood, and interpreted, by each and every composer) to a melody of affects. It would be illusory, likewise, to believe that it is nothing more than the subjective ebb and flow of tonalities. The incessant influx of affectivity, which oscillates from joy to suffering and from suffering to joy, reveals a mere approximation, a figure among others, of pure singing, of a singing without speech, the *Song of the Earth.* This song, a pure rhythmic matrix, was described by Paul Valéry as "empty rhythm," as kinesthetic elementary movement—similar to that of the body in walking, the silent source of the poem beyond the elaborated voice, which has been incarnated and set into words. It is a "universal" matrix that is susceptible of multiple symbolizing actions, among which spoken language holds a notable, but subordinated, place. For another type of humanity, this song might be able to, if not supplant, at least regenerate and metamorphose language. Music understood as "originary nature" *(Urnatur)* and "originary law" *(Urgesetz),*[94] "effaces and suspends *[aufhebt]* civilization as the light of the sun eclipses the brightness of lights,"[95] and it teaches us to consider language as powerless to "pull outside the most intimate ground of music":

> The cosmic symbolism of music resists any adequate treatment by language, for the simple reason that music, in referring to primordial contradiction and pain, symbolizes a sphere which is both earlier than appearance and beyond it. Once we set it over against music, all appearance becomes a mere analogy. So it happens that language, the organ and symbol of appearance, can never succeed in bringing the innermost core of music to the surface. Whenever it engages in the imitation of music, language remains in purely superficial contact with it, and no amount of poetic eloquence will carry us a step closer to the essential secret of that art.[96]

Pre-artistic music frees us from the weight of linguistic symbolic institutions, sets new symbols in play, enlivens us with joy. The ecstasy of the spectator of tragedy would be meaningless—and would be even nonexistent—if we started from words alone (words, Nietzsche says, are the libretto short of the opera), from mere action alone, if action were not sustained by music itself becoming ecstatic, climactic, in the rhythmic acceleration of "orgiastic music at its highest pitch."[97] Tragic joy can take place only when the spectator is suddenly immersed in the element of pre-objective musicality (from which 1. the heroes, 2. the myths, as "analogical sublime substitutes" of music, and 3. all the plastic forms draw their vital breath and their "meaning"). It is the magic of music or the "very voice of music"[98] that transforms the spectacle of annihilation into "superior pleasure." "That is why music is—above all—that which provides the spectator of tragedy with the surest anticipation that there exists a superior pleasure to which one gains access by means of ruin and annihilation; so that for him, in music, it is as though he hears addressing him directly *the very voice that emerges from the most hidden abyss of things.*"[99] This "voice" saves one from resignation to unhappiness: it "utters" nothing but the "spirit" of music, the joy of the eternal link between appearing and disappearing, between presence and absence.

Original music (heard and understood, yet not accessible to perception, because it is too bass or too treble, to reach the threshold of audibility) resides even beyond the couple Apollo-Dionysos. The Spirit links them, without marrying them or fusing them in Hegelian fashion. Dionysos, the principle of fecundity, is both Father and Mother; Apollo, the Son and Brother, is always naive and young, even after his sublimation; the third term, the ungraspable Spirit—always joyful, possessed with joy—operates the incessant linkage, it comes and goes from one to the other in the Game that links and transcends them. Strange Trinity of Joy!

The Spirit of music, which inspires the rhythms of the world, brings unity to a division or a plurality logically impossible to unify. "*Music* demonstrates how this entire moment in its diversity ceases to be experienced as dissonance."[100] (It is the same Spirit that is called later "artistic Will to Power," a force capable of subjecting the chaos of the greatest impulsive diversity to rhythm, to a regulated succession: it is Spirit exuberating with extra-ludicity and overflowing with plasmatic, shaping power).

But let us not forget that this Spirit rules over the wild cadences of immemorial festivals, that it likes to unleash magic without figure and without name, that it feels no respect for the most venerable traditions and the most solidly established offices. The music that it whispers in the ear is no soft and sweet lullaby; it is eminently dangerous. It destabilizes thrones. At all cost, Apollo must interpose pacifying images to heal the wounds that it causes and the incessant tearing-apart that it inflicts upon the principle of reality.

The two written, or at least orchestrated, performed musics—the Dionysian and the Apollonian—directly emanate from the music of the world. They are two competing versions of it. One could imagine—wrongly—a sort of hypostatic derivation of the three stages: primordial music → Dionysian music → Apollonian music. In fact both are equally ancient, in Nietzsche's view at least. They are two opposed, and complementary, interpretations of the Spirit of music. Besides staccato, syncopated rhythms, or a spellbinding recitative chant, there are sonorities that can be bass or shrill, overpowering or piercing, without measure. Recall the bass resonances of the third act of *Tristan*, where the audience hears echoed by the Dionysian gong the ramming strokes against the confines of the world, and where one feels throbbing against the head of the hero the deaf pulsating of the will in the proximity of death, the "echo of the immeasurable clamor of joy and suffering that arises from the immensity of 'the night of the worlds.'"[101] Recall also the first notes, which are symbolic of precosmic chaos, of *Rheingeld* (or of Haydn's *Creation);* or, closer to us, the massive, barbaric, orgiastic harmonies of the nuptial dances in *Le Sacre du Printemps*. The beautiful, more rarely sublime, geometrical, and contrapuntal architecture of Apollonian music is often aerial, playful, organizing and also akin to activity by the demiurge; for Nietzsche, this is the music of Palestrina ("the indescribably sublime and holy music of Palestrina"),102 Johann Sebastian Bach *("to hear his music amounts to being present when God created the world,"*[103] a verdict that he claims originated in Goethe). Later, however, although categorized under "Great Style" along with Schültz and Haendel as part of the "strong German fashion," Bach is called a "good civil servant," producing scores on demand. It is with some reticence that Nietzsche ranks Mozart's music in line with sublime Apollonism: Mozart is a "serene *[heiter]* spirit, solitary, tender, superficial,"[104] thus too Apollonian, which means here: too "frivolous," too city-like, too polished, too overflowing with the affectation and the oozing sociability of the eighteenth century. As a composer, Mozart did not discover his melodies by listening *(hören)* to the music of life as Beethoven, a Dionysian, did, but rather by contemplating *(schauen)* life from above;[105] in the end he was falsely joyful and serene, and deep down melancholy; in him we hear the last song from the good old times that have begun their agony.

At the time of *The Birth of Tragedy,* Nietzsche did not systematically distrust Spirit. Later, he says that "pure Spirit" is dumbness, because it is the plaything of the "great reason" which the body is, that "'spirit'" (duly bracketed!) is a "tool" *(Werkzeug)* in the service of the body,[106] that "the spiritual is to be kept only as the ciphered language of the body,"[107] or as its "sublimation"[108] ("spirit" is the sublimated double of the sublimity of the body, and its entire progress obscurely works toward the constitution of a *superior body),* etc. Perhaps nowhere so much as in the subtitle of the first edition is the word "Spirit" taken in such an exalted sense, and from such an enthusiastic perspective, that it comes to designate "enthusiasm" itself, the advent of a god within us in the Romantic sense, like Schelling's *Geist der Natur* (as in the *Discourses on the Plastic Arts).* Most often, "spirit" is reactive against life, afflicted with the "disease of ideality," as Mallarmé would later say, refusing its becoming-body *(Verleiblichung),* even though "*every spirit becomes* (or ultimately must become) *visible in the flesh [leiblich],*"[109] and even in this sense, Christian spirit has had beautiful and noble incarnations in human types. In the *Twilight of the Idols* we find one of the rare "positive" definitions of Spirit that, however, does not seem to be simply applicable to "the Spirit of music": "Under spirit I include foresight, patience, dissimulation, great self-control, and all that is mimicry."[110]

The immemorial cosmogonic and theogonic geniality, the mythico-poetic spirit, that is capable of inventing several orders of the world and espousing many contrary forms, this would be the *spirit of playfulness,* endlessly undoing the used vestiges, reshaping history, and reinventing the future. It would seem then, at first sight, that by itself alone the Spirit of music has no need for the tragic, no more than the Will to Power requires that its incessant movement of self-overcoming necessarily include the moment of tragic mourning.

Hence the question: Must all joy, even outside of the horizon of Greek theater, be always thought anew as tragic? The answer is *Yes:*

in spite of the apparent paradox, music, joy, and the tragic are linked indissolubly, just as in the core of music the major and the minor modes are indissolubly connected.

Nonetheless, major and minor are not on the same footing. By itself music is fundamentally gayer than sadder, as affirmative existence is. In Nietzsche's time there was not yet a nihilistic music, as opposed to the decadent novel and the plastic arts, already in the process of decomposing. Even the odes and the funeral hymns, the *Passions,* the *Requiems* (Mozart,[111] Brahms, Verdi, Fauré, if I may select some instances from *outside* Nietzsche's preferences!) exalt the listener and do not depress him, although they do not invite to *dance.* What Nietzsche reproaches Wagner's music with is precisely the effect of liming and stiffening the body. That is the reason why he opposes—for lack of a better option—Bizet to Wagner, as a sort of "ironic antithesis." If Wagner happens to be joyful (as in the beginning of the third act of *Lohengrin,* or in *Meister Singer),* his music is not an "apotheosis of dance," like Beethoven's seventh and ninth symphonies. Rather, Wagnerian music is a pompous course in metaphysics, a solemn seduction in favor of a new religion of the otherworldly, a melancholy and depressing meditation, one dangerously "hypnotic," "narcotic," on the frailty of divine destinies and the bourgeois tendencies of the heroes. As a reaction, Nietzsche voluntarily became blind to the *Wagnerian sublime.*

Every good music is a "cleansing of the soul,"[112] because it instigates dance in the body, prompting each and every part of our being to rise up and leap. Whether music makes us impassioned or sober, it heals by a homeopathic process distilling in us those sublimated and purified affects. "The word *melos* [song] means etymologically a process of softening, not because the song would be soft in itself (and there is many a sad song!), but because its effect after the fact is to soften."[113] Music pacifies all the dissonances of the world, by transfiguring them into tonal sequences: the dissonances are if not resolved, at least integrated within a necessary order. Music is sovereign mastery over the dispositions of our affects and this mastery cannot be realized outside artistic existence. In 1870, Nietzsche wrote to Hans von Bülow (Cosima's first husband): "I free myself up by means of a Dionysian tune,"[114] or, "you possess the Pythagorean secret of healing with 'good' music."[115] In 1885, he designated "good music" as "the best antidote,"[116] the miraculous balm and infallible remedy against disgust, fear, desire, boredom, frustration, anger, ressentiment, the mournful harshness of loneliness and disease, in short against every evil.[117] It is the medicine without nefarious side effect that leads extremely quickly to "great health." All good music actively sublimates suffering without negating or diminishing it, it *agrees* with it, it is a *Hymn to Joy*, to this spark of Apollonian beauty and Elysian beatitude, as Schiller has it.

*The Birth of Tragedy* calls Beethoven's *Hymn to Joy* of the ninth symphony a model of "good music," one naturally Dionysian. (Nietzsche himself composed *two* such hymns—and very remarkable ones, although too Brahmsian, to be sure, in spite of himself—on poems by Lou Salomé in 1882 and 1887, *Gebet an das Leben* and *Hymnus an das Leben.)* "Every one feels united with all men, as if Maya's veil were torn and there only floated tatters of it in front of the mystery of the originary One."[118] But in the last writings Beethoven does not remain the perfect model of joy. The pitiless critique of Romanticism takes this idol down. Beethoven's joy is too forced, hypertrophied, baroque: it calls for an emphatic sort of heroism, full of bloating. Beethoven, as Nietzsche says, is "both decadent and a beginning." He is a "hybrid soul," on the one hand very old, "who does not finish with dying," with saying goodbye to the old world, *and* on the other hand "a soul to come, very young and not finished yet with *being born*. His music bathes in the chiaroscuro of eternal mourning and of an eternal hope that stretches its wings."[119] True tragic joy and good music must be *measured and sober,* they must know how to finish the labor of mourning, they must know how to turn the page and be forgetful in an active mode, they must know how to affirm the *future* not as a hero that bulges his torso but as the "hero *on the night of an indecisive battle"* (that is to say, facing an uncertain sunset of the Western sun). This hero takes upon himself "the wounds, the loss of the friend ... this enormous sum of all kinds of bitterness," and on the "sunrise *of the second day of battle"* (in the new beginning, in the *da capo* of a new history), "greets the dawn and his fortune ... as the noblest of all ancient nobles, yet as the first born of a new aristocracy, the like of which no epoch ever saw or ever dreamt."[120]

Sober, classical, and restrained joy—like good music—is music and joy subjected to *rhythm*. But what rhythm? There would be much to say on the Nietzschean theory of rhythm and its evolution. All the texts postdating 1875 give preference to the rhythm of an Apollonian style, yet they no longer call the style "Apollonian," but rather *"great style, classical type":* they define it as concentrated plastic or musical art, which despises the fuzzy, the exuberant, the complicated, the merely pretty, the ephemeral; this art is interested in duration, *logical* continuity and *beauty* more than sublimity. The musical style that he calls for requires the future musician to evoke "the tension of the will, the infallible certainty that *chaos obeys, takes shape in, his voice."*[121] In the very latest Nietzsche *(Ecce Homo),* "classical" rhythm which informs chaos is referred to as one single thing in the artist's experience: "intoxication."[122] In intoxication, there is a connection of both the aspiration of Apollonian form to the sublime and the aspiration of the Dionysian disharmonious ground to a "taming" by means of form. Apollonian and Dionysian become "genres of *inebriation*,"[123] that is to say, of possession by rhythm: the first is "visionary" and more cerebral, while the second speaks to "the totality of sensibility," mobilizes the entire body, its nerves and muscles in quasi "hysterical"[124] frenzy. Inebriation, however, is not obsession, but *lucidity and extreme calm*. Pleasure, superheated sensuality, from now on belong *equally* to Apollonism (e.g., in Raphael, according to Nietzsche): "In Dionysian intoxication there is sexuality and voluptuousness: *this is not absent from Apollonian intoxication*. Yet it is necessary that between these two states there be a difference of *tempo*. ... Classical style essentially represents this calm, this simplification, this conciseness. *The highest feeling of power* concentrates in classical style."[125] The latter is no synthesis, however, because *the difference in tempo* of the creative rhythm remains. In one of his last letters to the musicologist Carl Fuchs, Nietzsche explicitly criticizes the falsely Dionysian rhythm of contemporary Dionysian Romanticism, which according to him is ruled to an excessive degree by the affects and the passions, and he insists on a *"distinction between the ancient rhythmic (founded on the tempo) and the barbarian rhythmic (founded on the affect)."*[126]"Rhythm in the ancient sense is the bridle that is put on passion on the moral and aesthetic level. In sum, our sort of rhythmic is in keeping with pathology, that of the ancients with *ethos*." [127] Here as well as in very many texts (dealing with music, poetry, the question of *style*—as in *The Gay Science*, in *Beyond Good and Evil* [Sections 28, 252, or 246], or in *Ecce Homo*) Nietzsche thinks of rhythm as the "measure of time": rhythm is a *necessary constraint*, a *tempo* that is carefully sustained, a regular and ordered cadence as that of waves, a periodic phenomenon. Being tantamount to self-determination and freely consented legislation, *rhythm must exert a constraint*, "the Greeks used to say that the hexameter was invented at Delphi."[128] Everything that lives has a rhythm, whether it be pertaining to the body or politics, to private or public life, to night or day, to memory or forgetfulness. Rhythm is "organic," said Hölderlin. It is this fundamental original rhythm, first called "The Spirit of Music," that each composer, poet, and writer must experience, receive, and *give himself* at the same time. Each must *want* the rhythm that is unveiled to him in the *Stimmung*. Metrics, regular units, long and short units, the codified alternation of foot set on the ground and foot raised from the ground, *thesis* and *arsis*, *dactyl* and *spondee, lento* and *presto,* are incontrovertible musical and linguistic requirements. Far from being the case that meaning "puts on" rhythm, it is rhythm that *makes sense.* "Misunderstanding the rhythm of a sentence is misunderstanding the very meaning of that sentence."[129] Rhythm is the irruption and originary quasi-organic inscription of meaning. That is why the *affective disposition,* the musical "state of soul," the high silent tonality, *calmness*, is articulation and *disposition* of meaning, shining forth of meaning. Nature's melody, the rhythms of the music of the world, unfold *in silence.* Only the joy of silent hours allows one to hear this inaudible, undetectable, yet unceasingly inspiring vibration of the world. *"Joy. Trinity of joy:* elevation, illumination, calm; unity of the three."[130] There is a muteness in the world that silently sings with joy and intimates a call to compose, to write, to think. "The greatest events are not the noisiest hours, but those hours of deepest silence... The world gravitates *in silence."*[131]

Hearing the Song of the Earth (the inarticulable common "origin" of music and poetry) is hearing rhythmic silence originarily made periodic, a rhythmic silence that is more ancient than any meaning. Nature itself seems to listen to it continuously, to listen to itself: "The pine tree seems to listen, the fur tree to wait—both of them without impatience."[132] Knowing how to remain silent is what Heidegger calls *Verhaltenheit,* attentive reserve: this would be the first quality of the musician philosopher, in contrast to the chatter of perpetual commentaries, to argumentative debauchery, and to the high points of dialectics. "The Pythagoreans invented a five-year silence, but not dialectics."[133] Thinking as an artist requires that one know first how to hear, that one allow oneself the resonance of musicality, the first *undulatory energy* of the cosmos: this musicality is then dispensed in gestures, in the dynamic of the artist-body, in the rhythmic of writing. Being available as *listeners* forces us to acknowledge the *relativity of language*. Indeed, language can and must be remusicalized, although we find it invaded by fixed stereotypes devoid of rhythm, by inert conceptuality, and by dull herd-like elocution. Rhythm may be brought back again to it. Yet even at its highest degree of intensity, i.e, of joy, in the poem, in the hymn, or in the dithyramb, language remains *tragically amputated,* tragically deficient with respect to instrumental, played music. Music speaks to the "inebriation" of the creative state of the will, a state where the will finds itself "jubilating or anxious unto death."[134] At such a point, natural sound becomes song or melody. By contrast, words and concepts are the imperfect residues of images, or the residues of the musical symbols of things.

Thought, therefore, translates only very imperfectly the originary rhythmic, the pre-worldly *[prémondain]* song because—by dint of its images and its sonic resonances of an originarily sensible impression—language has founded its symbolizations upon an extra-moral, incorrigible and irreversible lie. The key to the first metaphorization that set it to work is forever lost. The originary sensible impression cannot be translated linguistically, because the double metaphoric leap from a "nervous excitation" to image or sound, then from the sound-image to the concept, cannot be taken in reverse.[135] A fall of the vital excitation of the will into a symbol or an abstract metaphor, such is the essence of language for Nietzsche. And since "thinking" only occurs by connecting concepts (i.e., atomic units made up of sonic images devoid of soul or musical spirit), "the being of the thing is inaccessible to thought,"[136] and yet not to poetry and music. That is because the artistic *tempo* can *overturn* the entropy of language, can supply a new symbolic analogy *(Gleichniss)* for ontological Rhythm, can echo the strange ecstatic moments when a silent Voice is allowed hearing. Because conceptual language is in itself stillborn, more dead than alive, or a funerary edifice (i.e., "the great columbarium of concepts" evoked in *Truth and Lie)*, it must at all costs be remusicalized by singing, by the hymnal tonality, it must be recast thanks to the essential brevity of aphoristic expression. Aphorisms and fragments are the legacies of Novalis and the Romantics, but also of the stichomythia of the Tragics and the maxims of the French moralists. Their irruption means instantaneous revelation, *leaps* of meaning that compensate for, and struggle against, the "fallenness" of discursiveness. Aphorisms and fragments are shining bits of "eternity," the components of a mosaic without edges. They allow Nietzsche to "dance with chains" because it is such a difficult art to polish and to sharpen sentences of German prose, a prose that cannot sing, dance, or even have rhythm.[137]

The ontological Rhythm is always joyful, always reborn—it is the non-representable choreographic schema of the world; the unstable and non-intuitable Model of *everything that can be said,* written, thought, played, composed, sung, poetized, or put into aphorisms; it infinitely exceeds all its symbolic expressions. Such a demonic Rhythm does not lend itself to illustrations, which it makes appear insufficient, trivial and inadequate (as Nietzsche finds in the case of Bizet's "Noontime, Moorish dance, love").[138] This ontological demonic Rhythm foils, indeed is bound to foil, any attempt to conceive it and also does not seek its own parousia, as opposed to the Hegelian Absolute. But then in what sense does this Rhythm deserve to be called "tragic"? Being joyful in itself, is it not content being absorbed in its own play, building and destroying worlds, always young and regenerating, never jaded, never sad? And yet Nietzsche firmly maintains in the title of *The Gay Science* that joyful knowledge is tragic knowledge. *Incipit tragoedia.*[139] Tragedy begins (anew). The curtain rises on a new tragedy that is no longer a tragedy of the Greeks, of Wagner, or of Western nihilism.

One could interpret the renewed beginning of tragedy as Zarathustra's failure in communicating his doctrine: according to a posthumous fragment, he ends up going away alone with his animals (who remain a bit sluggish because the doctrine does not concern them) and dies alone. But in the widest sense, the tragic could not possibly qualify the destiny of one man, of any hero of history (or even the fictional Zoroaster), who returns to announce the end of ressentiment, the end of a thinking of time conceived as vengeance against time. In the broad sense, tragic is the being of *Nature,* thought as chaos, and our relationship to it; but more tragic yet is the funerary moment of the dusk of our world as it rushes toward night, as history seems to hesitate before a new beginning, proceeds gropingly, suspends itself because it is as blind as Oedipus and animated with the same excessive will to know.

Aren't Rhythm and Chaos taken together one contradiction among many that critics like to point out to disqualify Nietzschean philosophy? If the being of nature is Rhythm, it is also Order—be it complex and hidden. If the being of nature is Chaos, it is also from eternity if not disorder, at least absence of finality, or as Nietzsche says "not absence of necessity, but absence of order, articulation, form, beauty, wisdom, and of all our human aesthetic categories, whatever they be."[140] Nonetheless, we find in *The Gay Science* the idea that *chaos* as the gaping and abyssal opening, the pre-worldly crack or fissure, is *necessary.* The *necessity of the world* does not allow itself to be reduced within the categories of our human faculty of judgment, and therefore presumably in the end is neither beautiful nor sublime, neither wise nor possessed, is neither form-oriented *[formelle]* nor form-repugnant *[informe].* It escapes *our* finality, *our* perspectivalism, however multiple it may be. The counter-concept of chaos reveals, as Heidegger saw it accurately, *a negative theology.* The world as divine escapes us. Its divinity eschews those "human, all-too-human attributes" that we are tempted to assign to it. Its divinity worlds, plays the game-of-the-world, opens up … . Rhythm is the indescribable "schema"—always imitated yet inimitable—of its openness. As the intelligible character in Kant is the schema of the empirical character, Rhythm is the secret and inexpressible order that rules over the apparent order of "the laws of nature" and the great, fictional principles used by the sciences. Thus, the concept of chaos is not contradictory with the notion of an immanent order of things. It is a preventive concept, a handrail against the risk of *romantic* delirium, of *Schwärmerei,* of the delirious exaltation of intuition claiming to reach the Absolute. On this point, Nietzsche is close to Kant. Everything is "phenomenon," that is to say, for Nietzsche, "interpretation." The thing-in-itself is non-representable. Still it can be schematized, reached indirectly by means of the symbols: symbolism is inverted, because "everything imperishable is nothing but symbol." "To see the chaos" is an initial necessity of artistic creation, which does not amount to an intuition of chaos but means that the artist experiences more strongly the impulse to project *new* schemas to *unify* the diversity of forces. But rhythm, as revealed in joy, and originary productivity cannot attest, as Heidegger thinks, to the existence of latent preexisting forms in chaos. All there is—and that is "all" indeed—is the form-oriented power of *Phusis (die gestaltende Kraft):* there are no prior *Gestalten*, rather there is a *Gestaltung*, a shaping and ordering force that *intoxicates* us with *joy* when we move close to it.

Yet our relationship with this Power which bears us is tragic. Attached to it, dragged away by it, as though perched on the back of a tiger or a dragon, we must renounce *knowledge* otherwise than by art, that is to say, by means of analogies or impenetrable symbols, or else by means of a rare and instantaneous fusion that deprives us of the instruments and the procedures of *knowledge.* "Tragic knowledge," as it is defined in Section 15 of *The Birth of Tragedy,* remains the first and last word on the value of science. Science is spurred by a "sublime illusion" (hyper-Apollonism), a "delirious phantasm" that comes into the world with Socrates, the belief that by means of the principle of causality scientific thought is capable of discovering all mysteries, of piercing the secret of nature, and "of penetrating into the depths of things."[141] But *tragic* wisdom knows that the more science moves on as an endless vise, the more the enigma grows, the wider the shadows and the unknowable become.

The tragic joy of modern man, a long time after the death of Greek tragedy, belongs to a classicism that is equally removed from both extremes: the explanatory delirium of science and the intuitive delirium of the romantic worshippers of nature. Today such an alternative has given way to the opposition between, on the one hand, the mad rush to machinery—the endless vise of technology—and, on the other hand, the ecological dream, which even in its realistic achievements cannot slow down the irresistible devastation of the Earth. Knowledge without the least melancholy, knowledge which only artistic symbolization permits that "we have art (only) in order not to die of (scientific) truth"—that is the tragic.

Tragic is the mourning over the Greek scientific illusion. Not all have experienced it yet. Tragic is the loss—forever—of the Dionysian festivals of reunification with the One, the forgetfulness of the primitive Dionysian state of transfiguration of the world. Today's artists only deal with margins, and rarely cast light upon them. Tragic is the loss of "the long, the prodigious scale of light and colors"[142] that in the Greeks allowed the encounter of the highest divine joy and human delight in the most humble forms of nature. Tragic is the irreparable loss of the religions of the *secret*. Dionysos will no longer be reborn as an epochal god. Some will still have "god in the heart," that is to say a god according to their heart. But tragic is the expectation of a god still to come in the midst of the wasteland that grows in the implacable darkening of the world, and amidst the scarcity of celestial premonitions. Tragic is the twilight of the idols.

Yet joy remains because it is *not epochal*. Rather, in all times joy is the angel of those who hope in silence, the initiatory grace by which the gaping sight of the opening is firmly sustained. Joy remains as a calm force that is close to anxiety, as a gift for loving the work in process, without allowing us to recognize a Model. In its quiet calm Joy remains out of reach for the "madness and fury" of the times because it is—without our believing it—halfway along the path to the next Clearing; it is a "power that needs no proof, above the desire to please, a power to which there is no easy response, ... that rests *within itself.*"[143] In the smiling acceptance of fatalism, this joy continues with sobriety, greets existence with an unceasing *da capo,* and forgets in its extreme happiness that it is devoid of a proof for its future.

# List of Abbreviations

The texts most quoted by Michel Haar from the German or the French translations of Nietzsche are from:

*Kritische Gesaumtasgabe Werke,* the recently completed edition by G. Colli and M. Montinari, Berlin: Walter de Gruyter, hereafter *K.G.W.*

*Oeuvres philosophiques complètes* (henceforth *O.P.C.),* also contains the volumes of the *Fragments posthumes,* Paris: Gallimard. It is to this *O.P.C.* collection of Nietzsche's works in French that references are made, especially concerning *La naissance de la tragédie* (hereafter *N.T.).* Also included is *La Vision dionysiaque du monde* (in *Ecrits Posthumes* 1870-73)—hereafter referred to as *V.D.*

For the posthumous fragments the other edition used by the author is Kröner, edited by Alfred Baümler (with the title, *Unschuld des Werdens,* The Innocence of Becoming, in which a different ordering and numbering system has been followed than the one adopted in *K.G.W.),* in Kröners Taschenausgabe, Stuttgart: Alfred Kröner Verlag, 1956, 2 volumes, hereafter *K.*

The two texts the author uses for *The Will to Power* are:
The German *Wille zur Macht*, Kröners Taschenausgabe, Stuttgart: Alfred Kröner, 1956, hereafter *W.z.M.*. The numbering of the sections of *W.z.M.* corresponds to that of the English translation by Walter Kaufmann.
The French *La Volonté de Puissance*, trans. G. Bianquis, Paris: Gallimard, 1948, hereafter *V.P.*

Whenever possible, references are made to works of Nietzsche with a section number. In most cases, however, due to the author's selection of and emphasis upon a word, or a few words, it was not possible to keep the extent translations without modification. No abbreviation is used for these translations:

*The Birth of Tragedy* and *The Case of Wagner*, trans. Walter Kaufmann, New York: Vintage Books, 1967.

*The Gay Science,* trans. Walter Kaufmann, New York: Vintage Books, 1974.

*On the Genealogy of Morals* and *Ecce Homo*, trans. Walter Kaufmann, New York: Vintage Books, 1967.

*Beyond Good and Evil,* trans. Walter Kaufmann, New York: Vintage Books, 1966.

*The Will to Power,* trans. Walter Kaufmann, New York: Vintage Books, 1967.

*Twilight of the Idols* and *The Anti-Christ*, trans. R. J. Hollingdale, London: Penguin Books, 1968.

*Human, All Too Human,* trans. Marion Faber, Lincoln: University of Nebraska Press, 1984.

*Thus Spoke Zarathustra*, trans. Thomas Common, New York: The Modern Library.

*Daybreak,* trans. R. J. Hollingdale, Cambridge: Cambridge University Press, 1982.

*The Wanderer and His Shadow* and *Human, All Too Human,* trans. R. J. Hollingdale, Cambridge: Cambridge University Press, 1986.

*Untimely Meditations* (also referred to as "Considerations Out-of-Season"), trans. R. J. Hollingdale, Cambridge: Cambridge University Press, 1984.

# Notes

## Preface

1. They comprise five articles already published, revised for the present publication. "La subversion des catégories et des identités" (The Subversion of Categories and Identities) (1974); "La rupture, initialement acquise, avec Schopenhauer" (The Initially Extant Rupture with Schopenhauer) (1988); "La maladie native du langage" (The Native Malady of Language) (1978); "Critique et subversion de la subjectivité" (Critique and Subversion of Subjectivity) (1983); "Vie et totalité naturelle" (Life and Natural Totality) (1989); and three other unpublished texts: "Le renversement du platonisme et la nouvelle signification de l'apparence" (The Overturning of Platonism and the New Meaning of Appearance); "Métamorphose du divin" (Metamorphosis of the Divine); "La joie tragique" (Tragic Joy).

2. *Human, All Too Human,* I, Section 20.

3. *Twilight of the Idols,* "How in the end the 'true world' became a fable."

4. If "overcoming metaphysics ... requires the highest effort of human reflection," as Nietzsche writes in Section 20 of *Human, All Too Human,* it is because it is not sufficient "to look back on it with superiority," but rather one must—after taking the measure of its past greatness—still "climb back down a few rungs" and seek "to understand both the historical and the psychological *justification* in metaphysical ideas" [stressed added].

5. *N.T.,* p.32.

6. The beginning of an answer with respect to the "overturning of Platonism" is provided in Chapter Three. For a more systematic presentation of the relation Heidegger-Nietzsche see Michel Haar, *La fracture de l'histoire,* Douze essais sur Heidegger, Grenoble: Jérôme Millon, 1994.

7. *V.P.,* I: 90.

8. For Heidegger the overturning applies not only to Platonism, but also to Cartesianism and Hegelianism.

9 *Beyond Good and Evil,* Section 289.

## Chapter I
## The Subversion of Categories and Identities

1. In 1894, Lou Andréas-Salomé published the first and remarkable work on the philosopher, *Nietzsche in seinem Werke,* which exposes the three

great periods of his thought (French translation, Paris: Bernard Grasset, 1932; new edition by Gordon and Breach).

2. *Ecce Homo,* "Why I am so wise," Section 1.
3. *Ibid.*, "Why I am a destiny," Section 1.
4. *On Truth and Lie in an Extra-Moral Sense,* Section 1.
5. *Twilight of the Idols,* "What the Germans Have Lost," Section 7.
6. Letter to Fuchs, August 26, 1888.
7. *Beyond Good and Evil,* Section 186.
8. *The Genealogy of Morals;* II, Section 12.
9. *W.z.M.*, Section 693.
10. *K.*, II, Section 874.
11. *W.z.M.*, Sections 46 ff.
12. *W.z.M.*, Section 715.
13. *W.z.M.*, Section 692.
14. *W.z.M.*, Section 815.
15. *W.z.M.*, Section 619.
16. *Thus Spoke Zarathustra.*
17. *The Genealogy of Morals,* very last sentence.
18. *W.z.M.*, Section 715.
19. *W.z.M.*, Section 1.
20. *W.z.M.*, Section 269.
21. *Twilight of the Idols,* "How the 'True World' at last Became a Myth."
22. *Ibid.*
23. *W.z.M.*, Section 15.
24. *W.z.M,* II, Section 496.
25. *The Gay Science,* Section 110.
26. *W.z.M.*, Section 493.
27. *W.z.M.*, Section 333
28. *Ibid.*
29. *Twilight of the Idols,* "The Problem of Socrates," Section 9.
30. *K.*, II, Section 362.
31. *Ecce Homo,* 1 Section 6.
32. *Genealogy of Morals,* III, Section 27.
33. *K.*, II, Section 1270.
34. *K.*, II, Section 1274.
35. *W.z.M.*, Section 998.
36. *W.z.M.*, Section 822.
37. *Genealogy of Morals,* Section 341.
38. *W.z.M.*, Section 55.
39. *K.*, II, Section 1347.
40. *Thus Spoke Zarathustra;* "The Drunken Song," Section 10.
41. *Ibid.*
42. *Ibid.*
43. *K.*, II, Section 1343.
44. *The Gay Science,* Section 276.
45. *K.*, II, Section 1369.
46. *Thus Spoke Zarathustra;* "On Redemption."
47. *Thus Spoke Zarathustra;* "The Seven Seals."

48. *W.z.M.*, Section 617.

49. Letter to Burckhardt, January 6, 1889.

50. *Human, All Too Human,* II, Section 355.

## Chapter 2
## The Initial Rupture with Schopenhauer

1. *N.T., Fragments posthumes,* 1986–72, p.32.

2. *The Genealogy of Morals,* Foreword, Section 5.

3. *Considerations Out-of-Season,* III-IV, *Fragments posthumes,* 1874–76, p. 25. Nietzsche minimizes a distance that he has some trouble concealing: "I have found in him ... at the most a little mistake here and there"! as we read a few lines later in the *Considerations Out-of-Season.*

4. *K.G.W.*, IV, 3, 382. Fragment 309, "The Schopenhauer Effect."

5. *Considerations Out-of-Season,* third and fourth essays.

6. *Ecce Homo,* concerning the "Considerations Out-of-Season," Section 3.

7. At issue are the first versions of *The Birth of Tragedy,* specifically the two lectures given on January 18 and February 1, 1870: "The Greek Musical Drama," and "Socrates and Tragedy." *See Ecrits posthumes* 1870–73.

8. Letter to von Gersdorff, Basel, 28 September 1869 in *Correspondance,* II, Paris: Gallimard, 1988, p. 60.

9. *N.T.*, fragments of the 1869–70 winter, 3 (3), p.198.

10. *N.T.*, Fragment 3 (23), p. 205 (stress added).

11. *Ibid.*, Fragment 7 (165), p. 311.

12. *Ibid.*, Fragment 7 (198), p. 319.

13. *Ibid.*, Fragment 7 (202), p. 321.

14. *Ibid.*, Fragment 7 (157), p. 309.

15. *Ibid.*, Fragment 5 (80), p. 240–41.

16. *Ibid.*, Fragment 3 (46), 1869–70, "The Essence of Music as the Essence of the World."

17. See the first *Consideration Out-of-Season.* D. Strauss had accused Schopenhauer's philosophy of being "unhealthy and fruitless."

18. See *Fragments Posthumes* with respect to the *Considerations Out-of-Season,* IV, Paris: Gallimard, 1988, pp. 366–409.

19. "Schopenhauer relates to the world as a blind person to writing" (in *K.G.W.*, IV, 2, p. 465, Fragment 21 (13), end of 1876, summer 1877).

20. *K.G.W.*, III, 3, 105.

21. *W.z.M.*, Section 812.

22. *W.z.M.*, Section 821.

23. *N.T.*, p. 78.

24. *N.T.*, p. 153.

25. *N.T.*, p. 115 (stress added).

26. *Ibid.*

27. *The Twilight of the Idols,* p. 130 (underscored in the text). See also pp. 120–121.

28. *Ecce Homo,* about "The Birth of Tragedy," p. 285.

29. Preface to *The Genealogy of Morals,* Section 5.

30. *W.z.M.,* Section 453.

31. *Consideration Out-of-Season,* III–IV, Fragment 34 (43), p. 221.

32. *Ibid.*, (32), p. 216.

33. *Beyond Good and Evil,* Section 47.

34. But he is not the only one: one should also add the Romantic philologists Friedrich and Wilhelm Schlegel; the Goethean ones, Anselm Feuerbach and Otfried Müller; the historians and sociologists of Greek religion, Welcker and Bachofen; finally, the ideas of Richard Wagner and Franz Liszt on tragedy (see Andler, I, *Les précurseurs de Nietzsche,* Paris: Gallimard, 1958, 394–428).

35. Nonetheless, the reappropriations of Schopenhauer without distance or without drifting away from him are rare. This is not the case—notwithstanding appearances to the contrary—in dealing with the theory of music in Chapter XVI. In the fragments, the texts are often difficult to interpret, for we are presented either with critiques or with noncritical reading notes, even passages copied almost verbatim from Schopenhauer.

36. "Art is ... the joyful anticipation of restored unity" *(N.T.,* p. 84). Nonetheless, the word "joyful" is already contrary to Schopenhauerian orthodoxy: there is no joy, only infinitely repeated pain, in the will to live.

37. In Schopenhauer, the distinction between essence and appearance, which is that of the thing-in-itself and the phenomena, of the unique will and of the individuals, is governed by the Platonic opposition between the One and the Many. Let me quote a textfrom *The World as Will and Representation* (1: Section 63): "The world does not exhibit itself to knowledge which has sprung from the will to serve it, and which comes to the individual as such in the same way as it finally discloses itself to the inquirer, namely as the objectivity of the one and only will-to-live, which he himself is. On the contrary, the eyes of the uncultured individual are clouded, as the Indians say, by the veil of Maya. To him is revealed not the thing-in-itself, but only the phenomenon in time and space, in the *principium individuationis,* and in the remaining forms of the principle of sufficient reason. In this form of his limited knowledge, he sees not the inner nature of things, which is one, but its phenomena as separated, detached, innumerable, very different, and indeed opposed ... [He suffers from] his own individuality, involved as he is in the *principium individuationis,* deluded by the veil of Maya."

38. *N.T.,* p. 311. *K.G.W.,* III, 3, p. 211. Fragment 7.

39. *Ibid.*

40. *Ibid.,* p. 315, *K.G.W.,* III, p. 215, Fragment 7: *Weil der Wille nichts als Schein selbst ist und das Ureine nur in ihm eine Erscheinung hat.*

41 *Ibid.,* 313, Fragment 7 (170) (Nietzsche's stress).

42. *N.T.,* pp. 240–41.

43. *N.T.,* p. 115.

44. *N.T.,* p. 144. See also *Thus Spoke Zarathustra,* "The Drunken Song":

> *Woe saith: Hence! Go!*
> *But joys all want eternity—,*
> *—Want deep, profound eternity!*

45. *N.T.*, p. 115.

46. *N.T.*, p. 323, winter 1870–71, Fragment 8 (2).

47. *N.T.*, p. 282, end 1870–April 1871, Fragment 7 (117). Nietzsche claims in the same fragment that in Oneness, in the Will, the highest pain and ecstatic pleasure are *identical,* and that at this point of identity is artistic creation: "The will as highest pain generates an ecstasy out of itself *[aus sich],* an ecstasy that is identical to pure intuition and to the production of the work of art." The primordial One (as in Michel Henry!) takes joy from itself suffering in itself, or suffers from itself taking joy in itself.

48. *The World as Will and Representation.*

49. *N.T.*, p. 315.

50. *Ibid.*, p. 308.

51. *Ibid.*, p. 312 (stress added).

52. *Beyond Good and Evil,* Section 289.

## Chapter 3
## The Overturning of Platonism and the New Meaning of Appearance

1. *N.T., Fragments posthumes,* end 1870–April 1871, p. 1871. p. 308. *K.G.W.*, III, 7 (156).

2. *Fragments posthumes,* vol. XI, p. 391; *K.G.W.*, VII, 3, 40 (53).

3. *N.T., Fragments posthumes, p. 311; K.G.W., III, 3, 7, (167).*

4. *N.T.*, 315; *K.G.W.*, III, 3, p. 215, 7 (167).

5. *Ibid.*, p. 115.

6. *Ibid.*, p. 53.

7. *The Twilight of Idols,* see "The Case of Wagner."

8. *W.z.M.*, Section 567.

9. *V.P.*, 1: 205.

10. *Ibid.*, 1: 251; *W.z.M.*, Section 617.

11. Martin Heidegger, *Essais et conférences,* Paris: Gallimard, p. 91 (henceforth *E.C.*); *Vorträge und Aufsätze,* 3rd ed., Pfullingen: Neske, 1954, p. 79.

12. *Ibid.*

13. "The philosopher caught in the nets of language," *K.G.W.*, III, 4, p. 51, Fragment 19 (135).

14. Martin Heidegger, *Nietzsche,* 1: 242 (French trans. Klossowski, p. 190). In the first version that is given in the *GA* (vol. 45, 1985) H. Heimbüchel, the German editor, adds that this is the original text of the lecture course given in the Winter Semester of 1936–37, which is distinguished from the version published later (in 1961) by Neske, the latter being a "revised version" (*GA*, 43: 293). Heidegger by contrast *underscores* at the end of Section 28 (in an exclamative conclusion without verb) the following: there is in the "new interpretation of the sensible and non-sensible" *no twisting free* of Platonism, concerning which Nietzsche would repeat not so much the extreme terms as the fundamental inspiration: "Hence, no extraction, on the contrary!" (*ibid.*, 262). Thus it seems that the later Heidegger gained a more

nuanced position and that *for him the twisting free of Platonism*—if it cannot be considered granted—is *not for all that an irretrievable failure.*

15. *N.T., Fragments posthumes,* p. 312. The status of the contents of these fragments is often hard to interpret. We are faced at the same time with reading notes and with already elaborate sketches aiming at a critique of Schopenhauer, which Nietzsche did not systematize.

16. *N.T.,* p. 229.

17. *Ibid.*

18. See *K.*, II, 85 and *K.G.W.*, IV, VII, 3, p. 386. Fragment 40 (52).

19. "There only remains the shadow of a *right [Recht]* to speak here of appearance" (*W.z.M.,* Section 567), quoted by Martin Heidegger, *Nietzsche,* 1: 484.

20. A passage of Fragment 567 indicates that for Nietzsche the "view points" (those of forces, of the Will to Power) are true and must not be referred to as "apparent." I quote: "Perspectivalism *[das Perspektivische]* suppresses *[gibt ab]* the character of 'appearance'!" Let me mention that Klossowski makes a significant mistake in the French translation of this statement, when he writes: "Perspectivalism gives the character of appearance" (see French translation by Klossowski, *Nietzsche,* 1: 484, *Le perspectivisme donne le caractère de l'apparence).* Furthermore, the word for "appearance" is not here the German *Schein,* but *Scheinbarkeit,* which rather implies, or means, logical illusion, error in reasoning, sophism.

21. See "Essay of Self-Critique," added to *The Birth of Tragedy* in 1886, Section 2.

22. *E.C.,* p. 94.

23. Although for Plato *phantasma* (illusory reflection) is with *skia* (shadow) one of the two subdivisions of the *icon (Republic,* 510a), here we take *phantasma* as the general emblem of Platonic appearances because of its root in *phainesthai* (to appear, to shine forth).

24. Gilles Deleuze, *Logique du sens,* Paris: Editions de Minuit, 1969, Appendix, "Platon et le simulacre," pp. 292 ff.

25. *Ibid.,* p.303.

26. Gilles Deleuze, *Différence et répétition,* Paris: P.U.F., 1968, p. 167.

27. Here is the text: "a universe where the image ceases being secondary with respect to the model, where imposture claims to the rank of truth, finally where there is no more original, but an eternal scintillating in which the absence of origin is dispersed—in the explosion of the detour and of the return" ("The Gods' Laughter," *Nouvelle Revue française,* July 1965).

28. *W.z.M.,* Section 1067 (Fragment of 1885).

29. Martin Heidegger *Nietzsche,* II, Chapter 6 of the French translation ("La métaphysique de Nietzsche").

30. *K.G.W.,* VII, 3, 40 (53); *Fragments posthumes,* vol. XI, p. 391.

31. Martin Heidegger, *Nietzsche,* 1: 193.

32. *W.z.M.,* Section 567.

33. *Ibid.,* Section 568.

34. *Ibid.,* Section 566.

35. *Ibid.,* Section 572.

36. *N.T.*, Section 15, p. 106.

37. *The Gay Science,* Section 54.

38. Tragic wisdom presupposes a *difference* between life and knowledge, the critique of knowledge at whatever cost, the affirmation of artistic illusion as necessary and wholesome: "One must even *want illusion*—this is the tragic" (Fall-Winter 1872, in *Le livre du philosophe,* Paris: Aubier, 1969, p. 55). See also *Considerations Out-of-Season,* second essay, in *O.P.C.,* 2: 183, Fragment 19 (35).

39. Martin Heidegger, *Nietzsche,* 2: 254. Nonetheless, the echo of *aletheia* is extremely weakened. The initial *aletheia* has been metamorphosed, "perverted," to the point where its essence is completely occulted, in the identification or the assimilation of Being and Becoming in the midst of the Eternal Return—without however being annihilated. "Such a metamorphosis is tantamount to putting aside—and not to annihilating—its essence [i.e., the essence of truth]" *(Nietzsche,* 2: 19). This is why Heidegger can say—with a seeming contradiction—that in Nietzsche's thinking of truth "even the last echo of *aletheia* fades away" *(ibid.).*

40. *V.P.,* 2: 272.

41. *The Gay Science,* Section 54.

42. Fragment called "Recapitulation," Section 617 of *W.z.M.*

43. *E.C.,* p. 93. One must distinguish between "completion" *(Vollendung)* and "end" *(Ende)* in the sense where Heidegger says that "Nietzsche's philosophy is the *end* of Western metaphysics" (see *GA,* 44: 255). The completion is broader and deeper than the end. Whereas the end concerns the metaphysical principles, the completion concerns the totality in its entirety, i.e., the last epoch of History. When Heidegger talks about "completion" apropos of Nietzsche, he has in view "the completion of metaphysics" and *not the completion of the history of Being.* This latter completion has *merely just* begun. "The epoch of completed metaphysics is about to begin" *(E.C.,* p. 92). The ultimate completion *forgets, ignores* that metaphysics upon which it emerged: that is why it opens up the way to an extreme nihilism.

44. *E.C.,* p. 92.

45. Martin Heidegger, *Nietzsche,* 2: 19–23.

46. *Ibid.,* p. 314.

47. *K.,* I, p. 55.

48. *The Gay Science,* Section 107.

49. *Beyond Good and Evil,* Section 24.

50. *Ecrits posthumes,* Section 311, p. 134.

51. *V.P.,* 1: 76.

52. *Ibid.,* 2: 45.

53. Martin Heidegger, *Nietzsche,* 2: 16.

54. *Ibid.,* 2: 17.

55. *W.z.M.,* Section 710.

56. *Ibid.,* Section 842.

57. *Ibid.,* Section 818.

58. *V.P.,* 1: 330.

59. *The Gay Science,* Section 107.

60. *Ecrits posthumes*, vol. XII, p. 125 (2, 119).

61. *V.P.*, 2: 237.

62. To be specific, only between 1940 and 1946 (see the chapter in *Nietzsche* II entitled "La métaphysique de Nietzsche" of the French translation (pp. 207-66), a text not included in the English translation edited by David Farell Krell).

## Chapter 4
## The Native Malady of Language

1. *Thus Spoke Zarathustra*, "On Reading and Writing."

2. See especially the important fragment 12 (1) from the beginning of 1871.

3. *Ibid.*, p. 431.

4. *Ibid.*, p 61.

5. *Ibid.*, p 130.

6. *N.T.*, p. 65.

7. *Ibid, Fragments*, p. 431.

8. *Ecrits posthumes*, p. 280.

9. Emphasis added.

10. *The Genealogy of Morals*, I, Section 2.

11. *Ibid.*, I, 11.

12. *Ibid.*, I, 2.

13. *W.z.M.*, Section 545.

14. *The Wanderer and His Shadow*, Section 55.

15. *Beyond Good and Evil*, Section 289.

16. *V.P.*, I: 99.

17. *Ibid.*

18. *Ibid.*

19. See *Beyond Good and Evil*, Sections16 and 17, and *V.P.*, I, 65–79.

20. *The Genealogy of Morals*, I, Section 13.

21. *V.P.*, I: 82.

22. *Ibid.*

23. *Twilight of the Idols* in "The Wagner Case"

24. *Ibid.*

25. *Ecce Homo, O.P.C.* p. 277.

26. *The Anti-Christ, O.P.C.*, p. 234.

27. *Ecrits posthumes*, p. 289.

28. *Beyond Good and Evil*, Section 223.

29. *Twilight of the Idols*, pp. 146–147.

30. "Mallarmé, "Crise de Vers," *Oeuvres*, Paris: Gallimard, Pleiade, p. 858.

31. See *Thus Spoke Zarathustra*, "Of Salvation."

32. *W.z.M.*, Section 842.

33. See *De rerum originatione radicali*, 5. The "great style" is the art of obtaining a maximum of prolonged effects with a minimum "expense" of

signs; it is defined as "that which endures with few means."

34. *Nachgelassense Fragmente*, Colli und Montinari, vol. VII, 3, 305.

35. *Ecce Homo, O.P.C.*, p. 281.

36.*Ecrits posthumes*, p. 87.

37. *Nachlaß*, I, 188.

38. Every style of writing, as every language, has its own "metabolism" (*Beyond Good and Evil*, Section 289).

39. *Ibid.*,Section 190.

40. *Ibid.*, Section 191.

41. *Gay Science*, Section 354.

42. *Beyond Good and Evil*, Section 36.

43. *Ibid.*

44. *Twilight of the Idols*, "What the Germans Lack," Section 6.

## Chapter 5
## The Critique and Subversion of Subjectivity

1. *V.P.*, 1: 258.

2. *V.P.*, I2: 384.

3. *K.G.W.*, VII, 1: 25.

4. Martin Heidegger, *Sein und Zeit*, Tübingen: Neomarius Verlag, 1960, p.322; trans. J. Macquarrie and E. Robinson, New York: Harper and Row, 1962, p. 369.

5. Martin Heidegger, *Nietzsche*, French trans. Klossowski, Paris: Gallimard, 2: 241.

6. For example in Heidegger, *Essais et conférences*, Paris: Gallimard, p. 95.

7. *Ecrits Posthumes*, 1887-1888, *K.G.W.*, VIII, 2, 11 (73). O.P.C., t. XIII, p. 234–35.

8. *V.P.*, 1: 238.

9. *V.P.*, 1: 255.

10. See Descartes, *Discourse on Method* and *Meditations on First Philosophy*, trans. Donald A. Cress, Indianapolis: Hackett Publishing Company, 1980, p. 63.

11. Kant, *Critique of Pure Reason*, 2nd edition, section 17, B136.

12. *Ibid.*, Section 16, B135.

13. *Ibid.*

14. *W.z.M.*., Section 519.

15. *V.P.*, 1: 73.

16. *Ibid.*, p. 82.

18. *Human, All Too Human*, 1: 637.

19. *Ibid.*

20. *Cahiers*, 1: 861.

21. *V.P.*, 2: 384.

22. *Twilight of the Idols*, "Moral als Widernatur," Section 6.

23. *V.P.*, 1: 258.

24. *W.z.M.*., Section 480.
25. *Poèmes,* Kröners Taschenausgabe, vol. 77, p. 574.
26. *V.P.*, 1: 255.
27. *Ibid.*, p. 278.
28. *Ibid.*, p. 262.
29. *Ibid.*, p. 265.
30. *Ibid.*, p. 267.
31. *Beyond Good and Evil,* Section 19.
32. *V.P.*, 1: 265.
33. *Ibid.*
34. *Ibid.*, p. 253.
35. *Ibid.*, p. 268.
36. *Ibid.*
37. *Ibid.*, p. 267.
38. *Ibid.*
39. *Ibid.*, p. 279.
40. *Ibid.*, 2: 280.
41. See *K.G.W.*, VII, 3, 35 (35).
42. *Beyond Good and Evil,* Sections 16–17.
43. *Ibid.*
44. *V.P.*, 1: 280.
45. See *The Gay Science*, Section 179, "Thoughts are the shadows of feelings."
46. *K.G.W.*, VII, 3, 38 (1).
47. *V.P.*, 1: 239.
48. *Ibid.*, p. 274.
49. *Ibid.*, p. 265.
50. *Ibid.*, p. 272.
51. *The Gay Science,* Section 354.
52. *V.P.*, 1: 272.
53. See *V.P.*, 1: 316, "In 'pleasure' and 'pain' some judgments are already included."
54. *Beyond Good and Evil,* Section 19.
55. *Ibid.*
56. *Ibid.*
57. Although usage of the terms "instinct" and "impulse" *(Instinkt* and *Trieb)* has not been settled by uncontrovertable scholarly conventions, since *The Birth of Tragedy* Nietzsche uses *Trieb* to designate those "natural forces" belonging to *phusis* in the most general and elementary fashion (e.g., the Apollonian and the Dionysian), while he reserves the word *Instinkt* for an instinct that is both more specialized (instinct for knowledge, appropriation instinct) and more limited to a particular subject (to a given type of humanity), hence more socialized. Consequently, a pejorative connotation attaches to the word *Instinkt.*
58. *V.P.*, 1: 264.
59. *Ibid.*
60. *K.G.W.*, VII 3, 34 (57).
61. *Ibid.*, VII 2, 25 (374).
62. *Ibid.*, VII, 2, 25 (374). O.P.C., X, 126.

63. *V.P.*, 1: 263.
64. *Ibid.*
65. *K.G.W.*, VII, 1, 1 (70).
66. *K.G.W.*, VII, 3, 35 (68).
67. *V.P* 1: 248.
68. *Ibid.*, p. 268.
69. *Ibid.*, p. 255.
70. *Ibid.*, p. 256.
71. *Ibid.*, p. 249.
72. *Ibid.*, p. 256.
73. *K.* II, 171.
74. *K.G.W.*, V, 2, 12 (93).
75. *Ibid.*, VII, 2, 26, (262).
76. *V.P.*, 1:, 255.
77. *W.z.M.*., Section 678.
78. *Ibid.*, Section 520.
79. *Fragments posthumes,* 1887-88. *K.G.W.*, VIII, 2, 9 (30).
80. *Ibid.*, 199; 10 (136) (stress added).
81. *V.P.*, 1:, 228.
82. *W.z.M.*, Section 687.
83. *V.P.*, 1: 390 (stress added).
84. *Beyond Good and Evil,* Section 36.
85. *V.P.*, 1: 334, Section 815 (stress added).
86. *Ibid.*, 1: 216 (stress added).
87. *Fragments posthumes*, 1887–88, 343; *Posthumes,* 1887–88, 11 (374).
88. *K.G.W.*, VII, I, 4 (138).
89. *Beyond Good and Evil,* Section 223.
90. *Ibid.*
91. *K.*, I, 244.
92. Letter to Burckhardt, January 6, 1889.
93. *V.P.*, 1: 386.
94. *Ibid.*
95. *Le cas Wagner* ..., draft of a letter to Brandes, December 1888, in *O.P.C.*, p. 399.
96. *Ecce Homo,* "Warum ich ein Schicksal bin," Section 1.
97. *Ibid.*
98. *V.P.*, 2: 289 (stress added).
99. *Ibid.*, 1: 287.
100. *Ibid.*
101. Martin Heidegger, *Chemins,* first edition, Paris: Gallimard, p. 196.
102. Martin Heidegger, *Nietzsche*, 2: 232.
103. *Ibid.,* 1: 365.
104. *Ibid.*
105. See *The Gay Science*, Section 341.
106. See Heidegger, *Nietzsche* 2: 238.
107. With respect to this theme, I recommand the remarkable and exhaustive study by Wolfgang Müller-Lauter, *Nietzsches Lehre vom Willen zur Macht (Nietzsche-Studien*, Band 3, 1974, 1–60). I espouse very widely the

conclusions of his essay, in particular concerning two points: First, the author shows that it is possible to confer upon "the" Will to Power the unity and the universality of an "essence" or of a supreme principle in the sense of traditional metaphysics (see in particular the superb critique of Heidegger's position, page 23, note). Second, he shows that Nietzsche's perspectivalism as a philosophy of interpretation cannot be reduced to a form of subjectivism (which, however, does not mean that Nietzsche should be located outside of what Heidegger calls "the metaphysics of subjectivity") (see p. 13, note 32, and pp. 43–44, 59). This important article provides an impressive convergence of textual analyses and contributes to clarify the general problematic of the "subject" in Nietzsche.

108. Martin Heidegger, *Nietzsche,* 1: 116.

109. See my essay "L'énigme de la quotidienneté," in *Être et temps de Martin Heidegger,* ed. J.-P. Cometti and D. Janicaud, Sud, 1989.

110. Diels-Kranz, "Fragments des Présocratiques," Fragment 45.

## Chapter 6
## Life and Natural Totality

1. *Le Gai Savoir, Fragments posthumes,* 11 (197), p. 387.
2. *Beyond Good and Evil,* Section 227.
3. *Ecce Homo, O.P.C.,* p. 288.
4. *Beyond Good and Evil,* Section 188.
5. *Ibid.*
6. *K.*, 2: 269.
7. *Le Gai Savoir,* 11 (94), p. 345.
8. *K.*, 2: 267.
9. *Le Gai Savoir,* 11 (55), p. 258.
10. *Ibid.*, 392.
11. *Ibid.*, 11 (16), 319.
12. *Lettres,* 65, 12.
13. W.z.M., Section 711.
14. *The Gay Science,* Section 109.
15. *Le Gai Savoir,* 11 (211), 392.
16. *V.P.*, 1: 213.
17. *Le Gai Savoir,* 12 (111), p. 464.
18. *Ibid.*, Section 109.
19. *V.P.*, 1: 218.
20. *Ibid.*, p. 225.
21. *Ibid.*
22. *Ibid.*, p. 238.
23. *Ibid.*, p. 239.
24. *Ibid.*, p. 236.
25. *K.*, 2: 273.
26. *Ibid.*

27. *W.z.M.*, Section 968.
28. *Beyond Good and Evil,* Section 259.
29. *Ibid.,* Section 9.
30. *The Genealogy of Morals,* II, Section 11.
31. *W.z.M.,* Section 584.
32. *V.P.*, 1: 248.
33. *W.z.M.,* Section 853.
34. *Beyond Good and Evil,* Section 259.
35. *V.P.*, 1: 259.
36. *Ibid.*
37. *Ibid.*, p. 238.
38. *Ibid.*, p. 289. "It is it [the impulse] that makes that the world unfolds logically according to our judgments."
39. *Ibid.*, p. 262.
40. *W.z.M.,* Section 202
41. *W.z.M.,* Section 1067; V.P., 1: 216.
42. *Ibid.,*
43. *Le Gai Savoir,* p. 395; Book Three, Section 109.
44. Martin Heidegger, *Nietzsche,* 1: 274.
45. *Ibid.*, 443.
46. *Ibid.*, 276.
47. *V.P.,* 1: 117; *W.z.M.,* Section 711.
48. Martin Heidegger, *Nietzsche,* 1: 439–40.
49. *Ibid.,* 439.
50. *W.z.M.,* Section 1024.
51. *Ibid.*, Section 120.
52. *Human, All Too Human,* I, Section 508.
53. *W.z.M.,* Section 120.
54. *Ecce Homo, O.P.C.*, p. 271.
55. *V.P.*, 1: 248.
56. *Ibid.*, 2: 385.
57. *Ibid.*, 1: 257.
58. *Le crépuscule des idoles* (Twilight of the Idols), *O.P.C.*, p. 144; "Expeditions of an Untimely Man," Section 49.
59. *Ibid.*, p. 95; "The Four Great Errors," Section 8.
60. *V.P.,* 2: 152.
61. *W.z.M.*, Section 931.
62. *V.P.*, 2: 253.
63. *W.z.M.,* Section 708.
64. *Ibid.*, Section 617.
65. *V.P.,* 2: 229.
66. *Dithyrambes de Dionysos, O.P.C.*, p. 71.
67. *W.z.M.*, Section 1052; and see *Le Gai Savoir* (p. 529): "The Stoic says: Whatever happens, is good to me."
68. *Considerations Out-of-Season*, third and fourth essays.
69. *Ibid.*, second essay, *in fine.*

## Chapter 7
## Metamorphosis of the Divine

1. *Identity and Difference,* trans. Joan Stambaugh, New York: Harper and Row, 1969, p. 72, modified.

2. *Discours du Rectorat (Rectorial Address),* ed. Granel, T.E.R., 1982, p. 12.

3. *K.G.W.*, 17 (4), Section 5. See also Fragments Posthumes, 15: 272.

4. *Twilight of the Idols,* "'Reason' in Philosophy."

5. *The Gay Science,* Section 125.

6. *Ibid.*, Section 243.

7. *K.*, 2: 239.

8. *K*, 2: 337.

9. "The Enchanter," also translated as "The Magician" (see *Thus Spoke Zarathustra,* Section 65).

10. *Ibid.* One would have to wonder why Nietzsche inserts the same melodramatic complaint verbatim for Ariadne. "Does one know who Ariadne is?" See Dithyrambes de Dionysos, "Lamentation d'Ariane" ("Dithyrambs of Dionysos," 'Ariadne's Lament'), *O.P.C.*, pp. 57-63.

11. "The Ugliest Man" (Section 67).

12. *V.P.*, 2: 133.

13. *W.z.M.*, Section 708.

14. *W.z.M.*, Section 707.

15. *Dithyrambes de Dionysos* ("Dithyrambs of Dionysos"), pp. 70–71.

16. *W.z.M.*, Section 708.

17. *V.P.*, 2: 387; *K.*, 12: Section 168.

18. *W.z.M.*, Section 711.

19. *The Gay Science,* Section 357. Also quoted by Nietzsche in *The Genealogy of Morals,* 3rd essay, Section 2. (Emphasis added).

20. *V.P.*, 2: p. 46.

21. *Ibid.*, p. 47.

22. *Ibid.*, p. 105.

23. *Ibid.*, p. 13.

24. *V.P.*, 1: 300.

25. *Twilight of the Idols,* "Expeditions of an Untimely Man," Section 49.

26. *W.z.M.*, Section 1051; see also *V.P.*, 2: 374.

27. "It is only after the death of religion that the invention of the divine will take on all its luxuriance," *V.P.*, 2: 379.

28. Quoted by Morel, *Nietzsche,* Paris: Aubier-Montaigne, 1971, 3: 300.

29. *Beyond Good and Evil,* Section 53

30. See especially Section 111 of *Human, All Too Human,* "Origin of religious worship;" see also *Twilight of the Idols,* "The Four Great Errors," where at the end of section three Nietzsche writes: "The error of spirit as cause mistaken for reality! ... And called God!"

31. *V.P.*, 2: 234.

32. *K*, 2: 98.

33. *V.P.*, 2: 379.

34. *Ibid.*

35. *Fragments Posthumes*, XIII, 325 (11 {337}, 1888).

36. *V.P.*, 2: 375.

37. *V.P.*, 1: 252.

38. *V.P.*, 1: 294.

39. *V.P.*, 2: 372.

40. *K*, 2: 245.

41. *W.z.M.*, Section 1050.

42. *The Anti-Christ*, trans. R. J. Hollingdale, London: Penguin Books, 1990, Section 32, p. 154. Hollingdale translates: "*Denial* is precisely what is totally impossible for him."

43. *Ibid.*, Section 29, p. 151. "What are the 'glad tidings'? True life, eternal life is found—it is not promised, it is here, it is *within you:* as life lived in love, in love without deduction or exclusion, without distance."

44. *Ibid.*, Section 32, p. 154. "He cares nothing for what is fixed: the word *killeth,* everything fixed *killeth.* ... He speaks only of the inmost thing: 'life' or 'truth' or 'light' is his expression for the inmost thing."

45. *Ibid.*, Section 32, p. 155. "[He] stands outside of all religion, all conceptions of divine worship, all history, all natural science, ... all psychology, all books, all art."

46. *Ibid.*, Section 34, p. 156. "If I understand anything of this great symbolist, it is that he took for realities, for 'truths,' only *inner* realities—that he understood the rest, everything pertaining to nature, time, space, history, only as signs, as occasions for metaphor."

47. *Beyond Good and Evil* (Section 295): "not full of grace, ... *not enriched and oppressed as though by strange goods,* but richer in himself, newer than before, cracked wide open, blown opon and drawn out by a spring wind, more uncertain now perhaps, more delicate, fragile, and broken, but full of hopes that have no names as yet" (stress added).

48. *Ibid.*

49. *W.z.M.*, Section 1041.

50. *V.P.*, 2: 369.

51. *Ibid.*, stress added.

52. Edmund Husserl, *Ideas*, trans. W. R. Boyce Gibson, New York: Collier Books, 1962, note to Section 51, p. 142.

## Chapter 8
## Tragic Joy

1. This chapter has been slightly edited from the French (see notes 10 and 54). Both changes were approved by Michel Haar. (Ed.)

2. *N.T.*, p. 24.

3. *W.z.M.*, Section 1029.

4. *W.z.M.*, Section 851.

5. (to the point even of including beings taken either as a whole or in part).

6. *Cratylus*, 408c.

7. *N.T.*, p. 79.

8. *N.T.*, *Fragments posthumes,* 303.

9. Kant, *Critique of Judgment,* Section 23.

10. The original French text contained a reference to *Erschütterung,* as suggested in the interpretive work of John Sallis, who seems to find a connection between the term as it is used in Section 27 of Kant's *Critique of Judgment* and the aesthetic sublime in Nietzsche. However, in light of the fact that Section 27 purports to elucidate the *"mathematically* sublime" (in connection with astronomical distances), the interpretation prosed by John Sallis cannot be retained.

11. *K.*, 1: 186.

12. The same remark does not apply to Euripides *(Medea)* or Shakespeare *(MacBeth).*

13. *The World as Will and Representation,* Section 51.

14. *K.*, 1: 186. "That 'the hero is serene' has so far eluded the authors of tragedies."

15. *N.T.*, Section 9.

16. *Ibid.*

17. *Ibid.*

18. *N.T.*, Section 5.

19. *N.T.*, Section 9, p. 77.

20. *Ibid.*, p. 69.

21. *Ibid.*, p. 142 (stress added).

22. *Ibid.*, (Fr. 7 [123], pp. 291–92): "Dionysos possesses the double nature of a cruel and wild demon and of a benevolent sovereign, as *agrionos* and *meilichios."*

23. *Ibid.*, Fr. 1 [1], p. 160.

24. *Ibid.*, p. 53.

25. *Ibid.*, Fr. [128], p. 303.

26. *Ibid.*, stress added.

27. *Ibid.*, p. 47.

28. *Ibid.*, Fr. 7 [123], p. 292. This double nature can also be found in some of the *Fragments* of the last years, e.g., in *W.z.M.*, Section 1049, *"Dionysos:* sensuality and cruelty."

29. The complexity of these rites and myths was remarkably analyzed by Marcel Detienne in *Dionysos mis à mort,* Paris: Gallimard, 1977.

30. *V.P.*, p. 54.

31. *N.T.*, *Fragments posthumes,* p. 319.

32. *N.T.*, p. 48.

33. *W.z.M.*, Section 798; *Fragments posthumes,* 1888—89, 14 (36), p. 39.

34. *W.z.M.*, Section 799 (dated 1888).

35. *W.z.M.*, Section 1050 (dated 1888).

36. *Ibid.*

37. See Michel Haar, *The Song of the Earth,* trans. Reginald Lilly, Bloomington: Indiana University Press, 1993, pp. 146–47.

38. *K.*, 1: 391.

39. *Ibid.*, 390–91.

40. Especially B. Pautrat, *Versions du Soleil,* Paris: Seuil.

41. *N.T.*, p. 142.

42. R. Otto, *Le Sacré,* Paris: Payot.

43. See *K.*, I: 391.

44. *N.T.*, Section 22. All italics except on *Dionysian* and *tragic myth* are mine.

45. *Ibid.*

46. *Ibid.*

47. *N.T.*, Fr. 3 [54].

48. *Ibid.*, Fr. 3 [37].

49. *K.*, 1: 387 (stress added by Nietzsche).

50. *The World as Will and Representation,* Section 39.

51. Schelling, *Philosophie der Kunst,* Section 66.

52. First Duino Elegy.

53. See *Thus Spoke Zarathustra,* "The Sublime Ones."

54. The original French text mentioned the interpretive work of John Sallis (regarding *The Birth of Tragedy),* who claims that Deleuze's interpretation of the same text argues for a unification of the Apollonian and the Dionysian essentially Hegelian in style. But Deleuze actually claims something different: he views *The Birth of Tragedy* as Schopenhauerian in style.

55. Schelling, *Philosophie der Kunst,* Section 65.

56. *N.T.*, p. 153.

57. *N.T.*, p. 116.

58. *N.T.*, p. 103.

59. As a principle not only of the world of Appearance *(Schein),* but also of lightness *(Leicht)* and luminosity *(Licht),* the word *"das Scheinende"* often remains in the neutral. See *N.T.*, Fr. 3 [37], p. 207.

60. *das Leuchtende.*

61. Apollo is the principle that produces the mechanisms by which the will is mistaken about itself (see especially *Fragments posthumes contemporains):* illusions, dream, hallucinations or delirious phantasms.

62. See *N.T.*, Fr. 7 [122], *in fine.*

63. See for example *der Zürnende und Heitere,* 8 [12]. "the one who gets angry and the serene one."

64. *N.T.*, p. 149.

65. *N.T.*, p. 52.

66. *N.T.*, p. 144.

67. *V.D.*, 62; also Fr. 3 [12], "Apollo: the play with inebriation."

68. *Ibid.*, p. 60.

69. *Ibid.*, p. 53.

70. *Ibid.*, p. 61 (stressed by Nietzsche.).

71. Here I summarize too rapidly the remarkable Section 8 of *The Birth of Tragedy,* in which the essence of the theatrical phenomenon is described in terms of a possessed body and visionary projection, with fusional and corporeal unity, in the transe of the spectator and of the actor.

72. *V.D.*, 63.

73. *Ibid.*, p. 62.

74. *Ibid.*, p. 63 (stress added by Nietzsche).

75. *Ibid.*, p.64.

76. Many other "proofs" could be adduced in support of Nietzsche's argument: for example, the *skènè* was a location invisible to the spectator, withdrawm from *sight* and nevertheless the center of the entire drama; the palace, the cave, the location in which *most* of the action takes place, remain hidden. A messenger *(exangelos)* tells what took place *inside.* Double doors open toward the inside (see H.C. Baldry, *Le théâtre antique des Grecs,* Paris: Maspero, 1975, p. 72). Sometimes a special machine *(ekkyklèma)* a sort of bed on wheels, makes it possible to show a corpse to the outside, e.g., that of Clytmnestra, murdered by Orestes. But the *proscenion,* where the actors speak, is a *secondary* projected exteriority. It is Dionysos who pulls the strings from his hiding place: he is the center. By overturning this structure (in the *Republic,* books 6 and 7), Plato reversed both the essence of the theater and the thinking of the first Greeks, He destroyed their model for life. He made the *skènè* into the *topos noètos* (the invisible ideal of the *proscenion* or its "lunar" and weakened (as in mathematics) reflection). Most importantly, he turned the *theatron* itself and the *spectators* into the location for *doxa,* whereas for the pre-Socratics the *theatron* was the location of the highest truth and of the living incarnation of the *polis.* In addition, by dint of a sacrilegious reversal, Plato turned the *doxa,* which was the center of the *correct* gaze (the "theoretician" was the spectator then called "theoros"), into the shadow of the Chorus that moved to the music of the *orchestra.* After the overturning, the four dimensions of Greek theater *(skènè, proscenion, orchestra, public or spectators)* emerge as the four parts of the famous association: *ideas, mathematical entities, things or beings, images.* For Nietzsche, Socrates is the one who inspired this sacrilegious overturning of the previous Greek values.

77. *N.T.*, p. 71.

78. *Ibid,*

79. *Ibid,* p. 72.

80. *Ursprünglisch*

81. *Erlaüterungen zu Hölderlins Dichtung,* fourth ed., p. 25.

82. *V.D.*, p. 64.

83. *N.T.*, p. 143.

84. For reasons that we have presented in "The Initial Rupture with Schopenhauer" (Chapter Two).

85. Nietzsche quotes more than two pages of *The World as Will and Representation* in Section 16 of *The Birth of Tragedy.*

86. *The World as Will and Representation,* Section 52.

87. *N.T.*, Fr. 12 [1], Section 7, p. 431. This fundamental bass harmonic would be common to all languages.

88. *Ibid.*

89. *V.D.*, 67, Section 4.

90. *Ibid.*

91. *Ibid.*

92. *N.T.*, 430 (12 [1], Section 7).

93. *Ibid.*

94. *Consideration Out-of-Season,* IV, "Richard Wagner at Bayreuth,"

Section 6: "True music is a fragment of destiny *(fatum)* and orginary law *[Urgesetz].*"

95. *K.*, 1: 9.
96. *N.T.*, Section 6.
97. *Ibid.*, Section 21.
98. *Ibid.*
99. *Ibid.*
100. *K.*, 1: 41.
101. *N.T.*, 138. The quotation that attempts an abyssal reading of the abyss of the Dionysian sublime refers to the libretto of Wagner's opera.
102. *N.T.*, Section 19, p. 125.
103. *Human, All Too Human,* II,; *The Traveler and His Shadow,* Section 149.
104. *Ibid.*, Section 165.
105. *Ibid.*, Section 152.
106. *K.*, 2: 234; see also *W.z.M.*, Section 644; "Spirit is only a means and *tool* in the service of higher life" (stress added). The word *Werkzeug* recurs frequently, as for example in *K.*, 2: 117 and especially *W.z.M.*, Section 676.
107. *V.P.*, 1: 269.
108. *K.*, 2: 74.
109. *Daybreak,* Section 60.
110. *Twilight of the Idols,* "Expeditions of an Untimely Man," Section 14.
111. "Thinking of Mozart's requiem gives me pleasure," in *Fragments posthumes,* 1878, p. 388.
112. *The Gay Science,* Section 84.
113. *Ibid.*
114. *Correspondence,* 1869–74, Gallimard, p. 217.
115. *Ibid.*, p. 360.
116. *Fragments posthumes,* 1884–85, p. 400, 40 [65].
117. Enumerated in part in the *Fragments posthumes* for *Humain, trop humain,* 2: 395, 40 [16].
118. *N.T.*, Section 1.
119. *Beyond Good and Evil,* Section 245.
120. Let me be forgiven for fragmenting such a splendid text *The Gay Science,* Section 337, "The future feeling of humankind").
121. *V.P.*, 2: 337 (stress added).
122. See Heidegger's remarks in *Nietzsche* 1, first chapter.
123. *Ecce Homo,* "Expeditions of an Untimely One," Section 10.
124. *Ibid.*
125. *Fragments posthumes,* 1888, 14 [46], 14: 43.
126. *Dernières lettres,* (Last Letters), end of August 1888, p. 76.
127. *Ibid.*, p. 78.
128. *The Gay Science,* Section 84.
129. *Beyond Good and Evil,* Section 246.
130. *Fragments posthumes,* 1879, 2: 395, 40 [16].
131. *Thus Spoke Zarathustra,* II, "On Great Events."
132. *Wanderer and his Shadow,* Section 176.
133. *Le voyageur et son ombre,* in *O.P.C.*, p. 167.

134. See *Truth and Lie in an Extra-Moral Sense* and "The Native Malady of Language" (Chapter 4).

135. *Ibid.*

136. *Twilight of the Idols,* "Expeditions of an Untimely One."

137. *Fragments posthumes,* 1884–85, 44 [3].

138. *Fragments posthumes,* 1888–89, 16 [74].

139. *The Gay Science,* Section 342.

140. *Ibid.,* Section 109.

141. *N.T.,* Section 15, p. 108.

142. *W.z.M.,* Section 1051.

143. *V.P.,* 2: 373; and *W.z.M.,* Section 1051.

# INDEX